A Rainbow Division
Lieutenant in France

A Rainbow Division Lieutenant in France

The World War I Diary of John H. Taber

John H. Taber

Edited by
Stephen H. Taber

McFarland & Company, Inc., Publishers
Jefferson, North Carolina

LIBRARY OF CONGRESS CATALOGUING-IN-PUBLICATION DATA

Taber, John H. (John Huddleston), 1895–1986, author.
    A Rainbow Division lieutenant in France: the World War I diary of John H. Taber / John H. Taber ; edited by Stephen H. Taber.
       p. cm.
    Includes index.

    ISBN 978-0-7864-9990-8 (softcover : acid free paper) ∞
    ISBN 978-1-4766-2234-7 (ebook)

    1. Taber, John H. (John Huddleston), 1895–1986. 2. United States. Army. Infantry Regiment, 168th. 3. World War, 1914–1918—Personal narratives, American. 4. United States. Army. Infantry Division, 42nd. 5. Soldiers—United States—Diaries. I. Taber, Stephen H., 1953– editor. II. Title.

D570.33168th .T29 2015
940.4'1273092—dc23
[B]
                                                      2015031695

BRITISH LIBRARY CATALOGUING DATA ARE AVAILABLE

© 2015 Stephen H. Taber. All rights reserved

No part of this book may be reproduced or transmitted in any form or by any means, electronic or mechanical, including photocopying or recording, or by any information storage and retrieval system, without permission in writing from the publisher.

Front cover: Dough boy getting hit in battle (Donovan Collection, United States Army Heritage and Education Center, Carlisle, PA)

Printed in the United States of America

McFarland & Company, Inc., Publishers
  Box 611, Jefferson, North Carolina 28640
    www.mcfarlandpub.com

Stephen H. Taber
dedicates this book to
John H. Taber and
the brave men
of the 168th Regiment

In memory of friends and
colleagues lost on 9/11

Francis Noel McGuinn
Richard J. Cudina
Joseph A. Kelly
Anthony A. Rocha
John A. Sherry
Patricia Flounders
Joseph W. Flounders

—Stephen H. Taber

Table of Contents

Preface (Stephen H. Taber)   1

1. Over There   3
2. France   10
3. The Front   27
4. On the Line   35
5. Gas   61
6. Rest   74
7. Back Up   80
8. Away   99
9. Saint Mihiel Salient   111
10. On the Road   120
11. Paris   125
12. Back with the Company   129
13. The End   136
14. Germany   146
15. En Route to Paris   165
16. Back to the Rhine   172
17. Leaving Germany   187
18. On the Way Home   190

Chapter Notes   197
Index   199

French Trench Philosophy

Henri Raveau, a Paris businessman, and then a Sergeant-of-Engineers at the front in France, sent a friend in the United States the following amusing litany, which he said is very popular in the trenches:

"You have two alternatives—either you are mobilized or you are not. If not, you have nothing to worry about. If you are, you have two alternatives—either you are in camp or at the front. If you are in camp, you have nothing to worry about. If you are at the front, you have two alternatives—either you are in reserve or you are on the fighting line. If in the reserve, you have nothing to worry about. If you are on the fighting line, you have two alternatives—either you scrap or you don't. If you don't, you have nothing to worry about. If you do, you have two alternatives—either you get slightly hurt or badly hurt. If slightly, you have nothing to worry about. If badly, you have two alternatives—either you recover or you don't. If you recover, you have nothing to worry about. If you don't, and have followed my advice clear through, you have done with worry forever."

Preface

STEPHEN H. TABER

John Huddleston Taber, my second cousin, graduated from Columbia University in the class of 1917, and entered the army on May 12, 1917. He trained as a reserve officer, 2nd lieutenant, for a few months in Plattsburgh, New York, and later was assigned to K Company of the 168th Regiment (Iowa) of the Rainbow Division (the 42nd). The division was so named by Douglas MacArthur, as it was composed of the national guards of twenty-six states and the District of Columbia. It followed only the 1st and 26th Divisions in length of service in France out of the eventual 29 divisions sent there.[1]

The 168th Regiment consisted of the Regimental Headquarters, the Sanitary Detachment, the Headquarters Company, the Machine Gun Company, the Supply Company, and three battalions. The First Battalion had A, B, C, and D companies. The Second Battalion had E, F, G, and H companies. The Third Battalion had I, K, L and M companies. Each lettered company was led by one to two captains, six to ten lieutenants, and had around 250 men including sergeants and corporals. The regiments assembled at Camp Mills near Garden City, Long Island, New York.

Though the 168th had some interaction with the New York 165th, of which William Donovan commanded the First Battalion (Donovan later founded the O.S.S., predecessor of the C.I.A.), they were particularly close to the 167th Alabama both at Camp Mills and in combat.

On October 16, 1917, the 168th Regiment embarked on the *President Grant*, formerly a German merchant marine ship that had been sitting in New York harbor idle for three years, with other units. The ship was in terrible condition and was unable to keep up with the Europe-bound convoy and was forced to return to New York on October 22. The regiment then embarked on the *Celtic* in November. They would return home in 1919, disembarking from the

Preface

U.S.S. *Leviathan* on April 26. John Taber was demobilized from service on May 12 of that year, two years to the day after joining the army.

John mentioned only a few things to me about his time in the Great War. One was the terrible stench of 300 dead horses. He said he could still smell them at the age of 90. Another was a major not knowing how to read a map on a hillside. He related a story about his almost bumping into President Wilson in a revolving door in Paris. Finally he intimated that his Cousin Alice, distraught over the end of a relationship, jumped off a ship crossing the channel.

John Taber eventually assembled and wrote the history of his regiment, which was published in 1925. Given that he mentions that history often within this diary it was clearly on his mind even during his service, and one might assume that he relied, in part, on the diary to inform his writing of the regimental history. His history was preceded by Chaplain Winfred Robb's pictorial book *The Price of Our Heritage: In Memory of the Heroic Dead of the 168th Infantry*, published in 1923 and printed again in 2014.

This diary incorporated an earlier version written during the war and occupation on scraps of paper and the backs of envelopes; the piecemeal original was then transcribed by hand and fleshed out by the author to form the present work, after his return to the United States. The diary was part of the estate that was left to me, and finally I decided to transcribe and edit the handwritten account. As editor, I made only a few changes during the process of converting the diary to print; I chose to eliminate the daily entry of dates, and to use the contemporary format of "today" and "tomorrow," rather than his "to-day," "tomorrow," etc. The lack of accents on foreign names is true to the original, as they weren't included in the handwritten diary. Names of persons and places were verified, and I also made contact with relatives of Lieutenants Thompson and Doty for further information. While they are few, I have added notes where I felt that they would benefit the reader. Some of the pictures included were part of the diary, and others were found at the Donovan collection at the U.S. Army Heritage and Education Center at Carlisle, Pennsylvania. Many others that John had were lost to Hurricane Sandy. Most of the full names were gleaned from the regimental roster, with their final rank. I would like to thank Mr. Shannon Schwaller and Mrs. Marlea Leijedal of the U.S. Army Heritage and Education Center for their invaluable help. I would also like to thank Nimrod Fraser, author of *Send the Alabamians: World War I Fighters in the Rainbow Division*, for his advice.

John Taber died peacefully in his sleep at the age of 91 in 1986.

1

⇒ Over There ⇐

November 14, 1917
On board the S.S. *Celtic*

Last night Mother had dinner with me at the Garden City Hotel and we had quite a jolly time. I took her to the station and came back to camp with Scott McCormack (Lt., L Company) whose parents had gone to the city on the same train. Our baggage was all packed up in anticipation of an early start, so no one got to bed. I passed the night with a dozen others huddled around a stove in the supply sergeants' tent. It was very cold. Just before we left, orders came down to furl all tents, although the stoves were still hot, and as we marched out a little after five o'clock fires were breaking out all over camp. We entrained at Garden City where Bill and Jerry joined us in the last minute (Lt. William N. Lewis, K, Lt. Gerald O. Blake, K). At Long Island City we transferred to ferries, which took us around the island to the White Star Line Piers. After some delay our battalion boarded the *Celtic*. I had lunch and had time to write and post a few notes before we sailed. Marshall (Lt. Marshall C. Lefferts Jr., K), Bill and I share a good-sized stateroom, No. 139, convenient to the dining salon. I attended officers meeting in the smoking room after dinner and have since been writing here in the library.

The next day we are well out on the ocean headed north for Halifax. In addition to the Third Battalion of the 168th, we have on board some twenty Red Cross nurses and a few unattached officers. So there is lots of room for everyone, and the accommodations are so superior to the *Grant* that there is no comparison. We had boat drill in the afternoon, which due to previous practice went off smoothly. The men are kicking at the food, but they have fewer restrictions, and ever so much more space than on the *Grant*. Had a half hour's physical drill with my platoon and then turned them loose for the afternoon. The officers' mess is excellent. Each company has a table to itself. The rest of the regiment is in the *Cedric* and the *Aurania* in the same convoy.

I have been Officer of the Guard with little to do. Captain Hupp (Allen T., K) is Officer of the Day. Sighted land before Halifax, Nova Scotia,[1] and we are now anchored in Bedford Basin. We are to remain here until our convoy is made up. Not allowed to go ashore, so the best we can do is view it longingly from a distance. Boat drill, physical drill and fifty times around the deck with Noble (Lt. Heath B., I) have completed my efforts for the day. Played bridge with Miss Leonard, the head nurse, and Squibb (Lt. George Sampson) and Loomis (Lt. Lynn A.), two officers in the gas service in the lounge this evening. There is much jollification right now dancing and singing.

Still off Halifax the following day and I inspected quarters at nine. Had physical drill from ten fifteen to ten forty five, officers school from eleven to twelve thirty, non-coms school at two, and physical drill again from three forty five to four fifteen. This is to be our daily schedule so time won't hang heavy on our hands. A man from Halifax came aboard with a supply of Sam Browne belts and other equipment. When he left he said a belt was missing, so we got up a collection to reimburse him. Suspicion, unjust, I believe, is centered on one of our officers. I think it's merely a trick of the salesman to make money.

On November 18th our convoy formed up, consisted of the *Celtic, Cedric, Aurania*, a number of freighters, and an armed British cruiser, and steamed out about noon. As we neared two British Men-of-War, the crews, which were dressed up along the rail, gave three cheers for the American army and a band on one of them broke out with the "Star Spangled Banner." It made the thrills run up and down my back as we passed slowly by, all standing at attention. It was an impressive send off, and we thought it mighty fine of them. It makes me think we really have something in common with the English. As we got further out the band changed its tune, and we heard the faint strains of "Over There." And that's where we're headed for at last. We all stayed out on deck to catch the last (perhaps really the last) glimpse of America, and now we're all settled down for a comfortable voyage.

The day after we encountered fog and heavy seas as we passed over the Grand Banks. The ship is rolling considerably, and some are seasick, but my appetite is still first rate. The *Aurania*, which has been traveling five or six hundred yards to our rear, is bobbing around like a cork, a much smaller boat than this. Boat drill and regular schedule today. Bill Lewis has been confined to the stateroom for failing to exercise his men yesterday. He is very disconsolate, and I myself think the pun-

1. Over There

ishment a bit severe. However Brewer (Colonel Guy S., 3rd Bat. HQ) doesn't like him. Played bridge all evening with Squibb, Loomis and another officer.

The previous couple of days had fine weather and I played bridge one evening, however on the 22nd the sea kicked up in the morning and the boat rolled and pitched so during physical drill that the men weren't able to keep their footing and tumbled all over the deck. I now have two hours watch from two to four A.M. As I came in this morning I met Heath Noble walking up and down the passage because he couldn't sleep. Both he and Butler (Lt. Charles W., I) are having an uncomfortable time.

The following day I walked around the deck with Colonel Edwin B. Winans in the morning. He is inclined to be pompous, but can unbend and is interesting to talk with. He expects to be made a Brigadier soon. I had a regular routine today, and cards this evening.

The sea so lovely last night that I stayed up after my tour until the sun rose. An excellent amateur concert was in the lounge this evening followed by a dance. The twenty nurses are very popular as there are two officers to each nurse on board. While on watch tonight I got to talking with Vinton Bradshaw, a corporal in the First Platoon (K). He has an amazing fund of knowledge and is an exceptionally fine fellow. It's the first time I've ever talked to any of our men on equal footing. He forgot I was an officer and I forgot he was an enlisted man, as if it made any difference anyhow.

On November 25th we entered the danger zone, and extra precautions have been taken. No lights of any kind permitted, and we are not allowed to take off our clothes, or lose sight of our bulky life preservers. Our steward is growing apprehensive. He was on the *Britannic*[2] when she went down, and barely escaped drowning on another torpedoed ship. Marshall and I have been put on submarine watch, two hours on and six hours off, and relieved of all other duty. I like being out in the open, and prefer this detail to any other, particularly at night when everything is quiet but the sea and the wind. All we have to do is see that the lookouts are on the job. Censored a lot of letters, watched the gunners at target practice, and played bridge in off hours. This evening while we were playing in the lounge, the submarine signal sounded, and we made a common dive for the door. I beat Miss Leonard by a length and a half, very unchivalrous. It was a false alarm.

Monday and we are heading toward Iceland. The report is that we're coming this way because our escort hasn't shown up and we're maneuvering around to kill time. It was light until after ten o'clock. I have just come in from watch. It's wonderful out, but I'm too sleepy to stay up.

The next night I came in from my eight till ten P.M. watch. It is drizzling and the sea is running high, the best possible protection against submarines. We have left the freighters behind and are going ahead at full speed. The lounge is a gay area this evening, singing and dancing. I am going below to slip off my clothes (strictly forbidden) and get a bit of sleep before I go on watch again.

Belfast Harbor, Ireland

Met by four destroyers shortly after lunch, and sighted land within an hour, had a bit of excitement coming though a narrow entrance to the Irish Sea. What appeared to be a submarine bobbed up between us and the *Aurania*, which was running abreast of us not more than five hundred yards away. They immediately opened fire, and for a moment, we felt more in danger of their shells than a torpedo. Whatever it was disappeared as suddenly it appeared. In the meantime the captain received word of submarine activity in the Irish Sea and instead of making for Liverpool, put on full speed for Belfast, the nearest port. We dropped anchor about seven this evening and are riding peacefully in the harbor.

Belfast, Ireland
Thanksgiving Day

A freighter, said to be of our convoy, limped into port this morning with the greater part of her stern shot away. Evidently wasn't speedy enough to altogether escape our German friends. We had a special feast this evening by way of celebrating Thanksgiving. There are several cases of scarlet fever among the enlisted men.

Liverpool, England

We left Belfast about one in the afternoon of the 30th in a mist and a choppy sea, which by night became as smooth as glass and a brilliant moon made things more interesting. I was on the watch during the entire dash across the channel at top speed, and although nothing untoward happened, we were relieved to see the Mersey lights heave into view and to cross the bar just about mid-night.

On December 1st Earl Coons (Pvt. Earl E., K) of the First Platoon died of scarlet fever during the night. A pity that he should go that way. He is to be buried in Liverpool, and the others who are sick have been left there in a hospital. Heard that a South African liner was sunk just a few miles out shortly after we crossed the bar. After quite a delay we drew up alongside the quay and finally disembarked. Loaded right there into the train. We are making good time but haven't been able to see much as it got dark soon after we started. Stopped at Birmingham to get coffee for the men. We officers thought we were lucky to get baskets of lunch at three shillings apiece until we opened them and found them filled chiefly with nothing. Women have replaced men in every possible kind of work; shoveling coal, running locomotives, handling baggage. Cold in our compartment.

Sunday
Winchester, England

Arrived at half past one this morning, an eight hour trip. Not a light in the town, and I didn't see a familiar spot as we marched through on our way to the camp which is about three miles out. It was a weary hike, and there was no one on hand to receive us, so by the time we got our men stowed away, and into our own quarters, it was nearly daybreak and I was fatigued. All the men and half the officers are at Morn Hill, and the rest of us at Winnall Downs, about a quarter of a mile away. Both of them are desolate places. Marshall and I are together in a cheerless cell, heated, when there is any coal, by a tiny stove that emits prodigious quantities of smoke. There is no water in the building, but a marine orderly, whom no one has yet been able to find, is supposed to fetch it, and keep our rooms in order. However, the mess hall is quite close, and the food good, though insufficient. The men are on English rations, jam, hard tack, cheese, and tea. They are hungry, cold and dejected.

Scarlet fever has broken out again the next day, and a number of our men are quarantined. The battalion hiked to Winchester in the morning. Marshall, Jimmy (Cpt. James F. Cotter, K) and I went back this evening for dinner at "Ye God Begot Hostel." The last time I ate there was in June 1914 when Matthews and I stopped for lunch. This time the portions were so sparse we went to another place for a second meal. Not much to buy in town, and what there is sells at an exorbitant price. We bought some chocolates, but they were so vile (ersatz, I've no doubt) that we threw them away. Spent the remainder of the evening in the barrack of the Third Platoon simulating an encyclopedia for their benefit.

Taken as a whole, I have a fine bunch of men; just now they're rather down in the mouth. The Americans don't get on well with the English soldiers, there are a great many about here, and are quite disdainful of British methods.

The following day I piloted some of K Company on a sight seeing tour of Winchester, through the cathedral and the college. They evinced unexpected interest in the old things, particularly King Arthur's Round Table. Stayed in town for dinner with Jimmy and Brad (Lt. Glade T. Bradley, K).

We had a short hike the next morning. To conform to English custom, we keep to the left of the road. In the afternoon I went over to the Detention Camp, about a mile away. The prisoners appear to be comfortably lodged. Marshall and I went next door this evening for a game of bridge with Squibb and Loomis. In the course of conversation found out that Squibb was a S.A.E. at Harvard. Loomis is from M.I.T. Marshall was Alpha Delta Phi at Columbia.

Yesterday Scott McCormick suggested a trip to London, but Colonel Bennet (Matthew A., Rgt. HQ) promptly refused our request, so today we shipped off anyhow. No one seems to have missed us, so if we keep quiet, I don't imagine anything will happen. We got into town fairly early and wandered around until lunchtime where we had a passable meal at the Ritz. The city has quite a different atmosphere since the war, rather difficult to define the change, other than the general run down appearance of things, and the presence of so many uniforms. Very few Americans in town, and we carefully avoided those we saw. If we had been certain as to the regiment's movement, we would have stayed over night, but we were afraid to risk it. So after some shopping and more wandering, we got a bite to eat at an ABC restaurant and made for Waterloo station. There an English M.P. demanded our passes. I told him American officers didn't require them and he let us by without further ado. I don't know whether he was stupid or just kind hearted.

It appears that Major Brewer wanted me yesterday afternoon, and was quite wrought up because I couldn't be found. He told me that when I leave my quarters in the future I am also to leave word where I can be reached. It's cold, rainy, and dismal today. Went to the cathedral with Marshall and Bill. The place was like a huge cavern inside, the few lights being shaded as a precaution against aerial attack. An army chaplain discoursed at length on his experience with death at the front, the choir droned some lugubrious hymns, and collection was taken up, an altogether lively outing. The other two went right out and got drunk, and I am cured of church going, in England.

The company left camp in two sections Saturday morning, hiked to Winchester and entrained for Southampton, only a short ride. Marshall and Bill

1. *Over There*

went into town for lunch, and stayed so long that Tucker (Lt. William J., I, later Captain, L) and I who were left with the detachment on the quay didn't get any. But we found diversion in watching the loading, onto hospital trains of a large convoy of "grand blesses" (wounded), just arrived from France, which, of course cheered us all. I am glad to leave England. I feel as if I had been spending the past week in a morgue. Late in the afternoon we boarded a channel boat, two platoons of K, with Hupp, Marshall, Bill, Tucker and me. It is pitch black outside, and of course is raining, but the men prefer the open deck to the hold, as this ship is a cattle transport and the interior is permeated with a rich bovine bouquet. We were delighted to have a really good dinner served us in the tiny salon, as we weren't expecting anything. Evening pleasantly passed listening to hair-raising tales of trench warfare originating in the imagination of several British second lieutenants returning from a two-week leave in England.

2

France

Sunday
Le Havre, France

France at last. Spent the night comfortably on the floor of the dining salon in company with other officers, English and American. The two cabins were occupied by "officers of high rank." We slipped out so quietly, and had such a smooth passage that I didn't realize we had moved until I got up at four and found that we were already at Le Havre. After unloading we had some difficulty in connecting with the rest of the company who had crossed in another boat. Then we set out in a cold drizzle for this place, which some benighted person with a depraved sense of humor had designated "Rest Camp" No. 2. The officers are comfortable enough but the men have frightful accommodations, open sheds with cobble stone floors, and little food. It is a difficult problem to handle so many men, so I don't suppose the camp officials (this is run by the English) are really to blame. There are about ten thousand troops here, representing practically every allied army; Serbians and Russians, both in pitiful condition, Belgians, Indians, Portuguese, Italian, French, English and American. This afternoon an English Lt. Colonel gave a lecture on what to expect and be prepared for in trench warfare to the officers of our regiment. I gathered that the best thing one could hope for is a speedy death. The English have developed an expert type of joy killer. I haven't heard a cheerful word out of one of them since we landed on this side. If it is all so terrible, why not let us be happy in our ignorance until we have to actually experience it. Unless they are really trying to demoralize us, their psychology is faulty.

    Several trainloads of wounded from Cambrai[1] passed through camp the next morning. They say the fighting around there is quite fierce. Had an interesting talk with a young Serbian officer, who had been captured by the Austrians, escaped to Russia, and reached England via Archangel. He is now with numerous of his compatriots on his way back to the Balkan front, Salonika, I think. He talked of the debacle in Russia. One hears such discouraging comments from the English and French. Their morale is at low ebb and they are so sick of the war. I don't believe they really care who wins, if it only ends. Neither of them trusts the Belgians. They say they are treacherous and their army useless. Le Havre is the present seat of the Belgian government. As we are leaving sometime during the night, we're all sitting around the stove in the officers club, quite comfortable.

We left early Monday morning, each battalion in its own train. The Major stormed at the men and platoon commanders, and although the train was already on the "quai," and it was very cold, he made us stand around a long time. It was hard on the sick men, who are sticking with us so they won't be left behind in a hospital. Jimmy, Bill, Bradley and I are together in this compartment. A window is out, but we've stuck a shelter half in it, and tried to warm things up with a couple of candles, but we're about frozen, nevertheless. Our first stop was Mantes, where we all got a cup of coffee diluted with rum, and everyone cheered up. Major Brewer called on me to interpret the words and gestures of the sous-chef de gare, who gave us directions as to where and how the coffee could be procured.

Rimaucourt, Haute Marne

We were thirty hours en route and were all rather stiff when we unloaded here early this morning, the twelfth of December. Some new officers who have been in France since September, and who have been attached to the regiment, were on hand to show us our billets. Almost the first person I saw was Pardee, of my Plattsburgh Company. The men are distributed in various lofts and barns, all too well ventilated. I drew a clean room on the second floor of an old stone house. The maid was busy scrubbing the floor when I arrived. Bill Lewis wasn't so lucky in his room so he is coming in with me. Our landlady, a semi-invalid, is pleasant and solicitous as to our welfare.

Had a fine sleep in what must have been the most comfortable bed in the world, miles high and heaped up with feather beds. We are gradually getting straightened out. But the men's quarters leave much to be desired and they are very cold and uncomfortable. However they complain very little. The villagers appear to be anxious to do all they can for the Americans. My landlady heard me cough once last evening, and in a few minutes up came the maid with some sort of herbal tea for my "rhume" (cold). We, that is Bill and I, are eating with M company further up the street with Madame Gay. Rimaucourt is a picturesque village very much, I imagine as it was several hundred years ago. The one street is lined with houses that look as if they had always been here. The women, old men and children (there are no able bodied men except a few soldiers home with permission) clatter about in wooden shoes and quaint costumes. We can't buy anything in the way of food, and as the supply of petrol has given out, Bill and I are seated in front of blazing fire writing by candlelight. A few letters came in today. One was written in October when we first started out on the *Grant*.

It got much colder the next day and the men are suffering for although there is a tiny stove for each billet, there isn't any wood. Mme. Pillessout is selling us enough from her slim stove to keep our fire going in the evening or we would freeze too. She asked me in this evening and I had a pleasant hour, polishing up my French and drinking coffee. I also met Sultaine, the dog, and Taupette, the cat, important members of the ménage. Madame is from Epinal, and came here because she has a distaste for Boche bombs. Madame Lapierre, who does all the housework, is a Belgian refugee, quiet and meek. Scarlet fever has broken out again and the entire First Platoon is quarantined in the barracks next to the church.

Cold weather continues, and time hangs heavy on our hands. The men gather at the edge of the stream that runs through the center of town to watch the women pound their clothes in the icy water. It seems to hold a peculiar fascination for them. They think the French ways backward and strange, and it does seem modern ideas beat against the bulwark of French tradition and conservation in vain. Today the town crier and his little drum made their first appearance. After I inspected the billets, I held a class in French for ten of the more ambitious members of my platoon. As a result they can ask for in more or less perfect French, any number up to five, of glasses of red and white wine, and beer. Visited with Madame a while this evening and finished off censoring a stack of letters.

On December 16th a weather-beaten regiment of Algerian Tirailleurs,[2] woefully small in numbers, passed through the village in the morning, on their way from the front to their rest area. Very few young men, and they all seemed tired out. We unexpectedly got orders to move out by noon. Kit Lane, my orderly (Kit C., Pvt.), has come down with scarlet fever, and of course my laun-

2. France

dry was out somewhere. I finally found out from him where he had left it, and there it was soaking in a tub. I had just got the last of my belongings in my locker, and was closing it when down came another order to unpack. It looks as if we should be here several weeks at least, now. Pardee came in to see me in the evening. He has spent some time at the front, and is attached to our regiment as gas officer. Talked an hour with Madame, and am ready for bed.

Our new schedule went into effect the next day. Up for reveille, before dawn, at 5:45. It was snowing then, and has kept up, off and on, all day. Drilled all morning and hiked in the afternoon to Andelot, a village about three kilometers away. This evening a bunch of us reserve officers, Teddy Jones, Mac, Wallace, Noble, Setzer, Currie, and I (Lt. Theodore Jones, L; McCormick; Lt. Mahlon D. Wallace, L; Lt. Walter K. Setzer, L; Lt. John M. Currie, M; all second lieutenants) had an extended gripe fest, and we've decided to put in our transfers. We like our men well enough, but fail to see how there can be any real discipline or esprit de corps with the type of officers we have over us. All the second lieutenants are Reserve Officers. The National Guard simply doesn't speak our language. The hostility is slightly more veiled than at Camp Mills where Major Worthington (Emory C., 1st Battalion H.Q.) practically told the non-coms of the First Battalion not to pay any attention to the Reserve Officers. He drove Knowlton of C Company (Lt. Bernard W.) to attempt suicide at Camp Mills. We agree that he's a cad, and the most cordially hated officer in the regiment. Bennet (Col. Matthew A., Rgt. HQ) is a martinet, and as cold and unapproachable as a fish. Brewer is hard and unreasonable with an obvious partiality for the National Guard officers. I put in a good word for Hupp and Cotter (Cpt. James F., K) because they had always been decent to me, and Noble said that Dunn (Cpt. Lloyd C., I) had been fair to him. But not a good word was said for the C.O.s of Companies L and M, or for the Bradley, Christopher, Lainson triumvirate (Cpts; John C. Christopher, M, Percy A. Lainson, L). After getting that off our chests we felt better. But still can't understand why they don't realize that we are all here for the same purpose, and that we're willing to do our full share, and that it's not our fault we were assigned to the National Guard, instead of the National Army where we belonged. I suppose among the junior officers it's jealousy over our better education (we're almost all college men) and more up to date training, and I think they resent the fact we have the places they feel their own non-coms should have had. Well it's a mess, and mighty unpleasant for us. Sultaine and Taupette are keeping me and the fire company. It's quite late but Bill hasn't come in yet.

My roommate was a bit hilarious last night, and I didn't get much sleep, but was on hand at reveille. The stars were all out and it was bitingly cold. After drill I walked over to Andelot with Timothy (Lt. Christopher S., K), one of our new officers. He is an agreeable chap from Chattanooga. Tacked on to the tail end of our daily schedule now, is Officers School, held at Regimental Headquarters, very dull. Our superior officers took turns reading at us out of a book on trench warfare, which we all have anyway. If Colonel Bennet had any imagination at all, he would devise some means of making the meeting more interesting and profitable for us. Late evening, Captain Homer Davis (C), who is the ranking Reserve Officer in the regiment, asked the Colonel a question with regard to his company, and Bennet ignored him as completely as if he hadn't been there. That made us all hot, and today we hear that Davis has been relieved of his command, and is to be supplanted by an Iowa lieutenant. Our first mail came today. I got several letters from home, and an invitation from Cousin Alice to spend Christmas with them in Paris if I can get away. I'm afraid there's no chance of that.

On the 19th it was very cold, and unpleasant drilling on a windy plain. Tried a number of new formations. After Officers School this evening our griping society gathered in Mac and Wally's billet for a session. They live at the sawmill and have all the wood to burn they want, and are therefore likely to be much sought after. I induced the sawmill owner to sell me some, and brought it back with me in a wheelbarrow.

The next day it was freezing again. But to prove that you can't keep a good man down, while inspecting billets I came across Caroll Nelson (Sgt., K) bathing with the aid of a bacon can full of water he had heated over a tiny stove and the temperature of the place was about zero. The café being warm and comfortable is naturally a favorite gathering place. Many get tight but we try not to see too much.

Another uproar with us last night. I felt rather under the weather, and made up my mind to get some sleep, so I stayed in bed until noon. We had a fairly long hike in the afternoon. Talked till late with Madame Pillessout. She is very pessimistic as to the outcome of the war, but to show me that she wasn't lacking in patriotism, she brought out 25 thousand francs in Government War Loan Bonds. I shouldn't imagine that she possessed that much altogether, but these are thrifty people. Instead of depositing them in a bank she prefers to hide them in a secret place in her bedroom. Hear we are to move to southern France to complete our training, which is cheering.

M. Lapierre, who is sous-officer in the Belgian army, arrived last evening for two weeks permission and everyone is happy. He told me all sorts of interesting things about the Belgians, and the Germans when I went in for a chat with the family this evening. He is as loquacious as his wife is taciturn. Maybe it was the Mirabella we had by way of celebrating his homecoming. Frightfully cold.

On December 23rd I got some Christmas cables in the morning after going through a lot of red tape. Captain Hupp is sick in bed, but he is fortunate in having a fine billet and a kind-hearted landlady, Madame Huet, who is taking good care of him. She owns next to the chateau, the most pretentious place in town. Her husband, who is now dead, was for a long time Headwaiter at Louis Martin's in New York. The chateau formerly belonged to the Ducs Decres, but as Madame apologetically informed me that it had fallen into the hands of owners of a forge nearby. The building itself isn't much from the outside, but it has a pretty "parc" which runs down as far as our house.

I spent a long time at Captain Hupp's and while I was there Lainson came in and made himself most agreeable, and when I went downstairs the Major offered me some candy he had just received, Mon Dieu. I myself got a five-pound box of chocolates from Aunt Bessie. They were sent in a sealed tin container, and were as fresh as if just made. Several of our men arrested today for stealing wood. Personally I don't blame them a bit. John Currie and I walked over to Andelot in search of food and excitement and found neither. But great excitement here, Sultaine has given birth to one lovely pup.

It is now Christmas Eve. I had warning of an air raid last night, and heard some planes go over, but they may have been French. However it is unofficially reported that some bombs were dropped on Chaumont. So the plan to have a Christmas tree for the kiddies of the village in the "Place" has been abandoned, and the celebration is to be held in the church instead. Bought some trifling presents for the household today. There wasn't much to choose from. Later the Christmas entertainment was a great success. Chaplain Robb scoured the country to get a toy and some candy for every kid in Rimaucourt. The band played all evening and everyone had a good time. Madame Lapierre has just brought us some toast and bouillon because it's so cold, but Bill and I have built ourselves a roaring fire, and are very comfortable.

Christmas 1917

Although it has been quite cold all day, and the ground covered in snow, it hasn't seemed much like Christmas. To begin with the long hoped for mail didn't come, and we had nothing to remind us of home celebrations. And then, to the French, Christmas is merely a church feast day; all their celebrating comes on New Years. I had to explain to the family that we gave presents today instead of the first of January. They didn't understand why I left packages for them last night. But we officers of K Company created our own holiday atmosphere at a royal feast that Madame Huet personally superintended. She allowed us the use of her dining room, glass, china, linen, and silver and had her own cook prepare the meal. Captain Hupp was too sick to come down, but Jimmy, Brad, Marshall, Bill, Jerry, and I ate up all the soup, lobster, turkey, chicken, peas, potatoes, salad, cherry pie, cake, fruit, and coffee without any difficulty whatsoever, especially as it was washed down by a plentiful supply of Moet Chandon. We tried to persuade Madame Huet to eat with us, but she wouldn't come in until after we finished and the brought in a bottle of 1810 brandy, from which we all had a bit. The company had a good dinner, too, turkey.

The day after we had a trying day for we drilled in a snowstorm and the men got chilled to the bone and their feet wet. That wasn't so bad, but they have no way of drying them. The small stoves don't make enough heat to even warm their billets. However, they haven't had as hard a time as the troops from other units of the division who are hiking to an area south of us. For the most part they are equipped with the same light shoes that were issued them at Camp Mills in September, and of course there isn't a whole pair among them now. Those who could get it have bound up their feet in burlap. One chap who couldn't make it any further fell out and was sitting on our doorstep when I came back from battalion officers meeting. I took him up to my room to get warm. His feet were in a dreadful condition. He said there were many worse than he, and that a large number had fallen out along the way. They are all suffering from the intense cold. As there is only one ambulance to a regiment it is impossible to pick them up. Madame Pillessout gave me some bread and hot soup for him, and after he had finished I took him to the dispensary and saw him headed for the hospital in our ambulance. I don't see any excuse for the situation. Officers meeting unusually stupid, except that Worthington varied his program by remarking on the inefficiency of certain platoon commanders, and no one was left in doubt as to which ones he meant. By that time it had cleared off, and Heath Noble and I took a long walk. It is a magnificent night, crisp, a brilliant moon, and glistening snow. Then I came home and answered a few of the letters that came in today's mail, just letters, no Christmas boxes as yet.

The Major was up in ire at battalion officers meeting the following noon. He had what is commonly known as a crying drunk and raged at platoon com-

2. France

manders with unnecessary violence, but we're getting hardened to it. He looked so ridiculous that I couldn't keep from laughing which directed a verbal scourging on my lone head. He kept reminding us that we were now in the theater of operations. If we are in it at all, it's only in the peanut gallery, for we are so far away that if it weren't for the daily communiqués in the *Paris Herald* and *Le Petit Parisien* we wouldn't know a war was going on. One of the new officers, Lieutenant Sefton (Earle M., I) gave an interesting lecture on grenades in the schoolhouse this evening, thereby saving us from regular Officers School at Regimental Headquarters. Hurrah.

No drill on December 28th as the ground is deep in snow and it's still still storming. Spent a good part of the day with Captain Hupp. He is feeling a bit more chipper, is good-natured and has a sense of humor. Bradley and Marshall are packing up as they are to go to a British bombing school. The captain suggested my taking one of their beds up, but I like this place better. Bill and I had a pretty good dinner at the hotel this evening, and had quite a talk with two French officers who have been assigned to our regiment. Lieutenants Bentz (Leon) and Germain (Georges). The latter is recovering from his fourth wound.

-13 Centigrade

This being Saturday we had inspection instead of drill, and I am thankful for this is the coldest weather yet. Noble, Butler and I took a walk in the afternoon, and I spent the evening in Schaefer's (Lt. Walter B., L) room with Teddy, Mac, Bill, and Setzer.

I forgot to note that on Friday night after a meeting, Colonel Bennet asked a number of us to accept commissions in the National Guard, Currie, Noble, Marshall and me in the Third Battalion. He said that this being a National Guard organization, he had no authority to recommend other than N.G. officers for promotion. He also said he saw no probability of our being transferred. I most certainly don't want to give up my Reserve commission, and still if I have any hopes of promotion, I'll have to. I have talked the matter over with Captain Hupp, who strongly advises us to do it. He gave my name to the Colonel. Currie, Noble and Marshall have made up their minds, but I'm still undecided, as I should feel like a traitor to the rest of the crowd. When Captain Powell (Clifford, L) broached the matter to Teddy Jones, Teddy turned him down flat, so Bennet knew his attitude in advance and didn't ask him. I think it would have been better to wait. This morning Bentz gave a lecture on the Chauchat automatic rifle. Had dinner at the hotel with Bill, took a walk through the woods with Timothy, and spent the evening here with the family.

On the 31st nothing but muster this morning to everybody's delight, and nothing at all in the afternoon. Went through the chateau. Some beautiful, old furniture, but the interior of the building is on par with the exterior. Talked late with Mac and Wally in their billet.

Started the New Year wrong. I got peeved at Bill for the way he carried on last night, and now he's sore and has moved out. Well, I'll be glad to have the bed to myself, anyhow. When I went downstairs this morning M. Lapierre grabbed me and kissed me on either cheek as he wished me a Happy New Year. He managed to locate a cubic meter of wood for me and carted it to the house. Cost forty francs. Sawed it all up this afternoon. Had dinner at the hotel, Bentz, Germaine, and some First Battalion officers. Let three of my non-coms come up to bathe before my fire this evening. They heated the water downstairs.

The day after the New Year we drilled all day. That night Teddy, Setz, and I had a party at Mac and Wally's.

First Army Corps School
Gondrecourt, Meuse

Early the morning of January 3[rd,] without any previous warning we were notified to pack up immediately as most of the officers and a few non-coms have been ordered here to school. There was a great scramble to get our things together and down to the station in time. I gave the wood I sawed so laboriously to Farley (Sgt. Maxwell, K) to distribute among the sick of my platoon. We left at a quarter of eleven under Major Worthington who bellowed at us and made himself as obnoxious as possible. Arrived at NeufChateau at half past twelve and had to wait there four and a half hours for a connecting train. Had lunch at the hotel, and put in the afternoon taking in the sights. It has some picturesque spots and a couple of interesting churches. We met a band coming down a narrow street playing the stirring "Sambre et Meuse,"[3] and followed it to the Place Jeanne d'Arc where we heard an excellent concert. At half past seven we arrived at Gondrecourt, unloaded our baggage from the train onto trucks, and came out to school in buses. It's very cold and the place looks dreary and uninviting. All the 168th officers, with the exception of the three majors, are in one long Adrian barrack minus a floor, water or visible means of heating but plenty of fresh air.

2. France

Headquarters 168th Infantry
January 2, 1918

SO NO. 2

1. In compliance with SO No. 1, hd. 42nd Div. Jan. 1 1918, the following named officers and NCOs will proceed on Jan. 3, 1918, to Gondrecourt, reporting on arrival thereat to Commandant 1st Corps Schools:

(a) Section A. - Infantry School.

1st Lts.	2nd Lts.	Sergeants
Robert Ely	Claude A. Borland	Fred F. Youngman
Gerald O. Blake	Dan W. Brown	Mose Silverman
David W. Oyler	Heath E. Noble	Clifton E. Campbell
Albert K. Lucas	John H. Taber	James R. Dougherty
James F. Cotter	Theodore E. Jones	Everett T. McMurray
Charles O. Briggs	Scott McCormick	Harry N. Kendall
Ralph B. Ericsson	William J. Tucker	Orville C. Winter
Charles Tillotson	Ercell E. Douglas	Philip R. Koester
William B. Witherell	Howard L. McCall	Charles A. Miller
Frank McCoy	Warren E. Hunting	Everett I. Pugsley
William A. Kelly	Clyde E. Doolittle	Harry Widows
Solomon Rubel	Robert B. Thrasher	George W. Oaks
Frank B. Younkin	Francis S. Pearsall	Henry Henderson
Douglas B. Green	L.M.C. Adams	Owen C. Hawkins
Roy B. Gault	Andrew J. McKeon	Donald V. Ferguson

(b) Section B

Captain	Captain	Captain
Harry C. McHenry	Clifford Powell	Jonathan Springer
Glenn C. Haynes	Arthur J. Horton	Lloyd D. Ross
Edward Steller	Orville B. Yates	

(c) Section D - Trench Mortar and One Pounder Guns

2nd Lts.	Sergeants	Sergeants
Pryor D. Bates	William W. Pinkerton	Harry Ford
John Hutchins	Richard J. White	Walter J. Porsch

(d) Section C - Engineer School - Pioneers

2nd Lts.	Sergeants	Sergeants
Kirt M. Chapman	James E. Wedding	Alphe B. Young
Walter K. Setzer	Warren R. Lodge	Charles E. Ewin

(e) Signal School

2nd Lts.	Sergeants	Sergeants
Elmer E. Silver	F.F. Johanssen	Rex M. Sleezer
Charles W. Butler	Karl Vasicek	John R. Mahaney

(f) Field Officers' School

| Emory C. Worthington | Claude M. Stanley | Guy S. Brewer |

Major Emory C. Worthington being the senior officer will command the detachment from Rimaucourt
Major Claude M. Stanley being the senoir officer of the detachment from the 2nd Bn. will command that detachment until such time as they join the detachment from these Headquarters.

By order of COLONEL BENNETT

Paul I. VanOrder
Captain and Adjutant

Headquarters orders for officers and sergeants to go to school at Gondrecourt in January 1918.

Gondrecourt

It was -20 centigrade the morning of January 4th and we woke to find everything, including shoes, frozen stiff. But my sleeping bag was warm and I had a comfortable night. For this building, which must be 125 feet long, there are two tiny stoves, one at each end, but "pás de bois" (no wood). Jimmy and I tried to thaw out around a stove in the uncompleted enlisted men's Y. We later located the Officers' Y where I'm now writing. It is cheerful and comfortable, and at one end has a canteen where we can buy hot chocolate, cakes, etc. School doesn't start till Monday but we have to stay in Gondrecourt. Up until this session short leaves have been granted to Paris, but the last delegation from here cut up there, so we have to suffer for it. Down to the village this afternoon, a drab collection of muddy streets and decrepit houses. I talked with some German POWs working on the road, apparently without guard. They were all Wurttembergers (southwest Germany) and said they were quite content to be prisoners.

Jimmy and I scouted around the next morning until we discovered a platform that just fits in between our cots, and a shelf already provided with clothes hooks. So now that we purchased a pan for heating water (which we got outside), candles, and other household goods, we're ready to settle down. Equipment distributed today. Stacks of books and pamphlets and new Springfields on which we have already spent hours cleaning. Our mess is good, which is an agreeable surprise, and it's in the next building, which is convenient.

Sunday

We "subalterns" take turns getting up twenty minutes before reveille to make the fire so the others can dress without freezing. Though we have to make a big circle so that every one can get in. It is said this is the coldest winter in fifty years and it wasn't difficult to believe it when I crawled out of my nice warm cot to start things this morning. I am writing in the Y again. I don't know what we'd do without it for it is the only place where one can read and write in comfort. Met a couple men from the Fifth Plattsburgh Company. They have been assigned to the First Division and are here for the same course we're to take. The First, Twenty Sixth and Forty Second Divisions and a Marine regiment are represented here.

Work started on Monday, setting up exercises and close order drill carefully

2. France

directed by a regular Army officer, then a lecture, a tactical problem, dinner, more lectures and practice. I've been assigned to the bombing school, a two week course, which I think will be interesting. It rained, snowed and sleeted by turns throughout the day, and the outdoor work was disagreeable.

The next day I was pretty tired. A hard day's work. We can't do much studying by candlelight, and as it's so cold, and nothing else to do, every one is turning in early. Retired at the wild hour of seven last night.

Went to bed right after supper, and slept soundly till reveille at five, this Wednesday morning. Frightfully cold, and those who didn't have enough covers suffered during the night. Colonel Upton (Camp Commandant) gave Captain Horton (Arthur J., C) a stiff bawling out at drill.

It's January 10th and now we have mud to revel in, but the work agrees with me, and I have a wonderful appetite. So has Captain Powell, who tries to grab everything he can lay his hand on at the table. He, Horton, and McHenry (Cpt. Harry C., B) seem to think their rank entitled them to first service, and all of it, so we take especial pains to empty the dishes before they get to their end, three swine. Captain Haynes (Glen C., 2nd Bat. HQ), who sits opposite me, is quite a different sort and everybody likes him. We have a much better opportunity to observe our fellow officers here where we're all living and training together. Back with the regiment we hardly ever saw the officers of the other battalions except regimental meetings. With the exception of two or three other crabs, the bunch get along well, and the old antagonism seems to be disappearing.

I went in to town the afternoon of the 11th, after school with Jimmy. I bought at the commissary a pair of high-topped boots, which the mud makes necessary, and a pair of whipcord breeches. Teddy, Setz, Mac and I had dinner at the officers' club. The "club" is a privately owned restaurant which has been transformed by hanging out a sign "Café Americain," draping a flag over the doorway, raising the prices to a Paris level, and excluding enlisted men. We went afterwards to study at the village Y, as they have the advantage of a feeble acetylene system, but a chap was playing so well on the piano we listened to him instead.

To give us an idea of British methods, an English Sergeant Major directs our close order drill in the morning of January 12th. I rather think he enjoys having us officers hop about at his command. Anyhow we prefer our own way. The British is too stiff and exaggerated. An officer named Hazzard introduced himself to me after drill. He says his mother was a Taber, and we find we are cousins. The first week of school has been no vacation. All the drudgery of

Plattsburgh with discomfort and vile weather thrown in. I am writing in the Y where a good entertainment is in progress.

Got to bed at the late hour of 9:45 last night as I stayed up to hear all the entertainment. Today I am again at the Y. Some one is playing from "Springtime" on the piano. Spence, Johnny and I saw that together last winter.

January 16th was warmer and we gladly welcome the change. Have been working so tired the past two days. I've been too tired even to write up my diary before slipping into bed the first thing after supper.

Scott McCormick was killed on January 17th. Our section was rehearsing a trench raid in which he acted as my carrier. But the whole thing was over and we were walking back together. He said, "Jack, someone called to you." I turned around and he hadn't taken four steps when a tremendous explosion knocked me flat and something hit me on the back of the neck. I got up half stunned, and there was Mac on the ground. The grenades remaining in his sack had exploded, why, no one knows. He was still breathing when I got to him, but was unconscious and died in a few seconds. And a fraction of a minute we had been talking together. Others much further away than I were stunned and hit by fragments. If it had been C7 instead of O7 we all would have been killed. As it was my own escape was miraculous. Since it had to be, I am glad that his death was so merciful and quick but he is the first of us to go and the realization of what a grim thing war is has been very rudely thrust on us. He was an only child, and I feel most sorry of all for his mother. We are a sober crowd tonight.

Slept but little last night. But now that it's over, it's best to try to forget it, and to train the mind to face worse things without faltering. All the 168th officers were excused to attend Mac's funeral in the village cemetery one day later. The service was simple and dignified.

Teddy, Setz and I felt too blue to go back to camp, and stayed in town for dinner. While in the Y, I bumped into Bill McClure who is at the artillery school just a short distance from us. Just seeing him cheered me up no end. I'm going to have dinner with him on Sunday. Night exercise with a bored English captain in charge.

I had the exam that ended the grenade course the morning of January 19th. Got through it creditably, I think. I was interviewed by Colonel Morrow, the commandant of the Infantry School with regard to Mac's death. Tactical problem this afternoon under the guidance of "grandma" Welles (Major, 26th infantry). Went over to see Bill McClure in the evening to tell him I couldn't get away for dinner tomorrow. Met a bunch of his fellow officers of the 7th 7.

2. France

John H. Taber on January 29th in Gondrecourt during officer's school.

A. (1st Division). Mostly southerners and all agreeable. They have a very comfortable hut, but they say their mess is punk. Went into Gondrecourt to leave a ripped blouse (evidence of increasing proportions) with the tailor.

Sunday

We all spent the morning cleaning up; aired bedding, policed barracks, inside and out, scraped mud off overcoats and shoes, polished puttees, boots, and shoes, and cleaned guns. By the time I had got all my belongings back in place, and had shaved, it was dinnertime. Excellent concert at the Y in the afternoon. Read the *Life of Robert E. Lee* and then had supper "au club" with Heath Noble.

Last night Jimmy and Dan Brown (Lt. Dan W., B) came back from the village, tight as drums and very funny. Someone (McCoy, [Lt. Frank, E]), broke Captain Yates' (Major Orville B., 3rd Bat. HQ) cot, and he is raging about it.

Captains Stellar (Edward, G) and Haynes have been egging him on and we have an altogether merry crowd this evening.

On the 24th we had instruction and demonstration in trench construction, and other pioneer and engineer work, including demolition of entanglements, dugouts, etc. It was interesting and noisy.

Had tactical walk the afternoon of the 25th. Through field glasses saw an exciting airplane flight over towards Nancy. Several brought down, but it was too far to determine whether Boche or Ally. Went into town this evening with Hutchins (HQ company) (Lt. John) for a fine hot shower.

Got a letter from Captain Hupp via a French post today, January 26th. He has recovered and is acting as Battalion Commander. Tushek (Lt. Rudolph R.) has K Company with Bill Lewis and Timothy. Ten of us reserve officers had a dinner in Gondrecourt this evening, Setzer, Teddy, Cpt. Albert K. Lucas, Jerry, Tex Pearsall (Lt. Francis S., G), Rubel (Lt. Solomon, G), Tucker, Thrasher (Cpt. Robert B., F), Noble and I. We procured a room in a house, and the châtelaine thereof prepared us a most palatable meal. Our festivities lasted till ten.

On Sunday, the next day, I stayed in bed until after breakfast. Actually warm today and I sat out in the sun writing while my bedding aired. Everything calm and peaceful except for the distant rumbling of heavy guns. Eight sacks of mail arrived this morning for the 168th. We've waited for it so long, and there wasn't a thing for K or M. Our orderly didn't take the trouble to send our mail up to the ambulance that brought the other here. Ross (Cpt. Lloyd D., M) called up Regimental Headquarters, and made such a row, that they promised to send it over Tuesday. The others have been generous with their Christmas packages.

It's January 31st and we have been living and floundering in a sea of soupy mud and cold penetrating mist since Monday. Night exercises every day. Our Xmas mail didn't come after all and we've quite given up hope of seeing it until we rejoin the regiment. Gas instructions these past two days.

The first day of February and we had an all day maneuver, new and instructive, real barrage and everything. But we had a ten-mile hike to and from the practice area. I was reading here in the Y a little while ago when one of the last persons I ever expected to see came up to speak with me, Professor Siceloff, my erstwhile math professor at Columbia. Recognizing the symptoms of a homesick American, I didn't feel unduly flattered at his almost effusive greeting, but I was right glad to see him and have a talk. Being considerably above army age, he gave up his position to enlist in the Y, and arrived in France only a few days ago.

2. France

The following Saturday, we had pleasant weather for a change. Exam in tactics this morning. Our outfit has left Rimaucourt but we haven't yet found out the new station. Supper in the village with Setz and Teddy.

On Sunday I read and finished *Ruggles of Red Gap*,[4] amusing.

Monday, February 4th, there was a demonstration of machine guns and auto-rifles in action against pillboxes this afternoon, a diversion in addition to other work.

It's February 7th and there has been little change in the routine of the past few days with the exception of some entertaining lecture by Lt. Colonel Hutchinson of the English Regulars, quite a different type from the "temporary gentlemen" of English origin that have been foisted on us here. He is a veteran of numerous campaigns prior to this war, and was also in the retreat from Mons. Instruction in reading airplane photos and a lecture by Colonel Upton this afternoon. School ends tomorrow. Hurrah.

The final day and we finished up with a strenuous maneuver, "attacked" with the aid of machine guns, trench mortar, and artillery barrage and we have to consolidate the new positions we captured. Its hard work and we have to wear our overcoats. It has been a hard course, but I have learned a lot, and have again got into first-rate condition.

Mordor Haute Marne

On February 9th we got up at 3:30 in the morning as our baggage had to be at the loading stage at five, and we had to lug it there ourselves, quite a pull. Jimmy and I helped each other. No tears were shed as we left Gondrecourt, which is undoubtedly the General Headquarters of the world. The train ambled on never making more than 25 kph. We had a three-hour halt at Neufchateau and ours was a special train, we were able to leave all our stuff in the compartment. After a good lunch at the hotel a couple went up to the Base Hospital to see the nurses who came over with us on the *Celtic*. I hunted up Billy Levers who I heard was in Neufchateau with the Y but he was out somewhere and I didn't see him. We had no regular dinner, but had time at Chaumont station to buy bread, cheese and ham, which we ate by candlelight on an improvised table in our compartment. Jogged through Langres and arrived at Rolampont (Divisional Headquarters) at 11 P.M. Set out from there in "camions" (trucks) for the villages where the various companies are located. Our driver lost the way, but I fortunately had a road map with me and we were able to orient ourselves from that. Got into Mordor at 1:30 A.M. (the tenth). Every one in bed but Timothy who was on hand to show us our billets.

I stayed up to half past 3 reading some of the sixty letters that had accumulated in our absence. I was hungry for news from home, so I got up very late the morning of the 10th. I have a regular avalanche of mail, which includes three Christmas packages from London, two from New York, one from Locust Valley and one from Paris, but my box from the family hasn't arrived yet. However it doesn't matter much this late. Tush and I are together; in the next room, Marshall and Captain Hupp, and downstairs, Brad and Jimmy. Our landlady is the mother of the "curé" (parish priest). Captain Hupp seems glad to have us back. Says Bill has redeemed himself and has risen in favor, which statement seemed to disturb Marshall.

Mordor is rather a typical village, the few streets, all rather muddy, radiating from the church, and the houses made of stone, solid and unpretentious. However it is fairly warm out and it looks cheerful in the bright sunlight.

February 11th and I am writing from the walled gardens of our place. The sun is out warm and the buds are just about to burst. There is a delightful spring perfume in the air and I feel like a million dollars. We had a brigade maneuver today and whoever was in charge must have been completely obfuscated for we were never told what we were to do. So after wandering around aimlessly for a while, our brigade sat down on a grassy nook (or several grassy nooks) and took it easy. Marshall has taken under his wing a cute French kid, Louis Savy, who lost his father early in the war and whose mother was killed by an airplane bomb. He is now decked out in an American uniform. I'm letting him use my cot.

The evening of the 12th Louis gave a dinner to Captain Hupp, Marshall, Bill and me. He had arranged with a French woman to get up a really delicious meal, ragout of chicken, frites, salade and vin rouge, which we ate in great state before a large open fireplace in her kitchen. On the way home we stopped in to see the Major, who had just returned. The field officers went from Gondrecourt to the front near Reims where they spent a week with the French. He didn't tell us much of his experiences for he received the news this afternoon of the death of his father, and was feeling too blue. Have packed up my things as K is to be temporarily detached from the regiment, and leaves Mordor tomorrow. We don't know why we're going, or where, which doesn't make much difference, anyway. Have annexed an orderly, Skip Johnson of the Fourth Platoon, who is neat and unobtrusive.

The next day was en route on the "K Company Special" Chemin de Fer de l'Est. I got up late for breakfast with the company, but my landlady insisted

2. France

I come in and have some with her, cafe au lait and pain grille and much conversation. Although over seventy she does much of the work around the place, including her gardens. Her son, the "curé," is with the French army at Salonika and she has no other near relations. My Christmas box from home arrived just before we left, so I had it loaded with the baggage without opening it. Departed in trucks without Marshall, who has become Brewer's adjutant (unwillingly he says) and Louis, who has mysteriously disappeared. A train was supposed to be already made up for us when we arrived in Rolampont, but no cars were in sight, so Hupp demanded of the R.T.O. (Railroad Transportation Officer) a train of second-class coaches, of which there were a number on the siding. It was some time before the train was made up, our baggage loaded and we got under way. The officers have a first class carriage. I am in a compartment with Captain Hupp, Captain Hudson (who is in charge of our medical detachment) (William S., Sanitary Detachment) and Tush. Timothy, Bill and Jerry are next to us, and Brad and Jimmy in another. We have our kitchen aboard and four day's rations.

Another day and we are making slow progress as we spend most of our time on sidings. Stopped all night in the Langres yards, and were uncomfortable, as there is neither light nor heat in the train and our covering is locked in the baggage wagon. Tushek, in repose, takes up enough room for four men. Stopped at Neufchateau and Toul, and now we're held up just outside Nancy. It's about midnight and cold as the devil. Our last candle is about to go out.

3

The Front

Luneville, Meurthe-et-Moselle

Detrained here early the morning of February 15th, stiff as a board and sleepy. Major Potts (whose name befits his figure) (Allen, 42nd Div.) met us and led us to the Hotel des Bosques for a good breakfast. Captain Hupp, Captain Hudson, Jerry, Tush, and I remain here with half the company and the rest go a little further to St. Clement. Our company is to work for the Q.M. (Quarter Master) until the other units of the division come up. We are only three whoops and a yell from the front and numerous planes have been swooping around and stirring up our anti-aircraft guns. I have a peach of a billet, chez Ruse, a most pleasant family, in the Rue Guibal.

Woken up the next morning by a heavy bombardment up front. I could see the gun flashes from my window. More Boche planes over today, and we had to scurry for shelter when anti-air craft shell fragments rained all about us. The Boches were persistent and hovered over the city a long while. Jerry has left with a small detachment for St. Clement, and the others have moved on down to Baccarat. I've been made assistant to Major Potts. He's a blustering old woman with an exaggerated sense of his own importance and rank, but has been very decent to me so far. So far takes, in fact, insists on my riding back and forth to meals at the Vosges in his limousine. My office combines the duties of interpreter and telephone operator. At various intervals I call up the French "intendance" at the HQ of the French Sixth Army Corps when some thing is needed in the way of rations, forage, etc. (the French are helping us out until our own organization gets to functioning), and make periodic calls to the chef de gare and the R.T.O. to inquire about lost and delayed trains. The conversation goes something like this: I ring and a squeaky voice at the other end finally

3. The Front

answers "Allo, allo, allo, j'ecoute" all in one breath, then much buzzing followed by complete silence. After clicking away some time I am again connected with the intendance, and am told "ou nous a coupe." I then deliver my message and after merci-ing at both ends we hang up. Of course nothing is done about any matter until I have called four or five times. The same thing happens when I call the chef de gare, except that it takes longer to get the connection, and we are usually cut off two or three times in the course of one call. However that is practically all I have to do, as the time I'm taking to write this would indicate. Shepard (Cpl. Curtis E., K) and Morris (Cpl. Merle S., K) have been assigned to do clerical work. Captain Hupp and Tush are superintending the men at the "quai," and Major Potts fusses and fumes around, and gets terribly upset because he thinks the enlisted aren't punctilious enough in their saluting. He expects them all to stop work when he approaches and stand at attention until he gives the word. But no one takes him seriously.

Bought some good-looking lace for my mother, a "point" peculiar to the vicinity. My box from home had everything I could have wished for including a huge fruit cake that smelled so good I can hardly wait to get to the home and at it. Have arranged with Madame Ruse to serve some petit dejeuner of chocolate (which I furnish) toast and confiture. She will also care for my room, polish my boots and keep my fire up.

Sunday

Had a new job today. The "maire" has lent a fine house adjoining his own for the use of the Division Commander. It needed cleaning and partial refurbishment, and I was delegated to superintend it. What I won't be qualified for at the end of the war. The bathroom was complete except for a tub, so a Lieutenant from Division HQ staff and I scoured Luneville, but no bathtubs. So he'll have to content himself with sponge baths or a dry rub. Madame, the mayor's wife, a charming woman, invited us for tea. She said the last occupants of the General's house were Mrs. Crocker and Miss Polk[1] of San Francisco, who have done wonderful work in the reconstruction of Vitrimont. I got back to the scene of my supposed labors just as General Menoher (Charles T.) arrived. He was very affable and delighted with his quarters.

It's quite cold Monday, but with a fire going when I wake and when I return at night, and one (a bit smoky) in the office. It doesn't affect me. We are on the second floor of a big barn or warehouse. Among other junk stored there is an old battered electric piano with every possible sort of attachment, drums, cymbals, and what not. Having nothing else to do this afternoon, Shephard and Morris connected it up and entertained us all for fifteen minutes. It is dreadfully out of tune and makes a frightful racket and the different selections are almost undistinguishable. Major Potts heard it several blocks away and came boiling down the street to see what had broken loose. I got a severe lecture for letting them do it. At my age I should know better, he said. Then he sat down and told me his family history. He commanded the Richmond Blues and is some big frog in the Richmond puddle. Princess Troubetskoy[2] is his sister-in-law, and he's not particular that it's kept secret, also that he is the godfather of Kermit Roosevelt's child. I appeared sufficiently impressed for him to quite overlook my previous lack of judgment.

Had dinner at the Vosges this evening with a young French aviator. He turned out to be very agreeable, and we walked around town afterwards. The Germans held Luneville for about three weeks in 1914 and burned parts of it before they left. Others have been damaged by shellfire and bombs but not recently. However the greater part is intact, and I think it is a delightful city. The chateau, which is now used as Corps or Army HQ, once belonged to Stanislas[3] of Poland.

Some Boche planes very low over town at daybreak of the 19th, and the bursting shells directly overhead shook the house, rattling windows and put an end to sleep. Some of the more timid took to the cellar. Policed some sugar and white flour from the Divisional Supply dump and deposited it into the grateful hands of the Ruses. Captain Hupp and Tush have been out buying lace. He said he got a wonderful price for next to nothing. Had lunch again today with Lieutenant Brissac.

One battalion from each regiment goes into the line today, February 21st, the 165th and 166th near Luneville, the 167th, Ancerviller, and the 168th, Badonviller. They are brigaded with French regiments and the artillery divided up among them. The various units of the Division now scattered over a wide area, and it is no small job to ration them and keep them supplied with ammunition and other necessities. That is the function of this office right now. But soon the 117th and the regular G.Q.M. outfit will relieve us so that we can rejoin our command. The French made a large and successful raid to the Northeast at daybreak this morning. The guns woke me up, and I watched the fire for an hour from my window. Gave Mme. Ruse half of my fruitcake for the children and a little while ago a procession composed of Germaine, Suzanne and Marguerite came in to thank me and bestow blessings on my head.

3. *The Front*

Badmenil, Meurthe-et-Moselle

On February 28th, with many regrets we bade Luneville farewell and had a cold ride in trucks through St. Clement, Azerailles and Baccarat to Badmenil, a dirty, vile smelling city that has already been christened "Mudville." All the rest of the battalion, except the other half of K which is still in Baccarat, had been here several days, coming direct from Mordor. After some persuasion my landlady consented to clean up my room (it looked like it had been used for a chicken roost) and put fresh sheets on the bed. Then she cooked dinner for the Captain, Tush and me.

The detachments from Baccarat and St. Clement joined us the morning of March 1st. I have moved up with Captain Hupp and Jimmy. It's rather crowded as the same room serves also as an orderly room, but it's a bit more convenient and we all are sleeping on our cots, safer. Bill found us a mess in a dark little room across the creek, and the cook is a find. She states that she used to cook in the family of the Italian ambassador to Switzerland. Whatever her qualifications, she gave us a scrumptious meal this evening. It has been raining all day and the road looks like soup.

On Saturday, Marshall got the Major's horse for me and we rode into Baccarat and had lunch together. It suffered more than the German (Bavarian) occupation than Luneville. One district was completely destroyed. The famous crystalliere was also put out of commission by the Bosche. The town is dirty and cluttered up with Italian, French, and American troops. Little of interest architecturally.

Sunday

We three talked until late last night and I didn't get up for reveille. But I didn't get much extra sleep, for right after, Captain Hupp came in and turned my cot over. Went into Baccarat again with Marshall. We met a French military funeral outside the church. The civilians remove their hats and the militaires stand at attention as the cortege passes by, a pleasing refinement of custom. Saw Sergeant Pugsley who was one of my assistants on the *Grant*. He had just come back from the front for E Company's rations. Says things are lively there.

The company was reorganized today, March 4th. I had to fight to keep some of my men that Bradley and Blake tried to get for the First Platoon. The Captain backed me up, and I didn't lose any, but acquired some good ones. I have my old platoon, Bill has Marshall's, Timothy has Bradley's and Jerry keeps the First. I have made Farley my platoon sergeant. He is absolutely dependable, though perhaps a trifle too meticulous. Woods (Sgt. Merle) and Krebs (Sgt. Charles) have the two sections; they're both excellent soldiers, though Brad has opposed my recommending Krebs for sergeant. I am entirely satisfied with the bunch I have. At officers meeting this noon Major Brewer announced that the Third Battalion is to make a forward move on Wednesday. On that day the Second Battalion relieves the First, and we go into the support position. At supper with Teddy, Setz, Wally, Thompson (Lt. Hugh S., L) and Percy Lainson. I like the L Company crowd first rate.

The Major told us the next morning that B Company lost a number of men. Captain McHenry is the first of our officers to fall in action. Later in the day I got a more detailed account from Marshall. After a heavy bombardment the Boche attempted to raid the First Battalion at daybreak. They didn't take a prisoner and weren't able to even get in our trenches, our casualties were all due to shellfire. Some are depressed by the news, others "rarin" to go.

Neufmaisons, Meurthe-et-Moselle

It was a relief to see the last of Badmenil late the afternoon of March 6th. Had a short halt in Baccarat and then set out on a tiring hike for Neufmaisons, especially for the men who were shouldering the heavy Chauchats in addition to their packs. As we got on further, the road was camouflaged at points where it was visible from the front. Powell was afraid the Boche would see us and fire on us, made an ass of himself. The kitchen had gone ahead and when we pulled in at nine o'clock the cooks had a hot meal all ready for us. Got my men all stowed away in various lofts, and then made for my own billet. Captain Hupp and I have a little suite to ourselves, and the orderlies, Frankie and Skip, a room off Hupp's. All very comfortable and a vast improvement.

Neufmaisons

No work was scheduled for the 7th so that men could rest up. About twenty of my men are in the hay loft on the same floor, and below, right next to, and connecting with the kitchen, through which we have to pass to get "en haut" (upstairs), is the cow shed. Consequently the whole house has somewhat

3. The Front

of a mellow aroma. Neufmaisons is slightly less primitive, and not quite so dirty and forlorn, but I do wish the French would turn to some mode other than manure piles for front yard decoration. It doesn't offend their olfactory sense I suppose, but it must affect their death rate. Bradley and Jimmy live over the Café de la Verdurette, and Bill and Tim where we have established our "popote" (mess), Tush and Jimmy elsewhere. Had a cup of coffee with our landlady, a pleasant old lady, and her daughter, Marie, who sings in the village choir. We were joined later by a sergeant and corporal of the 117th Engineers, who have a room on the lower floor. The Corporal, Vantrot, speaks French and acts as interpreter between the family and Seargent Cosby.

The morning of March 8th the captains, Bradley and Timothy went up to the front to reconoitre our position. We are about 6 kilometers behind the front line. They stay there for two days, and then the rest of us go up. This afternoon we looked over the line of trenches we will man in case the Boche break through at Badonviller. We have christened the woman who runs our mess "Mathilde," have no idea of her real name, but she's a jolly old soul, and tickled to death at the attention we pay her.

F and M companies made a raid on the Boche late the afternoon of the 9th. Our batteries, augmented by some French guns, pounded the enemy positions for several hours before the attack. We had a splendid vantage point from the top of a hill just outside the village and watched the bombardment through field glasses with as little effort as if it were staged for our special convenience. Our guns were flashing from all sorts of unexpected positions, and until the smoke became too dense, we could see parts of trees, sprays of mud, and debris fly high into the air. I couldn't help but feel sorry for the poor devils at the receiving end, but before long we'll be experiencing the same thing ourselves. So far no news as to the outcome.

The bunch back the next day from the trenches, mud stained and tired. They had a lively time during the Boche bombardment, but none of them were hurt. Farley said that before he went up he had doubts about himself, but now that he has been under fire, he has perfect confidence in himself. And that has bucked me up, because I've been wondering how I should conduct myself too. M company got back late this afternoon. Our losses were light, with only a few killed, and not many wounded. Bernard Van't Hof (Lt., M) slightly wounded in the leg. Apparently the Boche were warned in advance, for though we penetrated to their third line, not a single one was found. Their first line was obliterated, and the woods through which it ran completely destroyed by our shellfire. Tomorrow Christopher and John Currie are to take over another party in the hopes of catching them by surprise and taking a few prisoners. Francis Bates (Lt., M) showed me a little notebook he had been carrying in his breast pocket, a piece of shrapnel had gone almost through and was sticking in it, rather close.

On March 11th when we were all at the table, a mule broke away from its moorings, dashed up the street and right into the mess shack opposite, where a number of Italians were getting dinner ready (there is a large detachment here). Terrified by the sudden and unexpected apparition, they came flying out the windows in all directions, and the cook landed plump in the garbage barrel. Then the mule, with its body still in the doorway, craned its neck through a window and calmly viewed the devastation with a sort of inquiring expression. The funniest damn thing I have ever seen, and we laughed ourselves sick.

4

On the Line

It's March 12th and I am at last at the front. Jimmy, Bill and I, and Sgts. Woods, Pace (Herbert W.), Twining (Merrick C.) and Hutchinson (Isaac G.) set out from Neufmaisons this morning, and followed, a camouflaged road to Pexonne, where Regimental Headquarters is located, and from there on into Badonviller. The gas alert zone is just outside Pexonne, near Fenneviller (totally in ruins and uninhabited) and at that point a sentry warned us to adjust our masks. Arrived without mishap and reported to Lt. Col. Claude M. Stanley at Battalion Headquarters. He gave us lunch and sent us to the trenches with a runner. The town is badly shot up and the troops stationed in it live in barricaded cellars. We took a communications trench (Boyau Central), leading off main street, and walked an interminable distance, ducking under cross pieces to H Company Headquarters in the support line. Things are well blown up there. Captain McHenry killed within a few feet of the dugout, and a couple of duds, one a 240, which we viewed respectfully, lying in the trench nearby. Lt. Hoar (George W.) in command, very nervous. Another interminable journey on treacherous duck boards through winding trenches finally deposited at G.C. 12 (Groupe de Combat), which Lt. McKeon (Andrew J.) is holding with a platoon from H Company. The garrison is a bit jumpy, as they're still new to the game, and the shelling and sniping keeps them constantly on their toes. Yesterday a sniper shot through the heart a runner who was standing at the entrance of this dugout. It was calm and peaceful when I got here, but McKeon and I had no sooner got started on a round of posts when things began to happen. The first shell that came over hit so close to the parapet that I went sprawling in one direction, my helmet in another, and my senses, God knows where. I was frankly scared, but relieved and a trifle surprised to find myself still all in one piece. There is some satisfaction in knowing McKeon was just as frightened as

Badonviller cemetery torn up by German shell fire. Donovan Collection, United States Army Heritage and Education Center, Carlisle, Pennsylvania.

I, and he had been out here three days. The trenches are in bad condition, caved in by shelling, and a foot of muddy water to help matters.

Neufmaisons

The rest of the night was quiet, except for occasional "rafales" (bursts) of machine gun fire, and a couple of false gas alarms relayed from way down on our right. The Boche sent up brilliant flares at regular intervals, but none went up from our side. I made so many rounds I could find my way about the post blindfolded.

After breakfast I met up with Jimmy in Badonviller and came back to Neufmaisons with him. Bradley is to have the First Platoon instead of Jerry, Major's recommendation. Company all ready for its first tour.

Badonviller, 1 Rue de Lorraine

Left Neufmaisons at three the morning of the 14th marching with a hundred yard intervals between platoons in case of shelling by the Boche. Arrived at Badonviller about 5 after an uneventful hike. And had breakfast right away, so we could relieve H Company before it got light. Brad holds G.C. 12 with the First Platoon, Tim (Lt. Timothy) is G.C. 11 with the Fourth, and Bill and I in support, he at P.A. 6 ("point d'appui" strong point) and I in town with Jimmy. We are to share a battered bed, minus mattress and covering, in the same room with Sergeants Hull (Carl E.) and Twining, Sanders (Cpl. Enoch A.) the company clerk, and two runners. Other non-coms are scattered about the house, which has been hit several times, but still in habitable condition. Shells are whistling down the narrow street in search of the batteries. Spent most of the morning in the trenches looking around, and this afternoon doing the town. Despite the fact it is half ruined, and within 500 yards of the second line trenches, there are still a number of civilians here, clinging to their foyers. They all carry gas masks, of course. This evening I went on a liaison patrol to the French post at G.C. 13. It is in a wood and looks more like a summer camp than a first line position. The captain in charge offered me some wine and I sat down and had a few minutes chat with him.

The next day I took out a working party to repair the C.T. ("collecteur trench," communication, connecting) between G.C. 11 and G.C. 12 this morning. A Boche plane flying low evidently spotted us, for soon after a score of shells came whistling at us. No one was injured, but it was unpleasant. This afternoon I went with Hupp to G.C. 11 to view their highly prized and odorous souvenir, the long since dead body of a Boche. While we were there the Boche began to shoot up the place. A shell made a direct hit on one of the auto-rifle posts and twisted the gun all up, but the crew made for a safer place the minute the shelling started and all escaped. On the way out Capt. Hupp slipped on a muddy duckboard, and hurt his leg badly. On liaison patrol again this evening.

Spent most of the following morning with Tim at G.C. 11. Fairly tranquil there, though the bunch over at G.C. 12 got a fair strafing. I got back to Badonviller just as an order arrived for a number of us to go back to Baccarat, or rather Bertrichamps, a village not far beyond, to witness a demonstration of liaisons between advancing troops and aero planes, which was executed by a battalion of French. Teddy Jones and I were so tired that we slept through the entire performance. We stopped in the hospital at Baccarat to see Vand't Hof. He is only slightly wounded and is getting along first rate, his croix de guerre was pinned up over his cot. There were some in the same ward who hadn't gotten off so lightly, an artillery officer in the next cot had lost both legs below the knee. After dark around nine we came back in a tiny Ford truck. Of course we had to run without lights and in attempting to make room for an ammunition truck coming from the other direction, we slipped off the road and rolled down an embankment. No one of us was even scratched, we just rolled it up again and went merrily on our way until a tire blew out halfway between Neufmaisons and Pexonne, so we had to walk the rest of the way.

March 17, Saint Patrick's Day

A day light raid by K and I detachments supported by some French late this afternoon. Captain Dunn was in command of the whole operation, but Jimmy actually in command of the attacking party. About four o'clock our guns started a bombardment of the enemy lines that lasted an hour, and then after a let up of half an hour, the attack. Again the Boche must have gotten wind of our intended attack, for not one was visible, and their artillery was very much on the job, and our men had a hot time coming back to our trenches. We lost a few men, more in K. Tubby Hall (Cpl. Leroy B.) got his rear shot full of fragments, and Doan (Pvt. Byron H.) had slight facial wounds. "Gertrude" Gerard (Pvt. Donald A.) had a wound of some sort or other. An incendiary bomb intended for a Boche

A raiding party of the 168th going over. Donovan Collection, United States Army Heritage and Education Center, Carlisle, Pennsylvania.

dugout struck a crosspiece, glanced, and exploded near Jimmy setting his breeches afire, but he was extinguished before any real harm was done.

On March 19th it was stand to from 4:30 to 6:30 A.M. and again at dusk this evening. My post is in the cellar of the chateau with Captain Hupp. Moderately heavy artillery throughout the day, and we have another warning of an attack and another report of spies. I was sent on a wild goose chase to the "faiencerie" (pottery) to find out who was signaling from a locality at ten o'clock this evening.

A few shells fell near us the morning of the 20th during stand-to on the C.T. just in front. The chateau where we are staying is in complete ruins, must have once been right good looking. The Germans used it as a hospital when they held Badonviller in 1914, and the sign "Lazarett" is still on the wall. They burned it to the ground just before they were driven out, and the walls have been further battered by shellfire. Had lunch at HQ. Marshall gets panicky every time a shell explodes. They were whizzing over regularly all day, and there was an aeroplane flight directly overhead, otherwise everything calm. Jimmy had a patrol out tonight and was going to take me along, but the Major says only one officer. I was curious to see what it was like, but I'm not terribly disappointed.

March 21st saw heavy bombardment all along the line in the morning, and shells have "siffle'd" over us ever since. For a while many of them came close, but we made up our minds not to abandon our orderly-bed room until the concussions blew the candle out. In a short while a shell hit the roof of the building directly across the narrow street, and left us in semi-darkness (the window frames covered with oiled paper in lieu of glass). We rushed out into the street to see who was hurt, and heard some one call out "Nobody here but me, and I'm all right," and there with his head stuck out the top window, Barbara Frietchie–like, was Fido Simpson (Sgt. Webster G.). So we retired to the damp depths of the shelter to await developments, expecting a bombardment of the town, which did not follow. Jimmy's patrol met with some excitement last night, but no casualties. Teddy Jones and his patrol ran into a party of Germans and had five men wounded by grenades.

Deneuvre, Meurthe-et-Moselle

A gas alarm raised in the middle of the night, and the next morning we stood-to, earlier than usual, because there were indications of an attack. We were relieved by the French and started back by platoons, the first leaving shortly after seven. I set out through the woods about nine, just when the Boche were unlashing a little hate on our batteries scattered in there, and at one point had to scramble some to avoid a messing up. The others on the road were spotted and had to indulge in a little sprinting practice. We consolidated forces at Neuf-Maisons and had a trying march to Deneuvre, a hambourg in the hill overlooking Baccarat. Tim and I had a tiny room, the size of a band aid-box. Prince Eitel Friedrich[1] used the house opposite here in September 1914.

Bru

We had a pleasant hike on March 23rd from Baccarat, about fourteen kilometers. I am billeted with Mere Toussaint, a quaint character, who looks like she stepped out of a book. A score of my men are in the hayloft behind my room, and as I have two beds here, I've given Farley one. He is suffering from rheumatism. Have a delightful view of a wide meadow backed by a wall of ever-

4. On the Line

American graves in Baccarat. Donovan Collection, United States Army Heritage and Education Center, Carlisle, Pennsylvania.

greens and cut through by a sparkling brook. It has warmed up, and the trees are budding, and the first flowers out. Everything is so quiet and peaceful. This is about as far as the Boche got in 1914, and the village is damaged somewhat, but not much. Right now there are a lot of men splashing in the brook, the first opportunity to really bathe since we left the States. Later the newspapers that have just come in are full of a huge Boche drive on Amiens. Things look dark for the Allies.

    March 24th and we hear that the French who relieved us at Badonviller have been raided and suffered heavy losses. Went to the little Catholic church with Jimmy, Tim and Tuck this morning. A number of Americans there. The acolyte and priest were obviously delighted at the munificence (comparative) of our contributions, a franc or two apiece from each of the soldiers. After dinner Tim and I walked over to Rambervillers, an interesting town, about four kilometers away. Took some pictures en route. Picked up some odds and ends at the Magasins Remmis which was open, although Sunday. Took in some sights and surreptitiously mailed some post cards home at the French P.O. Tonight at supper we were joined by 2nd Lt. R. Scott (Lt. Robert F. Scott) of the Second Training Camp, who has been assigned to K. He hails from Denver and is a good deal older than the rest of us. We now rank in order of age: Scott, Lewis,

Hupp, Blake, Cotter, Bradley, Tushek, Timothy and Taber. Hupp says he's going to put the officers in a platoon by themselves.

Supposed to drill four and a half kilometers the following morning, but it was such a fine day I turned my men loose in the meadow and let them play games or sun themselves in the grass. They were having such a good time that I discarded rank and dignity, and joined in on Duck-on-the-Rock and Once-and-Over. Got a lot of mail today and besides answering some of my own letters have censored over a hundred. Mere Toussaint showed me some letters two Boston youngsters wrote to her son, who is in the army. They "adopted" him and have been sending him packages since the beginning of the war, but now he is a prisoner in Germany. I gave her a big bar of chocolate to put in the box she is getting ready to send him via the Red Cross in Switzerland.

No drill on March 26th as we were expecting orders to move out anytime. Walked over to Jeanmenil with Tush and Tim to get clean clothes out of our lockers that are stored there, or rather dumped there, in front of Regimental Headquarters with the rest of the baggage. Tuck says that Frank McCoy of E Company is to be sent back to the States. He got panic stricken in the trenches, and made several unnecessary calls for barrage which resulted in casualties to one of our patrols operating in front of his G.C. Bill delivered today a box of candy his wife sent him for me, mighty thoughtful of her. Excellent band concert this evening, entire village turned out. Hupp is leaving for Gondrecourt early tomorrow. We had a sumptuous farewell dinner and wished him luck and better weather than we had.

The afternoon of the 27th an inspector, a colonel, came to interview me about the tents that burned in Camp Mills, way back in November on the morning we left. We disclaimed all knowledge of it, so he doesn't know on whom to fix responsibility. But it does seem disgusting that the army officials should send so much time and effort following up such a petty trail when so many more important things are neglected, but that's old time regular army for you. Orders came down to be prepared to leave at a moments notice, so I started right in to pack up. While I was on my way to return some boots I had borrowed from Tush, Major Brewer sent to my billet for me. He was a bit bleary and lit into me for not being on the spot when wanted, and said runners had been hunting me for an hour. He never did tell me what he wanted me for, but informed me I was under arrest and to confine myself to quarters. He said I laughed in his face just to be impertinent, which I most certainly did not do, but nevertheless that's why I'm spending the evening chez moi. Posted (Arrest of Officer without preferring charges. Officers will not be placed in arrest for light offences. Usually the censure of the commanding officer will be sufficient).

Deneuvre

My confinement was of short duration, for we left Bru early the next morning, and got here before eleven. I was put in charge of the baggage as punishment. The situation up North in Picardy has become so desperate, that the French are rushing all available troops to stem the advance, and instead of going back farther to complete our training, we return to Badonviller to relieve the French division which just relieved us. Had a billet to myself in a house with the M Company officers.

Deneuvre

March 29th and for some unknown reason we are staying on here. I spent the day in Baccarat and had lunch at the Café Du Pont with Jimmy and Brad. Met the Major on the way back, just as cordial as you please, without a word of reference to the other day. We established a temporary mess, with Billy Williams (Pvt. William H.), Ted's orderly as chef. The fried chicken he gave us for dinner would have been better raw.

Camp de Ker Arvor

On the 30th we had a mean hike in the rain via Baccarat, Bertrichamps and Neufmaisons to this place in the Foret des Eliex three or four kilometers behind Badonviller. Gustine (Pvt. Clyde P.) and Dot Garner (Sgt. Carlos) were tight when we set out, and I was cruel enough to make them walk back with me, at attention every step of the way. We landed here after dark, cold, wet and hungry. The men are in wooden barracks, and the officers in a barren shack with nothing to sleep on, as the baggage wagons, as well as the kitchen, all got stuck in the mud. A kind hearted French lieutenant shared what little food he had, but it only whetted our appetites. He and his orderly are now sleeping in the back half of the building, and my six confreres are courting Morpheus here.

Brad and Bill are attempting to find repose on two sheets of corrugated iron. The others are on the ground. While the wood lasted we enjoyed the luxury of a roaring fire in the enormous fireplace, and I am writing in the glow of the embers. I'm tired but wide-awake.

The baggage put in an appearance the following morning and we are comfortably fixed. We use the back room, which has a board floor for sleeping quarters, and the front for mess and general recreation. The company is satisfactorily lodged, each platoon in a barrack by itself. I slept all morning, and now that the sun is out, feel first rate. We are in a lovely forest and it is remarkably still, considering our proximity to the front. Had muster at two o'clock and after that I wandered about in the woods looking at the French batteries stationed around us.

Camp de Ker Arvor

It rained practically all day, April 1st. I stayed in doors, played pitch, read, wrote a couple of letters and was drawn into a general argument. Still another officer, also from the Second Training Camp, assigned us today 1st Lieutenant G.B. Noble. He seems to be very agreeable, is a graduate of Oxford (Rhodes Scholar), and has just come from a several weeks stay at the front with the French near Luneville. Had to relinquish Johnson (sans regret), as we must take our orderlies from our own platoon. George Woodard (Pvt. George M.) has applied for the vacancy.

It seems by the 2nd that we apparently have struck the rainy season, but no one really minds as we have sufficient food and cover, and are getting a good rest. Tim lent me Rex Beach's *The Barrier*[2] which I read at a sitting. Played cards for an equally long stretch with Jerry, Brad, and Tush, and spent some time in my platoon's barracks.

Cleared up on April 3rd and we have a wonderful day. Visited the officers of a French battery (75s) nearby. They have been in the same position for several years and have never fired a shot, as they are to open up in case of great necessity. So their positions being well concealed by natural camouflage they have never been spotted, and they've been leading an easy life, and enjoying it. We're lazy too, but I have no doubt that we'll make up for it later. I am reading the *Winning of Barbara Worth*,[3] didn't care much for the story but the descriptions are excellent. Rounded off the evening at pitch.

The next day I got up at 9:30 and sloshed back to Neufmaisons, it having

4. On the Line

rained during the night. My erstwhile landlady welcomed me with chocolate and cake, great luxuries nowadays, and wanted to know if she should get my old room ready. But after I got some clothes out of my locker, I had to come straight back to Ker Arvor. Noble left a bag in the storage room and lost everything in it. There hasn't been any guard put over the baggage and evidently those who chose went in and helped themselves. Our card game this evening interrupted by a gas alarm. It was all further up front, however, but the alarms are relayed for miles. My commission in the National Guard came this evening. I am the only one up. The rest are all asleep.

Sent out in charge of wood-gathering detail the morning of April 5th we are not allowed to cut down trees, but collect branches, and trunks splintered by shellfire, and naturally we had to go into an occasionally shelled area. We chose the wrong time today, and spent the greater time hugging the earth, more damn fire. There wasn't any use trying to get out, so we just lay low. All sorts of rumors are floating about. We were to go up to the front tonight, but plans evidently have been changed. We may be shifted up to the British front.

On a tour of inspection and discovery with Teddy Jones on April 6th found an observation post in a treetop, which commanded a splendid view of the front. Saw ten or a dozen shells light on Boyau Central, and when one or two whistled over us, we found something more interesting further away. Thought we would be moving today, but here we still are. Expect now to go tomorrow. Rain, as usual, but not much. Great discussion on the Irish question this evening. I'm violent against the English, and Noble just as much pro. The latter rather tied Tim up in his own arguments. Personally I have no use at all for the Irish Catholics. They are actually pro–German, and their driving forces religious prejudice and hatred of English. They don't give a snap for what happens to the rest of the world, America, France, Belgium, Italy, if only England is beaten.

Sunday
Neufmaisons

More rain. Waded out of Ker Arvor about half past one, and instead of going to the front, came back here. I am lodged in a not altogether tidy mansion, the last one on the road to Raon-l'Etape, swarms of children in the family. Farley is sleeping on my cot in my room. The officers of 7 Co. 117th Engineers have taken over Mathilde's for mess, but we found a good place across the street.

A Rainbow Division Lieutenant in France

In order to ensure promptness at meals we have instituted a fine of a bottle of champagne for lateness.

On Monday I drew the M.P. (military police) detail while we're here. A snap, don't have to stand any formations, and I have a capable force, so things will run themselves. My duties consist of an occasional inspection. The guardhouse is across the street from M. Marchal's where Tush, Noble and Scotty are billeted. Jerry put on a party for us after supper, this being his 28th birthday. Champagne and Muscat, all we could drink, a jolly evening. Brad, John Currie, and Teddy Jones have been detached from their companies to serve as B Scout officers. Either Tush or Jerry will have the First Platoon now. Farley came tumbling in pie-eyed a little while ago, but is now peacefully snoring.

The non-coms of my platoon got up a dinner for me the night of the 9th and didn't say anything about it until it was time to eat. They had the woman here to prepare everything, and we sat down at a long table in her kitchen. They had evidently taken great pains, and the meal was delicious; onion soup, omelets, chicken, frites, confiture, and fruit. Farley, knowing of the regulations forbidding officers to drink with the enlisted men, asked if I objected to having some wine. I ruled that the regulations did not apply in this case, and out came a dozen pints of champagne, already cooled. Secretly I was tremendously flattered at the attention, and I think it was mighty nice of them. I sat at the head of the table with Farley and Woods on either side, and Krebs at the other end, and Corporals Fulton (William E.), Neilsen (Herman), Nelson, Simerman (Wayne A.), Mack (Sgt. Mark L.J.), Dot Garner, and Ed Williams (Cpl. Edwin) in between.

On April 10th all but those on M.P. duty had to hike out to the trenches beyond Ker Arvor to look over the reserve positions. I had a lazy day of it. Spent the evening in the Major's room. He was affable and Chris, the Intelligence Officer, gave us a concert on the piano.

The next day it was bright and balmy. A man in the loft above shot himself through the foot with his rifle, an ugly wound. He says it was accidental, but undoubtedly self-inflicted. The doctor says that all malingerers have a sign, S.I.W., posted over their beds in the hospital. Mail.

Beautiful weather continues on April 12th and when I'm out I some times forget about the war. Airplanes have been actively flying behind our lines. Scotty late at supper and furnished the champagne. Vinton Bradshaw came to make a report to me this evening, and stayed till after taps. He is acting Sgt. of the guard. We had a long talk, a fine clean-cut chap.

Another fine day on the 13th, and Jerry and Scotty have been transferred

4. On the Line

to the 32nd Division. Jerry, happy, Scott, displeased. Have been offered the First Platoon, but prefer my own. Tush is to have it. He has been taking French leave whenever the spirit moved him, so tonight we gave him a good scare, and had a lot of fun over it. Yesterday he slipped off to Luneville pretending to see two of our men who were there on detail (one of them being Tut Anderson [Sgt. Otto F.], whom he reduced when he was temporarily in command of the company in January) saw and informed on him. Bill drew up charges of W.O.L. (Without Official Leave). Tim and I signed the Colonel's and Major's names to make it look official. And I had Walter Dickson (Cpl. Walter D.) and Archie Amons, (Cpl. Archie K.) who are on my M.P. force, serve it on him while we were at dinner. Of course we knew nothing about it, and were full of sympathy and comforting remarks as to the probable penalty. At first he affected an air of nonchalance and treated the affair lightly, but when he saw how concerned we all were, admitted that he was worried and sought advice. It was all we could do to keep him from going to the Major about it.

Sunday

Beautiful day. Brewer ripped up the platoon commanders at a meeting this noon. Two officers on horseback were hit by a shell on the road between here and Pexonne. One was killed. I think. In the evening Mathilde gave a party to the K Company officers; Tim, Bill, Brad and I were on hand, but the other three said they didn't know about it, and missed some good cake and wine. Grandpere chaperoned and Mathilde sang "Le chanson des saisons" and "Madelon"[4] for us, but her voice will never get her far.

Jimmy, Bill, and I went to Badonviller on the 15th to look over the positions we're to take. It rained all day, and was quiet at the front. Major Stanley gave us lunch at the Pink Chateau, Battalion Headquarters. Got back here late, and tired.

Rain, and more of it came down the following day. Company put in the day preparing for the trenches.

G.C. 12 C.R. Chamois, Badonviller

Pulled out of NeufMaisons at 2 A.M. on April 17th and had a silent march to Badonviller. Got there in good time, had hot coffee, and completed the relief of G.C. 12 at 5:45. Are manning only 5 posts, as the Boche consistently demolish Post No. 6 as soon as it is reconstructed and their aim is too perfect to make it worthwhile. To offset the decrease in posts I have borrowed an auto-rifle (A.R.) team from the First Platoon. Post No. 1 is held by an A.R. team, Moore (Cpl. Rennie L.), Kurtz (Pvt. Ray B.), Bob Drake (Pvt. Robert E.) and Vreeland (Cpl. Clifford C.); No. 2 A.R., Mack, Wagoner (Pvt. William H.), Rutledge (Pvt. Ralph A.), and Hutton (Pvt. Bert O.); No. 3 A.R., Lloyd (Pvt. Chris B.), Moyer (Pvt. George A.), Dickson and Draper (Pvt. Earl E.); No 4. A.R. Fulton, Lewis (Pvt. Russell J.), Kinselman (Pvt. Oral), and Sanders; No. 5 A.R., Simerman, Hamilton (Pvt. Fred B.), Beatty (Pvt. Leon M.) and Hagerman (Cpl. William). Gas Guards, Coss (Pvt. Floyd E.), Morgan (Pvt. Glen A.), Mintzer (Cpl. Lester F.) and Norman King (Pvt. Norman L.). Runners, Anderson and Woodward (Pvt. George M.), and Sgts. Farley and Krebs. All the posts are held by A.R. teams in addition to gas guards and runners. The other half of my platoon is holding G.C. 11 under Lt. Neale (Lawrence I.) of I Company. The trenches are in bad condition, mud and water above the knees in some places, and caved in from shelling. My dug out, constructed of elephant iron is about 5 feet underground, hardly proof against anything over 105. It is divided into two small rooms, one of which has two bunks which the runners and gas guards will share, and the other one but one, which the Sgts. and I will take turns at. I'm going to stay up all night and get what sleep I can in the daytime. A few shells and a couple of bullets from a sniper (unlocated) is all that has disturbed us so far. Have put in several hours trying to drain the water from the dugouts and trenches.

Went over to G.C. 11 at 3 A.M. on the 18th. I have given Neale some good men; Woods, Dot Garner, Bradshaw, etc., Sent in my report at four, and then stand to. Considerable bombardment to our left at that time. After breakfast I lay down for an hour and a half's sleep. Have fixed up the ammunition dump, which had caved in, checked up and sorted ammunition and pyrotechnics, worked on trenches, dug new latrines and inventoried trench supplies today. Tried to drain the trench but with the broken down pump we have, it is an impossible job. Over to P.S. 5 ("petite poste") to our left to look over the post held by Sgt. Pace and fourteen men from the Fourth Platoon. Considerable bombardment at G.C. 11 and the C.T. between us at three while Major Brewer was out here. Shive (Pvt. Peter), Ed Williams, Flannigan (Pvt. John H.) and Monroe (Mech. Ben H.) had to be sent to the rear for a shell burst in the trench near them and knocked them all out. The first three are badly shell shocked, and Ben Monroe's eardrums were ruptured. Last night Farley made a recon-

4. *On the Line*

naissance of our wire and reported it in bad shape, so I have sent out a wiring party tonight.

3 A.M. on April 19th

Have just come back from G.C. 11. It is so dark and slippery and winding and so many gates to open and close, that it took us three quarters of an hour to make the trip. Belardi (Pvt. Belardi Anichino) stands guard at the entrance to eleven, and I think every sound about frightens the life out of him, but he's ready with his bayonet when anyone appears, and I'd hate to have him misunderstand me, for he stands back in a recess and has the bayonet at your belly before he even challenges you. The accurate shelling of the Boche has made the bunch over there rather jumpy. One of the shells landed directly in the latrine. But the lighter spirits were amusing themselves by seeing how close they could come with rifle grenades to "Aunt Jane" (Blake, Private Leslie C.) who stands gas guard near the P.C. (Post of Command). He protested to me vigorously.

11 P.M.

Made an ineffectual attempt to have our telephone repaired, and to get a sufficient supply of ammunition, grenades, candles, and boots for the men. I went back to town for a short while and brought out the Y's supply of chocolate, cookies, and papers, which I distributed out here. Boyau Central heavily shelled this afternoon and a few dropped in our neighborhood. Our reprisal fire came at nine this evening and seems to have quieted our friends across the way. Our batteries turned loose on them with everything they had for half an hour's fierce bombardment. I heard a tremendous booming over at P.S. 1 in the middle of the afternoon and rushed over to see what was wrong. Sgt. Pace had gone into town without permission, and the bunch there were just throwing grenades for diversion. Went out with the wiring party after stand-to. Our garrison has been increased by two men in search of excitement. Kenny (Sgt. Charles J., Sanitary Department) of the medical corps who belongs really at P.S. 6, and an engineer corporal who finds life in Badonviller too tame. They're both anxious to stay, so I'm letting them. Just finished a cup of hot chocolate that Tut Anderson made, right good. We (Platoon Hdqs., Sgts., runners, and guests) eat our meal in great formality around the table in the dug out.

A Rainbow Division Lieutenant in France

Not a bad day on the 20th, and not much doing. A few German shells popping now and then, but no damage up to now. Colonel Bennet and Van Order (Cpt. Paul J.) came out on a fleeting tour of inspection. A shell hit a few hundred yards away, and their departure was prompt and hasty. Teddy Jones visited me a while this afternoon, and we made a sortie over the top to the patch of scrub oak. Found a sniper's nest and have trained a gun on the spot. Picked a flower in no-mans land, which I've already sent home. Right on top of the dug out is an apple tree in full blossom. The only whole tree anywhere near. But it's hardly safe to sit in the shade of the old apple tree. I climbed it after dark but couldn't see much. The nightingales sing in what's left of the woods across the way. All very incongruous. Lt. Neale has left G.C. 11 to join I Company, which goes in to the line further to the right, and Lt. Jarvis (Robert Y.) of L Company has replaced him. He built a fire too early this evening and a keen Boche observer spotted the cozy wisp of smoke arising from the ground and within a few minutes some twenty 77's lit plump on the P.C. Things had calmed down when I went over. Completed the wiring up of the gaps tonight.

The 21st proves to be a dismal day, a bit of rain every now and then. Went back to P.A. 6 in the morning to see Noble, and Tut and I had to squat in the trench for a while when a few shells were tearing up things in our vicinity. Explored the old abandoned trench down to the ruins of the farm house (Le Ferme du Haut d'Arbre) this afternoon. The trenches are at least five hundred yards apart here. Didn't discover anything new but tore my clothes on the barbed wire. Heard a grenade explode just outside the dug out this evening, and my first thought was that the Germans had got into our trenches. But Morgan, who was on gas guard, had seen a rat and threw a grenade at it. We had a little earnest conversation on the subject. Last night or early this morning "Cap Zig" (Pvt. Everett R. Zike) and Earl Beam (Pvt.) coming over on liaison patrol from G.C. 11 got confused in the darkness, and when they got to Post 1 G.C. 12 and heard snoring and someone talking German (as they imagined) they were sure they had walked into the German lines and tore back to eleven without ever reporting here. Our men at Post 1 heard them coming but when we appeared they were sure that a Boche patrol was in our trenches. I go out to eleven every night on the two o'clock patrol.

A lot of flares and firing over to our right during the night, and the morning of April 22nd we had bad news of the patrol that was the cause of it. Schaefer was killed and his body captured, and Bruce (Pvt. Elmer B.) of K Company is missing. Hear that they went in too far and were noisy. I was all keyed up for a raid when shells began to fall on us at stand-to this morning but it was just a

4. On the Line

salut d'amour. Jarvis has been relieved at G.C. 11 and I have put Woods in charge. He can manage it all right. We leave the trenches tomorrow. In a way I'm sorry, for I've really enjoyed my short reign of independence, and we haven't had such a terrible time. But it will be good to get away from the noise and suspense, and be able to wash and sleep.

Badonviller

The next day I went to G.C. 11 to turn the post to Wallace who relieved us at eight this morning. Got the platoon back to town without incident. Several of us are billeted in an evil smelling cellar on a side street. The company is also in cellars along the line. Bruce returned to our lines with considerable difficulty during the night. He got lost in no-mans land after the Boche opened up fire on the patrol and had to spend the day in a shell hole. I have slept all day.

Had to drag out of bed at 3:40 on the 24th to get to our alert positions for stand-to. My position is across the Neuviller road between the chateau and the faiencerie. Went out to G.C. 11 to get my message book, which I left there, and stayed for lunch (stew and coffee) with Wally. He tends strictly to business while in the trenches, and pays a great deal of attention to detail, but his men like him, and he gets the best of results. The recent rumor of spies in the vicinity and the continuing bombardment has necessitated the removal of the remaining civilians in Badonviller. The last went out today, they and their belongings loaded on U.S. trucks.

April 25th and up at 3:30 for stand-to, and stayed in position until 5:30. As soon as breakfast was over, we moved out for Ker Arvor getting in around seven. Then we had to stand around for Tushek, who had been sent ahead last to get our billets, was sound asleep in his old shack with some 1st Battalion officers. He was finally located, and we got our proper quarters. I am in a cozy, little rustic cottage with Marshall in the Pavillion des Officiers. Just room in it for our two cots, a table, and a small stove. We are in the woods just a short distance from our former quarters but this part with all the officers' cottages is much more attractive.

Ker Arvor

It was a fine sunny day on the 26th. We are messing with L Company, Percy, Teddy, Setz, Wallace, Tommy (Thompson), Wolcott (Lt. B.C.), Jarvis, and Powell. They all dislike Powell. Walked down to Pexonne with Setzer this afternoon.

Rode over to Raon-l'Etape with Marshall the next day. I had the Major's horse. Fifteen kilometers, chiefly through a magnificent forest. The Boche destroyed important parts of the town in 1914, the church of course. We had a good lunch at the hotel, and on the way out met Teddy and Setz. Couldn't get feed for the horses in town, so we left earlier than we had planned, and turned them loose in a field, and lay in the grass watching some peasants plow while the horses ate their fill. This evening in the Major's cottage playing the victrola.

Wakened by a heavy bombardment up front just before dawn on April 28th. One of the officers was very perturbed and rushed over to ask the Major if he should give the order to stand-to. The Major wasn't so alarmed, and I went back to sleep. Too disagreeable outside to do much, so I wrote letters, and read, and played the victrola all evening.

The sun came out bright the next morning and we had a lovely day. Walked up to Roche aux Cochons with Wolcott, and got a wonderful view down the valley into the foothills of the Vosges. The rock is on the edge of a cliff with a sheer drop of five or six hundred feet. This forest is an ideal place for a camp. Asides from its natural beauty, it is quiet and peaceful, and so well concealed from overhead observation that the Boche have never discovered it.

It sank in the next day that this is a delightful existence. Read, wrote, and

Lieutenant Christopher S. Timothy from Chattanooga, a friend of John's who died from machine gun bullet wounds, July 28, 1918. The picture was taken at Camp de Ker Arvor.

censored letters and walked about in the woods by myself. Like to get away from the rest occasionally, but one thinks more when alone, too much. Powell got terribly peeved at Percy's kidding at the supper table. The Major has become so amiable that one wouldn't recognize him as the Battalion Commander of Camp Mills and Rimaucourt. I really like him now. Played all the records on the repertoire before going to bed.

21 Rue Gambetta, Badonviller

Jimmy, Noble and I left Ker Arvor around ten this morning, May 1st, and in three quarters of an hour were in Badonviller. Douglass (Lt. Ercell B.) took us out to inspect our alerts positions, as we were to relieve C Company. In the afternoon our guns put out a steady stream of shells on the Boche lines, and while we were at the table this evening (with the officers of C) the Boche suddenly started in to shell the town. One man (Pvt. John M. Jennings of C) was killed in the street about fifty feet away, and numerous buildings were struck. We adjourned temporarily to the "abri" (shelter). The company arrived after dark, and we officers have taken over this house, which C Company has vacated. But instead of using the damp, poorly ventilated cellar, we're all sleeping on the second floor, Noble and I together.

Lt. Hugh S. "Tommy" Thompson of Company I, who was wounded three times. He was a childhood friend in Chattanooga of Lt. Christopher S. Timothy.

May 2nd and we're in the remains of a fine old house, and we're very comfortably lodged, but we sleep with gas masks, helmets, shoes, etc., handy in case we have to beat a hasty an ignominious retreat to the lower regions. Leigh Brown (Pvt. Leigh A.) (G.B.N.'s orderly) and Woodard have unearthed from somewhere, chairs, a large mirror, rugs and other decorations, which give our apartment a permanent look. We might just as well be at ease "en passant," for it won't last long. Flannigan has undertaken to run our cuisine, and thus far has done well. The other orderlies have salvaged a complete dinner set from the "faiencerie," and we now eat in state. Our house is close to the church, which has been totally destroyed. This morning a shell knocked off a little bit more of what's left of the tower. Even the mausoleums in the graveyard just above have been shot to pieces. Many war dead buried there. Twenty unidentified bodies, French and German in one common grave. It is lovely out today, and a resultant amount of aerial activity. Four Boches attacked one lone French scout and brought him down near Pexonne. The observer was killed by a machine gun bullet, and the pilot injured in landing. Continued artillery action, our guns have been throwing shells all day long.

Had a clean shave this morning of the 3rd. I was watching an airplane fight beyond the Hotel de la Gare, when a shell whizzed by and buried itself in the soft ground not thirty feet from me. Rather fortunately, it was a dud. It came so close that I felt the rush of air as it went by me. As it was the only one that came that way, I imagine that it was a shot intended for our batteries over the hill. Two deserters, Alsatians, came over to our lines this morning. Our boys gave them a good breakfast before sending them to the rear. A battery in back kept hammering away all night and didn't give us much chance to sleep. About 4 A.M. there was a tremendous bombardment to our left, that lasted till five. I went up on the hill behind the church to see what was up, but it was too misty to make anything out, a raid I suppose. We're having such wonderful weather that I hate to go to bed, even though I can hardly keep my eyes open. The stars are all out bright tonight and I took a long walk out past Village Negre. I was surprised to hear someone challenge me in French, and then realized I was behind the French sector. I gave the sentry a cigarette, which he smoked, while on duty, and exchanged views with him.

Went through the trenches at Village Negre on May 4th. The lines are closer than in Chamois, but the positions are much pleasanter as they are in the woods and hardly ever get shelled. Our guns kept up a steady fire all day, but the Boche were quiet.

Back to rainy weather again the following day, also more changing of residence to 89 Grande Rue on the road to Village Negre. We had to vacate the Rue Gambetta, as C Company came out of the line today and took over their former billets. This is not a bad place, however, hard wood floors, marble mantles and everything except windows, and parts of the back wall and roof. All our recently acquired furniture moved with us and we feel right at home. Noble and I are together again. The one drawback is that we face directly some 75's, and when they crack out in front, it makes a frightful racket.

4. On the Line

89 Grande Rue, Badonviller

May 6th is a fine day and we are all very lazy. Bernard (G.B. Noble) has been reading King Henry IV aloud to me this evening. He packs about with him a collection of Shakespeare, which he employs to counter-act the deadening effects of our present existence. Every two minutes the battery behind us sends a shell Germany-ward, and every two minutes it rattles and shakes from the foundations up.

On May 7th I had lunch with an agreeable company of French officers over in Chasseurs. They believe in taking life easy, and they have very comfortable quarters right in the lines, but then it is, and has been, very quite there. Bill came back from Baccarat in an exuberant mood tonight. He had a limousine from the J.G.'s department and invited us all to go back with him. Only Brad and Tim went, and they returned about ten minutes ago making more noise than the guns, which have just kicked up a rumpus.

Captain Hupp got back the next day well fed from Gondrecourt. He says all he learned was the college yell. Glad to have him back. Tim says it was so dark last night that they came all the way to Badonviller with the headlights on. Roughhouse after supper. Everyone is in fine spirits.

The Third Battalion relieved the First on May 9th, and K remains in Badonviller as support we've moved to the other end of town and are installed in the Pink Chateau. Our household goods followed right along, so Tim, Bernard and I are comfortably settled in a room on the second floor. Our dining room is directly beneath. It's rather gloomy as the windows are piled high with sand bags. The building has been hit several times recently. The most attractive feature of our new abode is the walled garden. It's somewhat plowed up and a couple of dud 77s are lying about, but there are enough flowers and trees to redeem it. I am in charge of the M.P. force again. The brig and the guardhouse are in the basement (there isn't much else left) of the Hotel de la Gare. The prisoners are sent out to the front line every day to repair trenches, and come back for the night. The number of transgressors has materially decreased since this new method of punishment went into effect.

May 10th and it's up at 3:30 for stand-to. Went with Cpt. Hupp through L Company's sector. Powell is scared to death with the mere thought of being so close to the enemy and keeps to the deepest part of his P.C. It's hard on his men for he makes them stay underground, though they're in the woods safe from observation. This is back in the second line. I don't suppose he ever goes all the way up front. Beautiful day. GBN called my attention to extraordinary mural decorations in a building on the edge of town. Stand-to from 7–9 P.M.

Being officer of the guard I don't have to get up for stand-to anymore, which fills the others with envy, but I didn't get any extra sleep the next morning, for the Boche dropped a bunch of shells on the C.T. a couple of hundred yards away just at that time. At eight o'clock they put some in town, demolishing a kitchen, and wounding several. Hear that charges have been filed against Brad on account of his conduct the night Schaefer was killed.

Sunday

Stormy day and cool. Went out with Blake's 37 mm team to watch them shoot up Boche machine gun positions, but a Boche observer spied us and we got shelled out ourselves. I broke the world's 220 record. It is blowy outside, and we have built a cheerful fire in the grate to warm us up.

Shelling in the night kept me awake, so after making a round of my posts, I came back to bed for a good sleep Monday morning. Rumors that we move to a more active sector. Picked up a handful of glass shrapnel, a recent offering from the Boche in Village Negre this afternoon. Makes a nasty wound if one hits a bone, for it shatters and makes complications.

On Tuesday the men all got cleaned up at a bath that has been rigged up across the street. Had a good hot shower myself. Made four rounds of my posts during the night and stayed up for stand-to. Heavy firing to the left at 4 A.M. More rain and new rumors of moving to a more active front. Our trunks are to be sent to a storage depot, and that does look like a move.

Last evening one of 155 batteries was attempting to register on the Boche lines, opposite G.C. 7 where they come close together. As direct observation is impossible, they were firing by map, and some one made a mis-calculation, for most of the shells fell in our own position. Word was immediately sent back to correct the range, but when they started up again Wednesday morning they were still falling short, and one went through the entrance of the P.C. exploding inside and killed Lt. McIlvaine (Francis A., M), Sgt. Hobbs (Clem, M) and Privates Hubbel (Max L., M) and McConnelee (Irwin O., M). There was one survivor who was blown out the rear entrance and horribly burned from head to foot. Went out there with Capts. Hupp and Dunn who were sent to make a report. The dug out was still burning, but the bodies had been removed. Nearby we found a dud 155 and that rather refuted the contention of an accompanying artillery officer that the shells falling on G.C. 7 were Boche, and not our own. The affair is all the more regrettable because it was due to carelessness. Teddy Jones was slightly wounded in the back this afternoon. He was pottering around in our own wire, and a sniper's bullet intended for him hit a steel post, ricocheted and went through his Sam Browne. The anti-tetanus injection caused him more discomfort than the wound, which isn't more than a scratch. Bill and I spent most of the afternoon reading under a tree in the chateau grounds. Weather perfect.

On May 16th I took time off today to go to Merviller, which is in the Alabama front line. Four years of shelling have reduced it to a jungle of battered walls. It's not exactly safe to saunter down the erstwhile main street, for the Boche sweep it with well directed machine gun fire the moment anything appears. Major Stanley had lunch with us today. He is from Corning and once was a member of K Company.

Neufmaisons

On Thursday GBN and I sent back to Neufmaisons to get a line on our reserve positions and get the billeting list. A hot and clear day. Got back at 4 P.M. Relieved by F Company at nine, and reached here at 10:30 P.M. A stupidity to make us go back and forth twice, tired.

1, Rue de Paris, Neufmaisons

It's Saturday, May 18th and GBN and I in a 2x4 room with a small window that looks out on the Ruisseau de la Verdurette, and a cow barn. As the stream serves as a general sewer for the village, the odors are sometimes strong. The company including officers is deloused at Village Indien this afternoon. In civilian life the necessity for such a process would result in social ostracism, here it is accepted as a natural condition.

Sunday

We overslept and at six Capt. Hupp sent a runner to wake us and threaten to send us on an engineering detail, which he was too gentle to do. We had an

A Rainbow Division Lieutenant in France

John H. Taber's Military Identity Card next to the same photo of him in Madame Kim's garden.

exclusive little party in our room this evening, GBN and I, Brown (Lt. Dan W.), Woodard and their guest, Rex Woody (Lt. Thomas L. Wood, 1st Battalion H.Q., later Capt).

On May 20th the Company was out on engineering detail but fortunately no officers required. GBN, Wolcott and I had a pistol shooting competition on the range this morning. I wasn't so very good. We gathered together some magazines and went up in the shady woods to read all afternoon. Take away the war and I would be completely satisfied with this existence. The latest rumor is that we go to the Somme. Hurrah. The Y woman has invited Bill and me for dinner. Later that night, Douglass (C Company), Wally, and Tommy came home with us after supper for a gab fest, and Billy Witherell (Cpt. William R., B) joined us later, lots of champagne and Bordeaux. George, Brown, and Rex Woody, who felt their presence indispensible, became loud and had to be deported, but the rest of the crowd was quiet.

On Tuesday we had a drill in the morning. After lunch I took the platoon out in a field beyond the village and let them do what they wanted. They found amusement in ducking each other in the brook (not the Verdurette). I joined in the rough house and got thrown in myself. In the melee lost my knife, pen, keys and some money. We reserve officers were once criticized for our aloofness towards the enlisted men. GBN says we've gone the Iowa outfit one

4. On the Line

better and are now actually Bolshevistic. But a little unbending now and then doesn't hurt. After making such changes of clothing as I could, most of my wardrobe in storage, I walked up to Village Indiens to sign for rations. Jerry and Scotty appeared on the scene during the band concert this evening. All the officers who were transferred to the 32nd Division have been re-assigned to us. They both enjoyed their outing and Jerry makes no bones about the fact that he doesn't care to be back at the front again. Good musical program at the Y following the concert.

Took my platoon up to the gas chamber for drill the morning on May 22nd. Pardee had them walk through tear gas without masks, and then put them through with phosgene. In the afternoon I had had charge of grenade instruction for K and L companies. One idiot nearly blew us all up. He had a grenade (C7) in his hand until it was about to go off, as it was, and then it exploded in the air. I'd rather put in twenty hours in the trenches than one with green men and live grenades. These were replacements who never had previous instruction. Another good concert by the 151 First Army band. Then beat Jerry and Scotty out of eight francs at pitch.

May 23rd had inspection at eight o'clock, relieved by some excitement. An L Company man shot his front rank man in the foot, an accident of course. Lay in the sun and took turns reading aloud with GBN in the afternoon. We had a great treat this evening, dinner with Mrs. Knowles, the YMCA woman. She, herself, is delightful, and an interesting talker. She has been about the world quite a bit, both before and after her marriage. Her husband has been, at times, minister to Romania, Serbia, Bolivia and Santo Domingo. The meal, which she cooked herself, was savory and delectable. Mlle. Feys, with whom Mrs. Knowles lives, helped us dispose of every trace of roast veal, potatoes, gravy, pickles, fruit salad, custard, doughnuts, cheese and coffee. At nine o'clock we started up the Raon Road for a walk, but an unexpected shower made us scurry for home. A brand new rumor out today that we go to the Italian front.

Spent an indolent morning on the 24th reading. After lunch GBN and I got up enough energy to walk up the hill to the observatory in the woods. We climbed up and got a wonderful view of the front through a powerful glass. The trench system for miles was well defined and distinct. We could make out Boches walking along a road which we figured by the map was nearly fifteen kilometers away. Took Mrs. Knowles out for a walk towards Ker Arvor and on the way home stopped in to see Madame Kim's garden. Notified this evening of promotion to first lieutenancy, the commission dating back to the

15th. GBN immediately sent out for some St. Emilion by way of celebrating the event.

14 Rue De La Rochotte, Pexonne

Up early on May 25th, and over to Pexonne with GBN to billet the company. Scotty came along for the exercise. The men's quarters are pretty good, but the officers' limited. So we have rented a room with two beds and an attractive outlook. An artillery captain saved us a trip by bringing us back to Neufmaisons in his car. After going up to sign for rations at Village Indien, we went up near the observatoire to read. Mrs. Knowles gave us some doughnuts when we got back and then we took pictures of each other and Mme. Kim's garden. No music this evening, so we sat and chatted with Madame Marshal. Eight letters in tonight's mail. Still light at 9:15 when the battalion set out for Pexonne.

Sunday

I was tired and slept until ten o'clock. Madame brought us a breakfast of café au lait and du pain grille, in bed. This being the Sabbath there are no details, and we had the day to ourselves. Our mess is not yet running, so again Mme. got us a meal, which she served in our room at one o'clock. Jimmy came in just in time to help us eat it; omlette, frites, salade, gelette. Brief officers meeting at which Scotty was notified of his transfer to M Company. At half past five the Boche suddenly opened up on our batteries in the vicinity, first with high explosives and then gas. It lasted two hours and was intense. We could see shells popping around the edge of the wood where one battery is in position. We got strong whiffs of mustard, and had an alert at 8:30. They are still sending over gas.

5

 Gas

Pexonne

The bombardment kept up all night. I was wakened at one in the morning Monday by a terrific explosion up front. Sounded as if it might have been a mine, and rocked things all the way back here. At the same time the Boche dropped nearly a thousand gas shells near town, and we had to get on our masks. At two o'clock our own guns got in action in earnest, and so many shells were whistling over us (over us, thank heavens), that it sounded like a winter wind. We didn't know what was up until daylight. The Boche made a large-scale gas attack on Village Negre, following it up with a violent bombardment and infantry attack. The explosion was the simultaneous firing of 1,000 electrically connected 10 inch projectors, and all that deluge of gas fell on the First Battalion without any warning, at a time when many of them were asleep. Before they had a chance to adjust their masks, the gas caught them. The raid was a complete failure, but the reports are sickening. Practically all of A Company was casualties, and many killed, wounded and dying. A steady stream of ambulances coming and going all day. Capt. Fleur of the M.G. Company (Edward O.), Lt. Green of A Company (Clarence R.), two Y men (who had a canteen in the trenches) and seventeen enlisted men were dead so far. Over a hundred have been taken to Baccarat hospital, and more to go. L Company has replaced A at the front, and GBN left this morning with First Platoon to relieve some other outfit. Wally went up with his company, and I took over the guard from him. Attended at dusk this evening the burial of seven men, including Gustine of my own platoon, in the village cemetery. It had to be held late, for the last time they had a daytime funeral there, the Boche attended with shrapnel. The service was impressive, but dispiriting, as I know most of us were wondering if before long, we would be the objects of a similar office.

The gas casualties increase. Many who did not know they were gassed have since collapsed. Reported that Lts. Severe (William E., A) and Priddy (Wellborn S., C) are dead. May 28th is a beautiful day and both Boche and French planes out in full force. Guard duty and censoring of letters took up most of my day, but I got in an hour at the Major's rooms with Marshall playing the victrola. Marshall was picked up by an M.P. in Baccarat the other day when he was a trifle too hilarious. As a result he is now under arrest, and is to be court martialed, but he thinks he'll come out of it all right. Trench fever is making the rounds of the outfit and fifteen of my men are laid up. Spent the evening with Capt. Hupp. He is under arrest too, for failing to have an officer present while the men were bathing, more assinity. He doesn't object so much to the confinement but thinks it is petty of Conkling (Major William S., Sanitary Detachment) who reported, and Bennett, who sentenced him. A good-sized mail came in late.

It just happened that I was standing at my window looking towards the front at one o'clock this morning of the 29th when a brilliant flash lit the sky, and an explosion as loud as Monday's indicated another projector attack. Immediately green rockets shot up all along the line, and I had just given the gas

The field hospital at Village Negre, Badonviller. Donovan Collection, United States Army Heritage and Education Center, Carlisle, Pennsylvania.

5. Gas

alarm, when a flood of gas shells struck the further end of town. One exploded at the feet of a sentry near the "faiencerie," and got him before he could put his mask on. In the meantime the Boche were shelling our front line, and fifty men, aided by a box barrage, attempted to raid G.C. 11.

They took no prisoners, though ordered to do so at any cost, but on the other hand left nine of their own killed, and five wounded in our trench. Wally has been badly wounded in the thigh, and Tommy gassed. A few gas casualties in our own First Platoon, but the total is not so great as in the previous attack. There were more deaths and wounds from shellfire, though. All this after the air service had reported the removal of the projectors, and the destruction of the emplacements by our artillery. But it is possible they reset them in another position. I got to bed at seven this morning and slept until noon. Powell has been relieved of the command of L Company and brought back to Pexonne to act as Regt. Claims Officer, in no sense a promotion. He said the reason that Tommy got gassed was that he lost his head and went up in the air as he (Powell) had always predicted. But as Tommy was up in the fire trench and as Powell kept to the bottom of his dugout throughout the entire business, I'm just not sure how he got such accurate information.

Decoration Day

K Company left for Badonviller this evening, but I was ordered to stay in Assis for the Memorial Day service in the cemetery. The village children spent the day picking flowers and arranging them in bouquets so that there would be one for each American grave. They marched in, "tous endimanches," bringing the flowers with them, and had a moving ceremony of their own, witnessed by the entire civilian and soldier population of Pexonne. There followed addresses by General Brown (Robert A.) and Colonel Bennet, and a prayer by Chaplain Robb. After that Capt. Davis, Lt. Bentz, Tucker, Ihrie (Lt. Charles I., 3rd Bat. HQ), and I went down the line decorating the graves. A salute by the firing squad and "Taps" concluded the observance.

On May 31st I was up at eight, bath and breakfast in my room. Trekked to Neufmaisons where I spent the morning and had lunch with Mrs. Knowles, real pancakes. Capt. Hudson brought us back to Badonviller in his car about three o'clock. Whizzed by as a salvo of shells hit the road behind us. GBN and I are together again.

Nothing new happened on June 1st except rumors of another attack. A message was intercepted on the T.P.S. ("telegraphe par sol") telling of the arrival of a large consignment of gas shells in Cirey. I hope it doesn't come off tonight, for I'm very sleepy.

Sunday

Another uneventful twenty-four hours. GBN and I had a little party in our room. One guest George Kalles (Pvt., K), GBN's orderly got slightly tight and entertained us extraordinarily.

Monday was an altogether delightful day. No attack last night, as feared, and I slept until nine. Dreamt that the reverse order in which we got up from the breakfast table would be the order in which we got knocked off. I took particular pains to get up first, then Bill, Jimmy, Jerry, Bradley, Hupp and Tim. I went over to Pexonne to see how the sick men were doing and on into Neufmaisons. There I helped Mrs. Knowles fry doughnuts, and ate as fast as she put them out. Heard a wonderful concert at the Y by a Mr. and Mrs. Rutherford, made a big hit with the men. GBN, who hadn't been able to get away as early as I, joined us there, and we all went to Mrs. Knowles for dinner. Mr. and Mrs. Rutherford, Mrs. Knowles, Mlle. Feys, GBN and I. We had a scrumptious meal (off Grandmere's best china which Mlle. Feys brought out of storage for the occasion), a very congenial party. Mr. Rutherford was giving a show in Pexonne, and brought us that far in the Y Ford. His wife wasn't allowed to go with him, too near the front for women. Played ball in the street after we got back, as it stays light until quite late. An entire regiment of French artillery has come to reinforce this sector, and I heard in Neufmaisons that a brigade of French storm troopers had come in. Either they are expecting trouble, or we are going to start some.

Badonviller

Walked around Village Negre Tuesday morning and lazed the rest of the day. Tush came home from school this afternoon, and GBN was host of a party in his honor chez nous in the evening.

Wednesday is a fine day, but I'm blue and out of sorts. Mrs. Knowles sent me a note and a big package of cookies by runner. Only two letters in tonight's mail. A patrol under Wallace was shot up last night.

5. Gas

On June 6th I was wakened about one o'clock by our artillery over to the right. Soon had a gas alarm and a quantity of phosgene drifted into town. I dressed, but went back to bed at four, and slept until eleven. Our company goes into the line tomorrow, and I'm to hold G.C. 11. Took Farley, Garner and Schuster (Pvt. Glenn C.) out with me to look things over this afternoon. It is in bad shape having been subjected to heavy shelling lately. But under present orders it is to be manned by a small garrison in daytime, and at night by a post of four men. If the Boche get in our own trenches, our own artillery will let a barrage down on them, and it isn't likely that any of them will escape.

Came out here in the afternoon of June 7th with GBN, and at eight took my detachment out to G.C. 11 to relieve the other gang, stayed for a stand-to, and back to P.C. 6 for the night. This is a new dug out, deep, and has six bunks, a great improvement over the ones out front. Have left Farley in charge of the night post on 11. He will sleep in town in the day. Frank Younkin (Cpt. Frank B.), of G Company, which we relieved is staying over twenty-four hours as per orders, and is sharing my bunk. Good-bye to sleep.

June 8th was a long tiresome day, out to G.C. 11 at 4:30 A.M. and back in at 9:30 P.M. One advantage is that we can come back along the road at night instead of making the long journey through the trenches. My garrison consists of three corporals, Garner, Neilson, and Mack; two runners, Tut Anderson and Glen Schuster; and Pvts. Fulghum (Milton D.), Ellison (Percy A.), Hamilton, Hines (Joseph), Vreeland, and Stimson (Sherman W.). Since Woods has been on brigade gas duty, Fido Simpson has been with my platoon. But as I have no need for a sergeant, at eleven, he stays at P.A. 6. Received a generous portion of Boche shells during the day. No casualties. The food detail was shelled on the way out and spilled most of our dinner, and all the water. Have put in a lot of work on the post. Collected a small stock of potato mashers, knives, and helmets, from the last Boche raid. Went into town after stand-to and got our mail. It isn't sent out to the trenches any more. GBN heated up some coffee when I got back. It's now midnight and I'm ready for bed.

Sunday

Didn't get up for stand-to, as GBN has to, and one officer is enough. Stayed in bed until four. George Kalles cooked me some eggs for breakfast, but when I attacked them with great glee, found that he had mistaken the sugar for salt. Got some more sleep after we got to eleven. The way we come out in the morning reminds me of a kid's game "Indian." After we relieve the night post, which is stationed in Collectuer Trench, we form a procession with a yard or so between ranks, and proceed up the trench. Me at the head, with pistols drawn and bayonets fixed. When we get to the junction one party goes to the right, the other to the left, and I to the P.C. We do have to be cautious, as the night guards don't leave their post, and it would be easy for a party of Bosches to slip in, and lay a trap for us. I'm not anticipating it, just prepared for it. Eight 77s dropped on us about ten o'clock, and twenty more between G.C. 12 and us. This post is practically isolated, and exposed on three sides, snipers are on work on two of them. If I had my way, I'd abandon all that part jutting out into no-mans land. There's no tactical advantage in holding on to it, and construct a new fire trench in a line with the others. This is undoubtedly the most disagreeable post in the sector, and owing to its accessibility and exposed position, the one always raided. Tush blew off a couple of his fingers while fooling with a grenade detonator this morning. He was explaining to his men at G.C. 10 the care to be taken in handling them, when the one he was holding up for inspection went off, taking his fingers along. "There," he said, "you see I wasn't careful." Some presence of mind. We are to be relieved in a couple of days, by the 77th Division, I hear.

Monday was disagreeable and cold, and a let up on both sides, so we've had some rest today. Went over to G.C. 12 for an hour to see Tim. No shells have landed there in a long time and it's in fine condition. After stand-to went into Badonviller with Tut Anderson, he's to be depended upon in an emergency. I am at present without an orderly having got rid of Woodard, who was neither dependable nor overburdened with courage. False gas alarm just as I was falling asleep.

Got up early enough on the 11th to shave and be on the job at eleven by 4:30. Spent several hours cleaning up tranches and policing dugout. Rats bad here. My posts are so far apart that they'd be able to render very little assistance to each other in case of trouble, but we've made each one as secure as possible. A sniper fired four or five times at Fulghum and me while we were looking over our wire. He uses a silencer, so we can't locate him, but anyway he's not a very good shot. Major Brewer, who was in a cheerful mood, came out in the morning with Captain Teddy Jones. They stayed for an hour or so in the afternoon. Got our daily gust of shells, and P.A. 6 came in for a brisk strafing. We are higher up than the support line and could see every shell land. GBN says that the Boche range is perfect, and they had to scurry back there. A dud lit in the traverse, where he was, and is still there, stuck in the side of the trench. A single shell dropped on top of the dug out in the middle of the afternoon while I was

5. Gas

asleep. Gave me quite a start, as there is only five feet of cover. But that didn't cause as much perturbation as some of our own that fell short. At dusk Neilson and I took a more extended trip through our own wire and the old abandoned French trenches beyond. We discovered the gaps the Boche cut, and the tape they used to guide them in the last raid, at least we hope it was for the last raid. We also came across a good-sized dud and two gas shells that I'm pretty sure came from a projector. I unintentionally stepped on the foot of a dead Boche, whose upper part was buried under six inches under dirt. I didn't notice until I felt something crunch under my foot. Went into town to get mail and when I got back, about 11 P.M. George had some bacon and eggs for me. GBN is to be transferred to L Company as they are short officers. I hate to see him go as we got on so famously together.

Colonel Tinley (Matthew A.), Colonel Mouvrey 39th Division and Major Brewer came out to G.C. 11 the morning of June 12th on a tour of inspection. Colonel Mouvrey was very cautious and thought it strange to stick our head up over the parapet. It was his first trip to the trenches. After piloting them around my post I took them over to G.C. 12 and left them in Tim's care. At dusk went again into the old French line. Thought we might be able to discover the sniper's nest, but only tore my clothes in the old wire. The Boche shelled Badonviller heavily at seven this evening with 77s. Our retaliatory fire on Bremenil came shortly after, and with 155s. But the other side tried to get last say and threw over about two hundred more as we were going back to P.A. 6.

Artillery fire all night but no unusual activity on Thursday. Finished Churchill's *A Far Country*[1] at the expense of much sleep. Tim came over from twelve to chat a while this afternoon. I think he has entirely gotten over his resentment at my promotion. I'm glad, for I like him, He is really a fine fellow. This evening while it was still light, Fulghum and I crawled out into no-mans land about five hundred yards (the lines are very far apart here) and lay there waiting to see what we could see. It was as quiet and as lovely as a summer evening at home, and the Boche trenches looked harmless and innocent enough. One wouldn't think there was so much potential ugliness and misery hidden in and behind them. The wind was coming our way and we could hear someone singing Schubert's "Wandrers Nachtlied" to the accompaniment of a stringed instrument, and it didn't seem a bit out of place. We had to come back then, as it was time to go to P.A. 6. L Company relieves an outfit of the 165th at Chasseurs tomorrow and GBN goes with them. I shall miss him like the deuce. He has been in line since the 27th of last month, and this will be his third successive tour without relief.

It's June 14th and GBN is gone and Capt. Hupp is now at P.A. 6. I have inherited George Kalles and brought him out to eleven with me. He fought in the Greek army during the Balkan war and thinks their tactics superior to ours. He illustrates by looking fierce and brandishing a knife. He does, however, admit the superiority of grenades. George is altogether epatant. He has brought Susie, his dog of indeterminate breed, out with him. She is having the time of her life chasing around after rats. George has made a gas mask to fit her. A few shells on us this afternoon. As far as I can see this is the only post to which the Boche pay any attention at all. The reason P.A. 6 was noticed the other day was that they had a working party out in full view.

Rained all day on the 15th, and for the first time I ate in the dug out. George has procured a side of bacon from somewhere (I have my suspicions but ask no questions), so we can have bacon and eggs whenever we want. In between rounds I have been wading through Dostoevsky's *Brothers Karamazov* and I feel so gloomy I think I'll give it to Suzie. Major Brewer came out with Lt. Watson, a frightened officer of the 308th infantry, trailing behind. Their outfit is going to relieve us sometime. No order is out yet, though our eight days is up tonight. More inquisitive but prudent officers out later this afternoon, all from the 308th.

Sunday

Captain Falinestock of the 308th spent the night at P.A. 6. As we were crowded I volunteered to stay up all night. Got through a couple of hundred more pages of Karamazov. Thought I could wake up for it this morning, but every time I dozed off, a message or a visitor came to wake me up. At ten o'clock Neilson on Post No. 1 saw two Boches crawling over the hill towards G.C. 9 several hundred yards away. He fired on them immediately and they ran back into the woods. A little later we heard considerable firing there. It appears that some of our men from G.C. 9 went out after them and walked into an ambush. Cahill (Pvt. Joseph J.), of the Second Platoon was killed, shot between the eyes, and Horton (Cpl. Floyd D.), who was with him, had to leave his body. Soon two parties, one from K, and the other from I, went out to recover it, and they walked into a far superior force of Germans. Five I Company men, and Teddy Lawrence (Pvt. Harold G.) from the Hdqrts. Signal Platoon (formerly from my own) are missing. They are the first captures the Boche have made from our regiment in the four months we've been here, in spite of all their raids. A runner

5. Gas

came out here with the warning of an attack and I drew in my posts temporarily according to order. General Johnson (E.M.) of the 77th came out with Capt. Hupp in the afternoon. He asked a lot of intelligent questions, and wasn't in the rush to leave that most inspecting officers are. Actually he told us a joke.

Nothing is new at the start of the week but rain and rumors. If the former keeps up much longer, the trenches will be in as bad condition as in February and March. There is little revetment here, and in places the rain has worn the sides down until it looks like an irrigation ditch. Our rumors are as follows: 1. A French outfit will relieve us tonight; 2. We are going to Paris to parade on the Fourth of July 3. Capt. Hupp is to be transferred to the H.Q. Company. The Major got out a very caustic comment on yesterday's skirmish, and jumped with both feet, and hard, on those concerned. Said among other things, that they acted as if they were on a rabbit chase.

Was up practically all night, and got but two hours sleep this morning,

Secretary of War Baker (right) with Alabama, the regiment aside the 168th. Donovan Collection, United States Army Heritage and Education Center, Carlisle, Pennsylvania.

the 18th. I haven't had more than ten hours sleep all told in the past four days, and feel a trifle shaky. Constructed two new shelters near the P.C. for the use of O. P. 1. While Hamilton was working there a sniper nipped his helmet. He appears to be close to our lines, so I have detailed a man to Post 4, hitherto unoccupied, to watch for him. With so few men, and such widely separated posts, it would be an easy matter for a couple of Heinies to slip in unawares. I can't spare any men to patrol the trench.

Just as I finished writing up my diary last night, or rather evening, for it was still light, the Boche started to shell Badonviller. We watched the performance from O.P. 1, which commands a view of all the rear of our sector. It was the heaviest bombardment I've yet witnessed, a steady fire for two and a half hours, mostly gas but some high explosives. At first they concentrated on the "faiencerie," but it soon spread as it increased in violence. For once the front line was safer than the rear, although I suspected them to open up on us any minute. They finally dropped a cargo of mustard and phosgene directly behind us, and anticipating an attack, withdrew my garrison to Collecteur to await developments. But the fire shifted to the Alabama line, and blew up two ammunition dumps behind them, very spectacular. A steady rattle of machine guns and small arms indicated trouble, and we found out later the Boche had attempted a raid and had been repulsed. Farley and his night watch couldn't leave Badonviller on account of the shelling, and after he had been over due an hour and a half, I sent the others in, keeping Schuster to stay on outpost with me. The belated detail arrived at 9:45 and we got back to P.A. 6 at 10:10. Had to keep our gas masks on all the time, by far the longest stretch we had to wear them. I went straight to bed after writing my intelligence report. At three this morning they started in again, centering on Chasseurs and Alabama with only an occasional one on us, but we had to get our masks on again.

This morning six Drachens (German observation balloons) are up, all this as a result of probable information gleaned from the recent captures. What information the prisoners were able to give must have been meager for even the officers know little enough about what is going on. But they probably scent a relief and are shelling the places where they think the most men to be gathered. We're prepared for a repetition tonight. Escorted the officers of the French outfit that is actually to relieve us tonight all over the post. They have just come from bitter fighting around Villers-Cotterets and Soissons, and are coming here for a rest. Mon Dieu. None of them speak English. The C.O., a first lieutenant, is a Corsican and speaks Italian. Have just received word that I am to stay over twenty-four hours with the relieving troops.

A postcard showing Baccarat before the war.

Neufmaisons
Chez Mlle. Marchal

We were just about to eat supper last night when I was ordered to withdraw immediately to P.A. 6. Our guns were to shoot up the Boche from six to eight, and retaliatory fire on our front line was feared. It was some show, gas, high explosives. shrapnel, and what not from the German front line back to Bremen. They confined their fire to our artillery and rear, killing several French soldiers and wounding a number of civilians back in Pexonne. Returned to G.C. 11 at eight, finished up our supper, policed the dug out, and then to P.A. 6 to wait for the French. Their arrival at eleven P.M. was coincident with a cloud burst, and it was after midnight when I got Lt. Bourdet and his men settled at G.C. 11. Replacements constitute three fourths of the company and some of them were very much frightened. Then I went to G.C. 12 and fixed up the platoon there. At two A.M. when I got back to P.A. Six, the last American had pulled out. I slept luxuriously until 7:30 this morning (June 20th) and had coffee in bed served by the French orderly. It took till noon to make the round of G.C.s 9, 10, 11, and 12, and straighten out their difficulties, translated the English orders, explained maps, etc., had dejeuner with Lt. Poli, the C.O., a five course meal, well cooked and served hot. Arrived at Battalion HQ in Badonviller at 5 P.M. as ordered, getting soaked en route. Heath Noble, Christopher, and Dolan (Lt. James H., D), who had all been kept twenty four hours in their respective company sectors, were already there looking for Marshall who was supposed to have waited for us and provided transportation to Baccarat. He had departed at three and left no word. Were unable to get either Regimental or Div. H.Q , and if it hadn't been for some French sergeants, who gave us crackers and coffee we would have gone hungry, as there wasn't an American in town. Giving us hope, we set out afoot at eight o'clock for Neufmaisons. The village is filled with troops of the 77th Division, and it didn't look as if we were going to get either food or billets. But Heath persuaded Marie-Louise to cook us dinner, which we ate at ten o'clock, and Mlle. Marchal has given us her best room for the night, she and I being great friends.

Baccarat

We drew lots for the single bed. Johnny Christopher won it, but Heath and I had a comfortable mattress on the floor. I had breakfast on the 21st at Mlle.

5. *Gas*

Marchal's. Said goodbye to our numerous friends who are genuinely sorry to have the 168th go. Mlle. Marchal said they always felt safe with us up front. Mathilde tearful and even Grandpere is downcast. Marie Feys said that Mrs. Knowles had left on Monday. At half past eleven we embarked on a truck for Baccarat. The men are lodged in the crystallerie, and the officers in buildings on the square. I got my cot set up just in time to learn that we leave this evening to join the rest of the regiment. They have gone ahead on foot, but because we're just out of the trenches (with a record tour), and because they've had a day's start, we are to travel in camions.

6

Rest

Thaon-les-Vosges

The Third Battalion left Baccarat around ten o'clock last night, jammed into fifty trucks. I was nearly jounced to death in a truck with about thirty of my men, and not a bit of sleep. The whole train got lost, and after having made a wide detour, arrived here at five this morning. Hupp, Jimmy, Brad and I had a refreshing breakfast at the hotel the morning of the 22nd, and then instead of turning in to sleep, we meandered about the town taking in the sights, the most impressive of which is a full bearded woman who presides over Le Café de la Femme a Barbe.[1] She looks like President Poincaré, only she is anything but dapper. General Pershing passed gradually through town in his limousine. I gave him one of my very best salutes, and being the only person on that particular block, know the one his return was especially for me. Capt. Hupp and I were billeted together, across from the Protestant church. We slept from eleven to 3:35 and had to scramble, for the company was scheduled to be at the "gare," prepared to entrain by four. We got there in time, and then had to hang around until 7:30.

Sunday
Aulnay-l'Aitre, Marne

We had a great trip, the men in boxcars, but more comfortable than if they had been in coaches. Not enough of those for officers, so some spread out their bedding rolls on the flat cars under baggage and ammunition wagons. I was on a detail at the last moment, and Bill saved me a seat in a compartment with

6. Rest

Wally, Setz, Teddy, Jerry, Eric (Lt. Earle Sefton) and John Currie. GBN and Eric entertained us on bits of Gilbert and Sullivan, and until we threatened to throw him out, Setz indulged us in a ballad or two. Altogether we had a merry party with plenty to eat and drink. I laid off the drink because I developed a rotten headache. At the first stop GBN went all the way to the last car to get me some aspirin, and had to stay there until the next halt, as the train went right on again. That fixed me up in no time. None of us had any idea as to our destination, Paris, Reims, and Chateau Thierry being the favorite guesses. We made remarkably good time, for a military train, through beautiful country, rich fields brilliant with poppies, and roses everywhere. We all slept a little during the night, but not much. Saw some huge camouflaged railway guns, one the "Elsie Janis"[2], and two German prisoner camps. These, and the battered condition and "abris" at the Nancy station were the only suggestion of war we encountered. Our route lay through Nancy, Toul, Neufchateau, Gondrecourt, and Bar-le-Duc to Vitry-la-Ville, where we disentrained at eleven this morning. Some of the officers, anticipating a longer trip, were unable to hike out with us at noon. Bill arrived on the baggage wagon. Tim succumbed on the road and had to be left in a cow barn. Brad, supported on either side, managed to keep up with us. We came through a lovely "pays" (country), neat villages, white houses covered with roses, and crimson poppies everywhere, trees, green and cool, and the sky, blue, but the sun was fearfully hot. Aulnay-l'Aitre is a gem, scrupulously clean and attractive. Captain Hupp and I share a pleasant little room, and Tim and Jimmy next to us. Across the street we've found an excellent place for our "popote." Battalion HQ is billeted in the chateau, which is dignified, but not pretentious. The parc however is lovely. This is the sort of rural community I used to visualize when I first read stories of France, so entirely different from the casual filth of Lorraine. Took a ride on the company bicycle this evening over to the next town. A lot of second-class mail in, all the books and magazines that have been sent me since Christmas came in a bunch.

On June 24th I was presented in the morning to the Marquise de Lasseville, who is the chateaulaine of the chateau. She is very agreeable and talked with me for half an hour. She was born in New Orleans of a noble family, and is about seventy, I think, and says she hasn't spoken English in forty years. She invited me to come in the parc whenever I feel like it. I took a bicycle ride through Coulvagney and St. Amand where I got weighed at the infirmary, 157 pounds with my clothes on.

The next day saw marvelous weather. Spent most of the day in the parc reading. Have at last finished *The Brothers Karamazov*, a powerful book, but even more depressing than *Fathers and Sons*. The marquis appeared as I put it down, and said in his opinion *La Vie Parisienne*[3] was better literature for soldiers than Dostoevsky, and I agree with him. He is very proud of his estate, and took me all over the place. The chateau is early Louis XIV. Their family name is Le Clere. Madame joined us after a while and we chatted for about an hour. He speaks no English. We had a regular meal tonight, no special occasion; fried chicken, cream gravy, new potatoes, asparagus, hot biscuits, salad, pie, and champagne. Our new cook, Happy Roberts (Cook Harry E.), is trying to make an impression, and he has succeeded all right. GBN, Teddy, Wally and I went out for a long walk this evening. L Company is all wrought up over Powell's return. They thought they had gotten rid of him for good. On the road we met Wally's uncle, who was coming over from a nearby town to see him. He is in the YMCA, but we had no idea where he was and was surprised and delighted.

Beautiful weather continues on the 26th. Teddy and I went up over the hill where we got a wonderful view of the Marne valley, miles of it. We studied the new drill formations together for a while and then walked over to an artillery range a couple of miles away. Then I took a bike and rode into La Chaussee, all before lunch. Followed that by a couple of rubbers of bridge with GBN, Teddy and Jerry. At four we had battalion officers meeting in the chateau parc, out on a wide lawn, between avenues of immense trees. Still feeling energetic I rode to Coulvagny and back to the chateau, where I met the de Lessévilles. Tucker joined us for a walk to the waterfall where we took pictures of each other (his Kodak, my films have given out). The marquis feels rather pessimistic as to the outcome of the war, and fears the next attack will come on Chalons, where they have a town house. If the Germans do break through, Madame will stay in the chateau with the daughter, who is "enceinte" (pregnant). In the evening I reformed the squads in my platoon according to new regulations. I was almost asleep when Farley staggered in, stewed to the gills. Despite his name he is a staunch mason. This evening he got it in his head that the Catholics were trying to assassinate him, and came to Captain Hupp, a brother mason for aid. But Hupp has fled, and Max is now snoring, and I'm thoroughly awake.

Our rest is over, and we can't complain. All are up at five at reveille on June 27th. Drilled from seven to one on new extended order formations, and all went smoothly. After lunch took a long ride out towards Vitry-La-Ville through La Chaussee, Orney and Pogny, and another after dinner to Coulagny. I'm getting all the exercise I need. The mail came in at 10 P.M. The first letter I opened was a cheerful one from Spence. The next from my mother telling me of his death in an airplane accident on the very day his letter to me was mailed.

6. Rest

My birthday on June 28th was uneventful, for I told no one of it, but we did have an unusually fine dinner. The marquis has invited me to dine with them tomorrow evening, but already rumors of a move are afloat, so I probably won't be able to make it. On that account GBN and I gave up a trip to Vitry-le-François, and I have spent the afternoon writing letters and sleeping instead. I try not to think of Spence, but every time I set my mind on any thing, it wanders back to him in spite of me.

Courtisols

Just before dark the order to prepare to move immediately arrived. The expected confusion and scurry to get equipment, kitchens, records, etc., ready. Also a great deal of speculation as to our destination and sudden move. One rumor had it that we were to return to Badonviller to recover our lines, which the Boche had been holding since a successful raid on the 77th the other day. Left Aulnay at 10:15 P.M. and marched, and marched, and marched. I began to think we'd never stop, and in order to prevent any of my men from falling out, I carried at least one pack, in addition to my own bag, all the way. We entered Courtisols at a quarter of six, a thoroughly tired, and foot sore aggregation. Bentz, who had ridden ahead in the Colonel's car, threw roses at the column as we came into the village. Gallic theatricism, but if the men had noticed the flowers falling at their feet, they were too weary even to laugh. I imagine we made 35 kilometers. No sleep for over twenty-six hours.

Later, I was writing while Tim and I were waiting for breakfast (we are billeted together), but I fell asleep before Madame brought it in. We got up to eat, however, and then to bed until five o'clock. Have found our popote at Brad's billet very satisfactory. After we filled up at the kitchen, Jimmy, Tim and I walked over to the next village, L'Epine, to view closer the church we can see from there. It is an imposing structure contrasting strangely with the plain little homes huddled about it. It is really quite lovely, delicate carving, graceful pinnacles, and gargoyles galore. The only criticism I can find is perhaps it is a bit too "fleuri." It was built in the latter half of the fifteenth century to commemorate the miraculous finding of a statue of the virgin and child which is preciously guarded inside. We expected to leave Cortisols tonight, but now it looks as if we might stay on some time. Some Italians here, and I saw some Arabs in L'Epine. We are the first Americans in this region. Courtisols is about seven or eight kilometers from Chalons-sur-Marne.

A Rainbow Division Lieutenant in France

Courtisols Ouest, Marne, 24, Rue des Petits Ayeux

June 30th and Tim and I had a hot bath here in our own room, and then joined Bill and Jimmy to go over to L'Epine, only a kilometer for church. There were more Americans than French in the congregation, and the priest made a most eloquent extempore address on the American ideal and war efforts. He said that the American success in blocking the Boche at Chateau Thierry had heartened the whole of France. Today I got a letter from Mac's mother. She is with the YMCA at Bordeaux, and wants to get with our regiment. Mary also sent a good-sized birthday check. Had a look at the men's reserve rations before lunch, and discovered that most of them had eaten theirs up. For this, the entire company, including officers, was confined to quarters, very much to our disgust, as it was a magnificent day. We got off after supper. Tim and I wrote letters and talked all afternoon in the little summerhouse. He's an awfully likable sort. He said he'd always felt uncomfortable about the way he behaved at my promotion. The chaplain had some sort of revival service out in the open this evening, and after much persuasion, four penitents "got religion." The whole performance made me sick.

On July 1st our new schedule begins again, up at five and drill at seven. The entire regiment marched to a field several kilometers away, halting twice en route on account of swooping Boche planes. Having arrived, Major Brewer assembled the officers of the Third Battalion and told us the maneuver we were about to go through was in reality a rehearsal for a show the Rainbow is to put on in conjunction with two French divisions. I found out from Tucker, who gets all the inside dope, that it is to take place near Olizy, southwest of Reims. It is to be a really important operation, and our brigade has the hardest job, to take a high, well-organized hill, and to consolidate the captured positions. Went through the maneuver several times. Stopped for lunch which was brought out from Courtisols and which we ate in the pinewoods. Back in town by 4:30, which gave GBN and me, time to bicycle to Chalons. Shops practically denuded as the city is frequently bombed, and I couldn't find anything suitable to send Mother for her birthday. Loaded op on fruit and vegetables for our mess, instead. My landlady gave me a short history of Courtisols this evening. It is of Celtic origin, very old, and the local patois and customs of this one village have persisted unaffected by surrounding changes.

Off to maneuver on same problem the morning of the 2nd. Several generals and French staff officers viewed the performance with evident satisfaction. Stiff resistance anticipated. A Boche plane brought down some distance away

6. Rest

as we were marching out. Came back to tour at noon, and took a twelve kilometer jaunt to Somme-Vesle with Tim. Five letters from home tonight.

On July 3rd we rehearsed attack again, but came in an hour earlier as the officers were to attend a demonstration of the use of tanks in infantry advance over at Chalons, the ones that were to support us. However it was called off, and we hear our entire show has been cancelled. The French have got wind of an imminent Boche attack on this front, and that the enemy is amassing troops right behind our objective. So instead of attacking we are going in as reserve for the French 21st Army Corps. We wrote letters, took a bath and a nap in the afternoon. Feel first rate.

Camp de Vautivet, near Suippes

Capt. Hupp was feeling under the weather last evening, so Marshall and I went to cheer him a bit. He perked up immediately and sent Frankie out for champagne. But before we had a chance to enjoy ourselves in came an order to leave instantly. That was at ten o'clock, and all the men were asleep, except those who had sneaked out of town and who we were missing when we left shortly after twelve. A miserable night, black as pitch, and a cold, steady drizzle. It was almost impossible to see one's file leader, and the column moved along like an accordion. We landed in this camp about seven the morning of July 4th. There is only one barrack for the company, so my platoon is out under the trees in their pup tents. We five (Capt. Hupp has gone to the hospital) slept in the tiny gas chamber and I got in a five-hour snooze. We don't move up to our positions until after dark. It is rumored that we're to be subsisted on French rations as we are far away from any American base of supply. "Bidons," pans, and other French equipment have been distributed among the men.

7

Back Up

Bois de la Cote

July 5th and here we are in the woods in a reserve position behind Souain about six kilometers to the north of Suippes. It was from here that the French launched their disastrous offensive in 1915. We are nearly five kilometers from the first line and have our own trench system with an excellent field of fire. The attack is expected any time within the next three days. It is reported that they have massed twenty divisions on this corps front. They'll have one fine time getting through as it is well organized in depth and there is a tremendous concentration of artillery to support the 21st French Army Corps (the corps d'elite) with whom we're now serving. The area around us is bristling with guns of every caliber and the terrain honeycombed by a labyrinth of trenches hacked out of the solid chalk, which from our position shows up distinctly. We left Suippes about nine last night, and though we had a short hike, there was some hitch in the arrangements. We didn't get settled in our proper place until midnight. The company had to sleep out in the open. There was a good elephant iron shelter for the officers, but the baggage wagons weren't allowed to come up, and we had no bedding rolls. So I slept out in the open between Sgts. Farley and Woods, two blankets for the three of us. Aside from the fact I nearly froze to death, and woke stiff as a board, I passed a comfortable night. Up at five and spent two hours with Jimmy looking over our positions. As it is absolutely necessary to keep the Boche ignorant of the presence of reserves, we have to be careful about exposing ourselves. The country is very uninteresting, all chalk and scrub pines, which afford little cover. So we have to camouflage all the tents. There is a battery of 105s, not a hundred yards away, and another of 75s right behind us. To the front there is still more artillery, and heavier guns to the rear. Considerable

7. Back Up

aerial activity this morning. I think the French brought down a Boche, but I didn't see him land. Warned in the afternoon of a gas attack, which didn't materialize. Our baggage has come up now, and all of us, Jimmy, Brad, Bill, Tim and I are housed in our rainproof shelter. Happy has established our popote in an adjoining shack and all is very good.

At 12:30 the morning of the 6th we were ordered to stand-to in our combat positions. The French had made a raid somewhere in the neighborhood and learned from their prisoners something was up. Anyhow we were to be on the alert at 4:15. Our guns, and we must have a million of them, opened up on the Germans, and kept a drumfire until broad daylight. In the meantime we all waited calmly enough, and got as cold as possible, without actually freezing. The men were tired to begin with, as most of them had already been working on an engineering detail for several hours, when we were alerted. Due to some mix up, we were made to stand-to until seven, hours after any probability of an

American doughboys loading heavy artillery. Donovan Collection, United States Army Heritage and Education Center, Carlisle, Pennsylvania.

attack. Alabama, with whom we connect up on the left, withdrew at dawn. We slept all morning and had dinner served us in bed at one thirty. Eight letters from the states. Went over the M and L sectors, which adjoins ours to the left, in that order. I Company is behind us. I then went back to Battalion Headquarters to watch a battery of French 155 howitzers in action. I stayed there for supper. I think the French are really anxious for the Boche to start something, for they've never been so well prepared for an attack, and everyone is confident of walloping them. Running through our camp, parallel with the front, is the old Chaussee Romaine, the main highway that the Romans constructed between Reims and Verdun.

There was heavy fire from our side all night. It is a lazy morning on the 7th. Wrote a letter or two and censored as many as a hundred. One man, in describing this particular region to his family said, "The meanest trick the allies could play on the Boche would be to hand it over to them." Officers meeting at 7:30, after which I played the victrola an hour. Setz is jubilant for he is to go back to the states as an instructor, expects his order tomorrow. Supposedly an officer is to go every week for the next four months. Looks as if we might get out of here.

Heavy artillery fire again last night. The Boche return scarcely a shot. It may that they don't want to give away their battery positions, but they're taking an awful lot of punishment. Their planes, too, are keeping out of sight. Another idle day. Our artillery put on a show from four until six this evening, intense fire. I watched it from an O.P. in a tree on top of the hill. The French first line comes in for a retaliatory blowing up. Tommy came back from the hospital today, and he and Percy have been spending the evening with us.

On July 9th Bill and I walked over to what was once the village of Souain, two kilometers to the east of us. The destruction is complete. No two walls of the same house standing, and nothing but the outline of the 13th century church. The poppies grow in profusion all over the trenches and make a brilliant contrast to the glaring white of the chalk. This entire section is nothing but a network of trenches for miles and miles. The Germans hold the more commanding positions, except up towards Reims, where the Montagne de Reims dominates the whole front. It is shelled almost continuously, and we can see the spurts of dust and smoke as the shells explode. The atmosphere is very clear, and the visibility remarkably good. One of our own six inch shells burst prematurely overhead this morning. Fragments flew all about, but no one was hit. Meeting at Battalion HQ this evening. It rained and I got soaked on the way back. I stopped at L Company P.C. to say goodbye to Setz, who has just left, lucky devil.

7. Back Up

Up early the next day, and took two platoons back to bathe. Haven't done anything else today except to read *La Tentation de St. Antoine* which Bob sent me from Paris. I've had enough of this indolent life and will be glad when we get to doing something.

Exceptionally heavy artillery fire in the night and the French pulled off their daily coup de main at 11 P.M. They've made a raid somewhere on this corps front every night for the past two weeks. The Major bawled us out the morning of the 11th for sitting around doing nothing. I think he did it on general principles, for I don't know what there is to do other than sit down and await events. We certainly can't drill. Tim and I walked over to see a plane that came down in the rear of the Alabama line yesterday. We thought it had been shot down, but it appeared undamaged, so it must have been engine trouble. Later, a solution for our inaction has been evolved. We are to dig C.T.s. So this afternoon the men have been hacking away at the stubborn chalk. Teddy and Tucker were promoted to first lieutenants today and Captain Hupp has arrived from the hospital.

On July 12th in addition to the usual artillery rumpus we had a gas alert at 2 A.M. None near us, however. Worked on C.T. all day and spent evening with L Company bunch. An entertaining French artillery lieutenant there. His chief ambition is to acquire a comprehensive vocabulary of American slang. Raining, but we're dry here.

On the 13th the French directly in front of us made a coup de main at 2 A.M. We were in the midst of the 126 guns (so an artillery officer told us) that joined in the barrage and the racket was considerable. Sleep was out of the question, so I went to the edge of the woods to watch the front. It was livid with star shells and signal rockets, a really beautiful sight. Sat around all morning. Had a haircut and a shave (George Moyer, coiffeur). The lieutenant commanding the 75 battery behind us has invited us for dejeuner tomorrow. We started a poker game this evening, but the arrival of the mail broke it up. Philip wants to go on leave with me and will go anywhere I suggest. I've written him that we don't know what that word means up here.

Sunday

Alerted at eleven last night, just as I finished writing. The attack was looked for at midnight. Routed out our platoon and made them dress, but we didn't have to stand-to. We lay down until something should happen, and when I came to, it was already daylight, and yet no attack. No work today in honor of the French Fete Nationale. Had a delightful time at lunch with six French artillery officers. They are a jovial crew. We avoided all war talk, and enjoyed ourselves.

The long waited for offensive broke the morning of July 15th, and we've had a taste of real warfare. At 11:45 last night, when I was on my way with a detail to stock up at the ammunition dump, I intercepted a message that the Boche bombardment would open at twelve. Before we got back our own artillery had let loose with a tremendous roar. It seemed as though every gun had fired at the same instant, and in a second the sky was lit with gun flashes and bursting shells. I'd never conceived of such a thunder of sound. The reports from the nearby batteries were deafening, but we could still distinguish the steady rumble of the heavier pieces to the rear, and the shriek and whistle of the big shells as they went over in a solid stream. But all this was dwarfed by the fury of the Boche bombardment that commenced fifteen minutes later. They first drenched the area with gas, so impeded by masks, there was great difficulty and confusion in getting the company into the dug out. While checking up my men I heard that Beatty had been hit and was lying out on the road where he had attempted to throw across a barricade. There was nothing to do but go out for him. I was too scared to remember much, but shells were bursting all about. I was knocked down once. I couldn't find a trace of Beatty, and found out on my return to the dugout that Fido Simpson had brought his body in. He was killed instantly, as was Killian (Pvt. Albert S.) who didn't have time to get out of bed. Heiden (Pvt. Lawrence E.) lost several fingers but managed to help bring in Glines (Pvt. John A.) who was badly wounded in the chest. Carrol Nelson was wounded too and was the first one to volunteer to go out after Beatty. In a short while the dug out became so foul that the candles went out, and a match would flicker for only a moment. We had to keep the curtains down for account of the gas. Glines, who was lying in the upper gallery, had a difficult time in breathing and loss of blood made him so thirsty that he drank up every bit of my water. George Kalles was badly wounded in the side and had an arm broken. He sent for me to say goodbye and to give me Susie. He was adjusting her mask when he was hit. Pace, Johnson, Douglas (Sgt. Grover C.) and others were wounded. We had a dressing station at the far end of the upper gallery, open on one side, and hardly even splinter proof. Here we fixed up the wounded as best we could. At six o'clock we got word that the Boche had broken through, were advancing rapidly, and we were immediately ordered to combat positions. In a way it was a relief, for the dugout was impossible, but on the way out, over the open, we had four or five more casualties. Bill and Brad are holding our front line, Tim

7. Back Up

and I directly behind. However all my automatic teams are up front. I spent some time there, and wished I hadn't gone. The bombardment continued until nine o'clock, just nine hours of it.

Many of the guns around us have been put out of business, and all the ammunition dumps blown up. Practically every one of the tents was struck. Shortly after one o'clock I saw Lt. de Champigney, who was my host at lunch yesterday, come in on a stretcher with both legs blown off. A large group of Boche planes (I counted over thirty) flew very low over our lines machine gunning our men in the open trenches. We find now that the Boche did not break through. The French abandoned their first positions as planned, and are holding everywhere. Four infantry battalions from our own division are up with them. It's now 12:30 and I'm writing while all this is fresh in my mind, in a dugout where I have part of my platoon. The spirit of the men is marvelous. They're laughing and joking as if we were at a picnic. No news from the rest of the outfit, except that Tommy and John Currie have been wounded and that I Company has been badly hit. The casualties in our own company are five killed, Trimble Curry (Pvt. Trimble C.), Jack Short (Pvt. John) and Louis O'Dell (Pvt. Louis E.) struck by shells this morning and about twenty seven wounded (includes seven gassed). Expect the bombardment to resume soon.

7:40 P.M.

We had several hours' respite during which the men went out to gather up their equipment. Our shelter wasn't hit and our impediment is intact. The Boche are at it again, began about six, and are sending over some big ones that shake the dugout as if it were made of cardboard. But for the first time since I've been under fire, I feel really safe, for this goes down thirty feet in the solid chalk, and it would take a good sized shell to demolish it. The enemy planes have been very active all day. They go around in groups of six, except the large group, which we hear is Richthofen's famous circus. The French aviators are courageous enough. I have seen plenty today to prove that. But they are so few and fight against certain death. I got two hours sleep this afternoon. Bread, butter, and good hot coffee came up from the kitchen.

On July 16th the news is very good. The Boche have made practically no gain from Chateau Thierry to the Foret d'Argonne, and their "Friedensturm" has been an absolute failure. We heard that an entire division opposite was so badly shot up by our unexpected bombardment that it had to be replaced before the zero hour. Their casualties must have been enormous, ours were bad enough, and the French lost heavily. Three divisions were employed in four attacks directly in front of us. The shelling continues and the numerous Boche planes are diligent. Schuster and I were fired at by a flock of 17 or 18 while we were alone in the open C.T., very annoying. Last night a shell got four or five litter bearers. Killed Arthur Peach (Pvt. Arthur), blew off Fulghum's legs, tore the calf off Rhodes' leg, (Pvt. Orien H.) and wounded King (Pvt. William J.) in the stomach. Dutch (Fulghum) displayed the greatest grit during the dressing of his wounds, giving us directions and urging us to be cool. Neither he nor King can live. Casualties in K now, 6 dead, 31 wounded, and 7 gassed. We all got some gas. My throat is quite hoarse from it. The other companies have lost in about the same proportions.

Up all night. Our artillery kept up a violent fire to which the Boche replied in like degree. The 17th has been comparatively peaceful. The kitchens have been withdrawn ten kilometers, so our meals are few and far between. We are on the wrong side of the wind, and the odor from three hundred dead horses, all gassed in the artillery park that is being gently wafted in our direction is not refreshing. Policed dugout and ground around the post this morning.

Slept seven hours last night. The next day I shaved and cleaned up in general. Fine day. I tried sitting out under a tree to enjoy the sunlight, but the shower of anti-aircraft shrapnel drove us under cover. Now it's raining.

Ordered to move out at eleven o'clock last night, totally unexpected. In the dark no one could find his equipment and the confusion would be hard to equal. At the last moment we had to lug all the ammunition back to the dump, half a kilometer away. Then just as we were to march out, the Major told me to stay behind to look after the salvage. It was a rather vague order, but I discovered that three trucks would soon arrive to cart it off. I waited with the detail for the trucks to appear, and as the French started a lively barrage, I lay down on a board with a piece of canvas as cover, for a little sleep. I got up at eight, policed the area and separated the salvage, a mean job. Jimmy Bonham (Cpt. James C., Rgt. HQ), who has been left to collect and sort the ammunition, and I commiserated together. Our two details are the only Americans left here, and we don't know where the trucks are supposed to come from, or where the outfit has gone. We have nothing to eat, and it looks like we might stick here until the end of the war.

Camp de la Noblette

The trucks finally put in an appearance at eight last evening, and we had a trip at ease to this camp, between La Cheppe and Chalons. A number of

7. Back Up

bombing planes were hovering over La Cheppe as we came through, and we missed five or six bombs just as we cleared it. The anti-aircraft guns at Chalons put up a lively barrage around the city, so the Boche must have been attempting to get in there. Couldn't locate the officers (it was nearly midnight), so I unrolled my bedding roll where I found it, in a room with the Second platoon sergeants, and off to sleep. We are camped on the locale of Attila's defeat and my first duty this morning was to settle a dispute as to date of the battle. I decided in favor of 451, which sounds right. Eight letters in the morning's mail, which I've had all day (July 20th) to answer. I hear that Lts. Veasey (Edward J., F) and Hunting (Warren B., D) were killed back at Div. HQ on the 15th. Ihrie was wounded too. We think our present destination is Soissons.

On the 21st I walked over through Cuperly with Heath Noble to take a look at a Boche plane that was brought down the other day. It was nearly stripped by souvenir hunters. This afternoon, GBN and I wandered off in the other direction. The regiment moves tonight for Courtisols.

Courtisols Est., Marne

I drew eight replacements last night from Indiana and Alabama, a good-looking bunch. Left camp at 9:30, a gorgeous moonlit night. About eleven a squadron of bombing plane overtook us, and we wondered why the Major didn't halt the column, for we undoubtedly showed up very clearly on the white road. I was walking at the rear of the company with Capt. Hupp and Hull. Signals were going up on all sides of us, and I remarked they must be pretty close. Hull said "There's one right over us," and it was so low we could make out the pilot. At that moment we heard a whish and three tremendous explosions as he dropped the bombs in succession. Fortunately his aim was bad, and they landed in a field fifty yards away, abreast of I Company. No one was wounded, but it gave us a jolt. The men didn't wait for orders to fall out, they just scattered. A mule team with a heavy combat wagon at the rear of the column stampeded, and rushed up the road like mad, increasing the general confusion and nearly killing a number in its path. By that time bombs were dropping on Chalons, signals going up everywhere and anti-aircraft guns booming, and a good time was had by all. While the planes were still humming around us, we started out again in columns of squads. We fell out once more into a wheat field when they buzzed too close. We came through L'Epine to Courtisols Oueste and found our old billets had been grabbed by the Second Brigade, so we had to trudge

Trench scene of a dug-out splinter-proof shelter. Donovan Collection, United States Army Heritage and Education Center, Carlisle, Pennsylvania.

7. Back Up

on four kilometers further, and just as we drew in here three bombs fell on the other end of town. I was glad to fall into bed at 3 A.M. and slept all morning. I have a comfortable billet with a motherly old woman whose every other word is "mon pauvre garcon," and who over charged outrageously for the dinner she cooked for us officers. Rode over to Courtisols Ouest to call on my former hosts. They are all cheered by the failure of the Boche offensive and the great success of the allied attack, which started on the 18th. Captain Hupp and Twining stayed in my room till eleven, talking of one thing and another.

On the train

Left Courtisols at 3 A.M. on July 23rd and marched in a drenching rain through L'Epine to Chalons, arriving there about six as all the people were returning home from the municipal wine cellars where practically the entire population has slept since the Boche started to bomb the city every night. It was an odd procession for they carried their bedding and valuables in whatever vehicle was available, baby carriages, hand drawn wagons, etc. We entrained at Coolus, a small place five kilometers beyond, at eight o'clock. Have been having a comfortable trip and in with L Company. Have passed through a rich agricultural district, which has evoked favorable comments from our many farmer representatives. While we were halted at Esternay, two trains of wounded Britishers from the Reims front, all stretcher cases, passed through. We went within four kilometers of Paris, close enough to see the Tour Eiffel and then turned off in the other direction towards Chateau Thierry. Demonstrative crowds along the way and on the bridges cheered and waved flags as we went by. The Americans seem to be very popular right now, and maybe we need cheering.

Jaignes, Seine-et-Marne

The next day we detrained shortly after three in the morning at Trilport, a small place just the other side of Meaux. It took till four to unload our combat weapons, baggage and kitchens, and to gather the outfit together. Then with the promise of a short march we set out gaily on what proved to be a three hour's hard march up hill and down dale to Jaignes, a delightful village, set way up on a hill above the Marne. I have drawn the prize billet of all this time, a well-furnished room overlooking a pretty garden surrounded by feathery trees. We thought we were going to be here at least twenty four hours, and although I've been sleepy and tired all day (we got little sleep on the train) I thought I'd wait until tonight for a good long snooze. Now I wish I had taken advantage of the inviting bed for I've just been told that we leave tonight. However I've had a good bath, and have changed my clothes. Later we had a sumptuous dinner chez Capt. Hupp, roast duck, fresh vegetables, and champagne. We're all packed up, and waiting for the trucks.

Foret de Fere, Aisne

Left Jaignes at midnight in a French camion train driven by colonials, Anamese, I think. One particular truck had seats, and as there were only six of us, five officers and Patton the Y man, we had a really comfortable trip and managed to sleep a bit en route. I woke up as we were going through Chateau Thierry, but it was too dark to see much. At six on the morning of July 25th we were dumped out in the road beyond Epieds, which was captured yesterday by the 26th Division. Shells were dropping in a field a few hundred yards away, several airplane fights were in progress, and the sky spotted with bursts of anti-aircraft shrapnel. In front of us was an over turned German gun of large caliber, and some dead bodies, and in the distance puffs of smoke and shots of flame from exploding shells. It looked like an exaggerated chromo of a civil war battle. The 26th Division, which we are to relieve, has had heavy losses. We came through a wheat field strewn with the bodies of the 101st Infantry. They were mowed down by machine gun fire and there hasn't yet been time to bury them. From there we hiked into these woods, encountering more bodies; mostly Boche, captured field pieces and all manners of equipment. We have been waiting here all day. The First Battalion goes into action tonight. Wonder what it will be like.

Last night after we had all lain down in a bunch to sleep, the Boche began to search with good-sized shells for a battery in the neighborhood. They were uncomfortably close to begin with, and kept gradually edging closer and closer until its very last one struck a tree about twenty feet up, right in the center of a score of us. Jimmy and I were sleeping together or trying to. The concussion knocked the breath out of us, and a shower of fragments whistled all around. One hit Jimmy on the wrist, the handle of my pistol was sliced off, my helmet cut in two, my canteen knocked to pieces, and I got a scratch on the forehead. But Allen Hanft (Pvt.) sleeping on the other side of Hupp within arms reach of us was instantly killed, as was Leo Kenyon (Pvt. Leo N.), directly across, and

7. Back Up

Barr (Pvt. Chauncey W.), Sutton (Cpl. William M.) and Graham (Pvt. John B.) (joined July 18). Seven others were wounded, Livingston (Pvt. John B.) seriously. After the wounded had been taken care of, and the dead moved, we transferred our position across the road. Having nothing better to do we employed ourselves in making splinter proof shelters. When Jimmy and I had just completed ours we were ordered to move. It was then raining so no Boche planes to observe our movements. We advanced, a file on each side, up the road. Every one rather sober, not knowing what to expect. Captain Hupp was in a bad way, having been completely unnerved and shaken by the explosion last night. When we left the road for the woods again we walked into a checkerboard fire of 6 inch pieces. The shells created great havoc with the trees and made it uncomfortable for us all. I was leading our company when one burst to our right killing an I or L company man directly in front of us and wounding Glen Schuster, my one remaining runner, behind me. We continued to advance however, meeting wounded of our Second Battalion on their way to the rear. We soon left the shelled area but the companies further back, especially the Machine Gun Company was hard hit. Three or four First Platoon were shell-shocked but are staying on with us. We halted a kilometer further on, within supporting distance of the Second Battalion, which was meeting with stiff opposition ahead. We have taken up positions along an old ditch and are prepared for the night. Captain Hupp, still very nervous, has just gone over the plans with us. Detail from the kitchen brought up bread, molasses and coffee.

Bunked with Sergeant Woods. It rained and our narrow ditch soon filled with water, and we got soaked through long before morning. At daybreak on the 27th we advanced to the edge of the forest, and about noon moved over to the right to wait for the First Battalion to move out. French cavalry groups are reconnoitering the area ahead, a number of our 2nd Battalion dead lying near us, and the men haven't been exactly cheered by the accounts that the surviving members of the battalion have given them. The Croix Rouge farm, where they lost so many, is a couple of hundred yards to the left front of us. Major Brewer is going up and down the line singing "Old soldiers never die" though I'm sure he doesn't feel any too lightheaded himself.

When the First Battalion cleared us yesterday we set out in columns of twos along the woods, much German ammunition, neatly piled there. Whether orders were changed or whether it was due to the fact that Worthington didn't know what he was about, we went ahead of the First Battalion and formed into combat groups as soon as we struck the open. We had no sooner appeared than a battery on the heights of the other side of the Ourcq let loose on us. Our

A Rainbow Division Lieutenant in France

Captured Germans (seated in front) from the battle of Chateau Thierry and the Ourcq River. Donovan Collection, United States Army Heritage and Education Center, Carlisle, Pennsylvania.

company was in the lead, and the first shell lit into the Fourth Platoon, got ten men. We could see the guns flash, and after that first shell, every one dropped flat as soon as the gun fired, and then after the shell exploded went on. It was nerve-wracking business, as they all fell right among us, but no one broke the formation, a wonderful exhibition of discipline. Had many casualties at this time, Wallace (Pvt. Floyd E.), of the first, was badly wounded, and Vinton Bradshaw, his corporal, went to his aid. The next shell killed them both. Lost an exceptionally fine man in Bradshaw. We soon hit a patch of woods and were safe for a while. Then we came into the open again and advanced though shell and machine gun fire to a wheat field within a few hundred yards of the Ourcq. A number of my men were hit here, Simerman, Hagerman, Hamilton, Rennie Moore, among them. Ahead of us near the bridge the shelling was intense. We had no artillery support there, or until after we had been in position some time today. We finally got control of the bridge, and as the Major was about to order the advance (we had fixed bayonets), the outfit on our left (Major Donovan's Battalion of the 165th) withdrew, and, so, with our flank exposed, we, too,

7. Back Up

were forced to retire. Can't explain their withdrawal, as we were getting as much punishment as they. The Boche accompanied our retirement to the reverse slope of the rise, about five hundred yards to the rear, with a well-directed shower of gas and high explosives. It was getting dark and we commenced to dig in. At this point Capt. Hupp and Marshall went to the rear, gassed. Major Worthington, exhausted and terrified, appeared from somewhere, and Major Brewer, who had been yelling at me to get the company together, although there were two officers senior to me, now ordered me to dig a hole for Worthington. I let Worthington hunt a hole for himself. And Woods, Brown, and I chose a big one, a 240, in which to spend the night. Shells whistled and dropped around us continuously and I had a good many wounded to attend to. It was truly a dreadful night. Means (Pvt. Orville B.) was killed by a direct hit that blew him out of his hole, and badly wounded Bentley (Pvt. James A.) and Barr (Pvt. Carl H.) (two of the replacements I got last week) who were in with him. He let out the most horrible shrieks and kept calling for a stretcher-bearer. But he died before I could do anything for him. We carried Bentley and Barr, both very husky, to the bottom of a hill near a brook to dress their wounds. They were evidently in great pain but never let out a whimper. About three this morning Major Brewer got orders from General Brown to cross the Ourcq at dawn of July 28th and capture the opposite heights. George Woodard heard the message in transmission and immediately developed such an attack of cramps that he declared he couldn't move. But I made him come along and later saw him dodge a shell in a most agile fashion. Bradley went ahead with a detachment to secure the bridge and then we advanced towards the river, screened by a heavy fog. K was on the extreme right with L to our left. After crossing the river we fixed bayonets and deployed into skirmish line. When the fog lifted we encountered severe machine gun fire and then shelling. Tom veered off to the left with his platoon and was shot in the abdomen. As we advanced a man fell at every rush, Moon (Pvt. Albert J.), Art Bray (Pvt. Arthur E.), Ed Williams, Stinson, Mintzer, Greenway (Sgt. Clyde W.) and Flannigan added to the casualties of my platoon. There isn't much left of it now. We halted and re-organized on a line running from the mill (Moulin de Caranda) up over the lower part of Hill 212. Flannigan was brought in a little while ago, so weak from loss of blood I'm afraid he'll die. Every time we send out a stretcher, the Boche follows it up with a 77, which he is using solely for sniping. We are holding a wide sector thinly. Jimmy and Brad have the remnants of the 1st and 4th Platoons behind a fairly high bank to the left, and Bill and I along a row of trees and bushes on the edge of a brook. When I read "On a bank by the Ourcq," I didn't think I'd be contem-

A Rainbow Division Lieutenant in France

Soldiers of Company C, who captured the enemy at the battle near the Ourcq. Donovan Collection, United States Army Heritage and Education Center, Carlisle, Pennsylvania.

plating it for the first time, sitting in a wheel barrow, minus its wheel, stuck in the mud of one of its tributaries. But that's where I've been sitting for the past hour writing, and watching 150's explode in the swamp behind us. They send up great geysers of mud and make a lot of noise.

Some troops of the 110th infantry (28th Division) dug in behind us late yesterday afternoon, but pulled out during the night, and moved over some distance to our right. Saw a large number of Boches forming for a counter-attack on the high ground a kilometer in front of us but before they got started our artillery which is last in on the job, broke it up with some accurately placed shots, and they all scampered back for the woods. Have moved out to a German machine gun pit slightly in advance of our line, excellent observation on all sides. Woods is in here with me. The enemy has now trained an 88 on us and every now and then another man is wounded. There are only 75 effectives left in our company. But the 1st and 2nd Battalions have suffered more than we, only 120 men in the four companies of the first. It's July 29th and we've had no food since leaving the Foret de Fere, reserve rations gave out some time ago, and most of us are getting weak. The men look haggard and sunken eyed, just

7. Back Up

when we are most in need of dependable men. Sgts. Cruise (Eugene B.), Farley and Hull have been ordered back to school at Langres.

An 88 lighting entirely too close yesterday caused me to stop writing, and nothing much more happened, except such a kick about the food that we finally got some from the kitchen this afternoon, also some of the "sick" men who were back there. Up until today we've been getting machine gun fire from the church tower in Cierges, but our artillery has blown it up, Red Cross flag and all. I think the 28th Division captured the town today. I saw them make an attack yesterday and get driven back. Two men in Bill's platoon were wounded by an 88 that dropped on us. And Harker's arm was blown off at the shoulder (Pvt. John T.). At the present moment Woods and I are confined to our pit, for a Boche machine gun has our exact range, and every time we make a move, over comes a stream of bullets. We've busied ourselves digging in under the sides and ends, so we are now not only protected from shrapnel but can lie down as well.

Shelling, which I'm beginning to think will never end, keeps up again on the 31st and is gradually thinning our already depleted ranks. Many, too, have been made sick by drinking the only water available, right here from the brook, and heaven knows what's in the upper end of it. Fifty under Tush, who returned yesterday from the hospital, went to outpost Sergy last evening. Hear they met with hard luck. This morning a group of us were standing behind the bushes watching one of our planes, which was flying very low. But when it bore down on us with his machine guns wide open, we realized it was no ally, and dove for safety. He paid for his daring, for a number of our planes were in the air, and he was brought down a few minutes later north of Cierges. Later, at noon, I was sent for by Major Brewer. I reported, all prepared for some unpleasant mission, but instead I have been made adjutant to Col. Tinley for the period. He is in command of the troops in the field. Our P.C. is right in the front line, a hole dug in the bank of the Sergy road, near the base of Hill 212. We were shelled out at two o'clock. Mangled bodies minus heads and limbs still unburied in the field behind us. About three, troops of the 32nd Division appeared on the crest of the hill behind us where we had so many casualties, and we watched them as they walked into heavy shellfire. They advanced through us at an angle up over Hill 212 where the Boche opened up on him with everything he had, and cut them up terribly. We took turns widening and deepening our shelter, so that we now have a fairly habitable, light proof P.C. Percy tells me that Jerry claims to have been gassed and went back the first day, but they all think he is yellow and not gassed at all. Major Brewer came flying in late this afternoon. A shell just brushed by him so close he felt the rush of wind, and just dove in.

```
At P.C. Hill 212
31 July 18  4.45 p.m. (By JHT)
To C.O. 168th Infantry
Thirty second advance with same results. Shelling this position, shrapnel,
high explosive, and small amount gas. In another hour position will be
overcrowded with remnants of 42nd Div. and 32nd Div. making slaughter easy
for Boche.   Tinley


At Hill 212
5.25 p.m. 31 July 18
To. C.O. 168th Infantry
Maj. Matthews 125th just received word his Co. K Capt. has been hit, company
roughly handled and halted. C6.M 126 unable to move forward. M.G. nests
are still in Felger and Planchette. need artillery on same bad bad bad.
All our roads here congested, Boche planes directing H.E. fire on our
positions. No harm done us. We are comfortable, but congestion increases.
They could use sacrifice 75 possibly. Tinley


At Hill 212
5.35 31 July 18
To C.O. 168th Infantry
C.O. 3rd Bn. 126th just rec'd message from a Lt. of Co. M (MG?) they are
nearly all annihilated no ammunition. Capt of M Co. hit. said to have their
lines to edge of Bois Planchette possibly road 186(220) 213. casualties
very heavy. Our artillery apparently now operating from Courmont.
```

Communications from Hill 212 as the 3rd Battalion is holed up.

Hill 212

Excitement aplenty. Last night a Boche aviator flew up and down the line dropping large sized bombs, but did no damage, except to our nerves. After that a shell struck a German small arms ammunition dump ahead of us and it has been crackling away ever since. The 32nd Division made another forward move this morning (August 1), and wounded and prisoners have been coming back this way. I was called on to interview two machine gunners. They both wore Red Cross brassards (it appears they all do) and were too frightened to give any information, so the Major (of the 32nd) sent them on back. Shells continue to rain down on our position. I was knocked down by an 88 on my way to Major Stanley's P.C. It knocked me breathless and scared the wits out of me. And this afternoon another 88 exploded on the road in front of the ditch where Col. Tinley, a Colonel of the 32nd Division, and I were sitting. It was so close that it is a marvel we weren't all blown to pieces, but we were low, and the force of the explosion was away from us. Col. Tinley says it's the narrowest escape he's ever had, or heard of. In spite of this we are in comparative safety, for the slope of the hill protects us somewhat, behind us it's much worse. Saw a stretcher party hit as they were on their way to the first aid station with a "blesse" (wounded), all killed.

7. Back Up

Nesles

Advanced today, August 2, through Sergy stopping long enough to sample a case of excellent Tokay which Col. Bennet discovered and distributed and then on through Nesles to the Foret de Nesles. Met with only light shellfire en route. Ate lunch under a tree near the old Tour de Nesles. After the line was established came back with Col. Tinley to the village, which like Sergy, is mostly in ruins. We were left in peace, and it is about time as the regiment had 1,453 casualties, so far in this fight. The Boche are retreating so fast that we've practically lost contact with them but we will remain where we are for the night.

Foret de Fere

Back where we started from. The Fourth Division relieved us late last evening. I came ahead with two regimental runners. Had a long, muddy hike in the dark and got in several hours before the regiment. Captain Von Order (Paul I., Rgt. HQ) was waiting along the road. With him was a new officer, Lt. Doty (William D. Doty III), who has been assigned to K Company, and who piloted us to our proper area in the woods. We relieved the HQ kitchen of a generous helping of bread, butter, and molasses before we turned in. One of the runners, an F Company corporal, shared his blanket with me and we were soon asleep. Now that we're out of immediate danger, minor discomforts annoy us. There are dead horses and other evil smelling things about us, the flies are abominable, and cooties bothersome. No way to get rid of them. When I took my pants off (the first time in two weeks) I found my right leg clotted with blood from a small shrapnel wound, I don't even remember getting. It was already healed up, but I had it painted at the dispensary and am entitled to a wound stripe. Nothing to do today but rest. Our baggage is not to be found and I'm bunking with Woods and Krebs in their pup tent.

Sunday

Policed a portion of our battlefield today, up to the Ourcq. Looks decidedly different when no shells are flying about. The Boche have left numerous quantities of ammunition all over the place. Played the Major's victrola this evening. The lines are so far away that we get only a faint rumble of guns. The flies are almost unbearable. If we don't move out of here soon, we'll have trouble.

On August 5th we are just learning how badly we've been hit. In our Battalion, Heath Noble and Bernard Van't Hof have been killed, and today we got word that Tim has died of his wounds, Eric, Captain Dunn and GBN were wounded, and with Hupp, Lefferts, and Blake gassed, we are short of officers. But the 2nd Battalion is worse off than ours, and Brad has been transferred to F Company, and Teddy Jones to H. Rubel, a good officer, was killed early in the fight, and Douglas Greene (Lt. Douglas B., H) was sent back in dying condition. GBN was hit in the arm. Soon our outfit won't be recognizable. It will be difficult to replace the men we have lost. The weather has been disagreeable, and nearly all those left are sick, probably from the water. Mail today.

August 7th and it has been raining for three days. Still in the Foret de Fere. All anxious to leave and wondering why we are kept in this pestilential hole. The flies and odors are obnoxious. We'd like to know what's going to be done with us. There are rumors of our returning to the line.

8

Away

Verdilly, Aisne

On the tenth at last we have put the fly infested swamp behind us, and what a relief. Marched here via Beuvardes and Epieds and are to camp in the open.

Nothing but the occasional hum of a plane to disturb us last night. It was clear and quite cold, so I was glad to share Jake Schmidt's (Pvt. Jacob) and Eddie Bray's (Pvt. Edward C.) blankets and tent. Eddie was being my orderly. But the next day it was hot, and we had a hard march. Along the way French reservists were already harvesting the grain in the field that have been in German hands since early June. We came through Chateau Thierry. There are evidences of wanton destruction and thorough pillage, but isn't as badly shot up as I expected. But Vaux and Le Thiolet, two villages this side of it, are leveled, not a habitable place left. The civilians are returning to the countryside, many of them to a pile of ruins.

Coupru is dirty, battered and practically deserted. Bill, Tuck, Doty and I are billeted on the second floor of a building, which is at least rain proof, though there are no windows. In the absence of furniture, we have set up our cots. Took a fine hot bath in the shed this evening, changed all my clothes and feel like a million dollars.

Coupru

Had the first real sleep since we left the Camp de la Noblette. I am having my dirty clothes boiled, this being the twelfth. We move from here soon. Hurrah. Doty and I took a long walk over to Lucy-le-Bocage and Bouresches this afternoon. Caught a truck back as we went further than we intended. He's a mighty nice chap.

Coupru

The next day's program consisted of resting, reading, and writing letters. The 166th gave us a fine concert. Another 2nd Lt., Mohn (Robert D.), assigned to us today. First impression hardly favorable.

Sainte-Aulde, Seine-et-Marne

Set out from Coupru about noon, August 14th, and had a short hike, no more than 10 kilometers, and the country lovely all the way. This is a delightful spot, untouched by the war, perched up on a hillside overlooking the Marne and the magnificent valley beyond. Our house is the summer villa of a Parisian aristocrat, and while most of the furniture has been carted away, we are very comfortable. Jimmy and I are together, and Tush and Doty have the room next to us. This afternoon we four and Mohn went swimming in the river, which is only two hundred yards away, and had a great time. Sent a detail over to La Ferte-sous-Jouarre this evening for food. They brought back a quantity of fruit and fresh vegetables, and lots of wine. Spent the evening out on the balcony, writing letters and enjoying the scenery. It was unbelievably calm and peaceful until a nosy Boche plane came snooping around and stirred up every anti-aircraft battery in the vicinity. The moonlight is lovely, and I'd like to stay up longer, but we may move tomorrow. I am now second in command, and have had to relinquish my platoon to Mohn. I have had it eleven months. Tush takes the First, and Doty has Tim's.

Sainte-Aulde

Got up before reveille on the 15th and watched the sun rise from the balcony. The men enjoying a well earned rest in decent surroundings, no drill or details. I wandered about the village this morning inspecting billets, and ended up in the church, which is the most originally decorated edifice I've seen. Catholics so often ruin a lovely structure by sticking in a lot of junk. This church would be quaint in its simplicity, but for atrocious statues, bleeding hearts, banners, and walls and pillars plastered like a crazy quilt with odd bits

8. Away

of brilliant wallpaper. After lunch rode a horse with Tucker (now Battalion Adjutant) to La Ferte. Passed through Chamigney, and stopped to look at the chateau. La Ferte is a fine town, at present very much overrun by the Americans, temporarily lodged there. We did some shopping and had something to eat at the bakery. As we were mounting our horses, some one in a passing motor called out to me. It was Ray Thompson, who is an officer (1st Lt.) in a balloon company which he says has been with our division ever since we first went into line. Walt Reed is an officer in the same outfit. A number of our men have returned from the hospital, among them our cook, Happy Roberts, who was gassed in the Champagne. This evening Doty and I took another long walk. I think he is a fine fellow. He grows on one, was a Sigma Phi at Hobart, and like GBN, was married just before he sailed for this side. He came over with an ambulance company of the 27th Division, and was sent right to officers' training school where he got his commission, and has never been under fire.

Jimmy and I went to church the next morning, and I must confess the weird decorations commanded more of my attention than the mumbling priest. Spent the remainder of the morning on the balcony, reading and writing. Bruce, of the 1st platoon, drowned while in swimming this afternoon. Dragging gave no results, so we tried half a dozen grenades, which were also inefficient. Chaplain Hatch (Lt. Roscoe C., Rgt. HQ) came over to bury him, but as there is no corpse, is going to stay with us until it appears. Went for a horseback ride with Tucker after supper, and nearly ran a Frenchman down.

Last night's slumber disturbed by planes dropping bombs on or near La Ferte. On the way back a plane dropped a souvenir or two on the railroad across the river from us. The anti-air craft guns barked out, and made a great rumpus. Hot all day. Officers meeting in the afternoon, after which Doty and I had a good swim.

Went to church on the 18th again with Jimmy. It was the occasion of the first communion of ten youngsters, none of them old enough to know what it was all about. Has tried to rain all day, but has finally cleared off and is cool once more. We leave tonight via La Ferte for a destination unknown. The Major said that Italy was rumored again, but the general impression is that we're to go somewhere between Chaumont and Neufchateau, perhaps to Rimaucourt.

On the Train

Bruce's body came to the surface around six o'clock last evening. I chased all over the place to get permission from the burial director. He wasn't found, so we just appropriated a plot in the cemetery. It was particularly impressive as we stood in the brilliant moonlight, with all that lovely country spread out beneath us, while Chaplain Hatch recited the burial service from memory. We marched out of Sainte-Aulde at one this morning (the 19th) and arrived at La Ferte station about three. It was still moonlight, and as the station had been a favorite target for night bombers we were prepared for unpleasantness. But none came over, and all went smoothly. We K officers have a compartment to ourselves, and have brought enough good food to last us a week. Have had a first rate trip. Passed through Chateau Thierry, Epernay, Vitry-le-François, St.-Dizier, Chaumont, and Langres.

Chaumont-la-Ville, Haute Marne

Disentrained at Breuvannes at ten last night. I was sent ahead with the billeting detail, and hiked in here at one A.M. on August 20th and spent three quarters of an hour trying to find the town mayor, and finally got things arranged, on paper. But everyone was tired and cross when the battalion pulled in an hour later, and things got terribly balled up, but now they're all straightened out. Lucas, supported by Haley (Cpt. William M., I), made a terrible stir because there was a pile of horse manure in the corner of the barracks assigned to the I company officers. I suppose they would have had me clean it up. Briggs (Lt. Howard B., HQ Co.), too, was dissatisfied with his billet, all this at three A.M. I told the bunch to go to hell. The only one who had reason to complain was Major Brewer, and he said he was all right. This morning I found him in an excellent place, and all the disgruntled ones have been pacified. The men are in clean new barracks with plenty of room; each company has a large mess hall, and there is a good Y building and infirmary. We (K) are wonderfully situated, Jimmy and I together at the "mairie" (town hall), a big comfortable bed in a pleasant room, connecting with our dining room. Madame Gabrielle, our hostess, insists that we use her table linen, china, glass, and silver. Such luxury. To mention not the least of our conveniences, we have to but step out of the window to reach the cabinet. Tush and Mohn have a room over the café, and Dor (Doty) is further down the street.

The following day and Happy fairly beams in the large and well equipped kitchen and if he continues to serve such meals as we've had for the past two days, we're all bust. Madame keeps the dining table and the dresser in our room supplied with flowers. Every thing is so fresh and clean. Her husband is in peace

8. Away

times, the village schoolmaster, "institutier," but at present is in the Engineer Corps. She is extremely kind to us and has two cute youngsters, Serge and Nadine. Dor and I amble around the country this afternoon.

Played pinochle with Tush, Dor, and Mohn until late last night, and I've been sleepy all day on the 22nd. Very hot, and no one has any energy but we were all cheered last evening, by the news that leaves were to be granted, 48 hours in Paris. I put in for mine and wrote Monty, I'd meet him there on the third of September. The first contingent, which left this morning, got only as far as Langres, where they were turned back. We now hear that all passes have been withdrawn. That may mean a return to the line. But I'm going to make the most of our surroundings while it lasts. Tucker told me tonight that Jimmy is on the list to go home, and that the Major said I'd get command of K Company. Jimmy and I have been good friends and I'll miss him, but I can't deny I'd like to have the company. However, I'm not over optimistic.

It's been too hot on the 23rd to move today. Have been thoroughly listless. Tush, Dor and I played cards a while after dinner, and then when the sun got low and it cooled off a bit, Dor and I set out for a constitutional. But we hadn't got far before the storm that's now raging turned us back. I'm going to answer a few letters and then turn in.

Out for setting-up exercise the morning of the 24th. Have been eating too much and getting sluggish. Having no platoon, I have every opportunity for being indolent. Read in the forenoon, and had charge of the men's mess. In the afternoon went over to Regimental Headquarters at Blevaincourt to get replacements for the battalion. They are fine looking men, National Guard and troops from Texas and Oklahoma, but we drew only fifty-nine for the entire battalion. Tommy reported in from the hospital while I was waiting in Van Order's office. He was quite knocked out by the news of Tim's death. They had been friends for years. I thought of course he knew about it, and made some remark about how badly we all felt and then caught a glimpse of his face. Tush went over to Vittel this afternoon. It is out of the divisional area, and he has no pass, but he wanted to go to a dance, et voila. It took an hour and a half to induce Dor's landlady to sell us a chicken for tomorrow's dinner. Not until we resorted to jollying did she capitulate, and then for a good price.

Jimmy and I retired at 9:30 last night and didn't wake up until 6:30. The finest sleep I've had in months. This morning John Currie, Wiener (Lt. Frank W., M), Doocy (Lt. Elmer T., M) and I started a fire in the bathhouse, pumped the tank full and took a first rate hot shower. First time I've felt absolutely clean since I don't know when. Changed all my clothes and thought I had rid myself of the last cootie, but an hour later found another one. However I've long since ceased to be squeamish, and dirt and vermin don't bother me nearly as much as at first. We planned to have dinner at two, so I arrived with notepaper, some Centuries and Harpers. Dor and I climbed to the top of the hill over looking the village. Lovely view on both sides. From where I'm sitting I can see the steeples of nine different villages. It was so quiet at noon that we could hear all the bells. Later we descended to a most delectable repast; fried chicken, cream gravy, hot biscuit and apple pie. Tommy dropped in for dessert. He got three wounds in the Champagne and was taken to a hospital near Chalons. The Boche bombed it every night for two weeks following their attack and the patients were in constant fear of death. This afternoon the battalion had a memorial service for our dead in the orchard across from the barracks. The band came over from Blevaincourt and played well. Col. Bennet, Col. Tinley, Major Brewer and Happy Hatch (Chaplain) made addresses. Jimmy has received official notification that he is to go home, and wants to stay with the outfit. Drill starts tomorrow.

On August 26th I get the latest news now that all vacancies of captains are to be filled by captains of replacement units over here, so goodbye to any chances I might have had. Drilled from 7:30 to 10:30. In the afternoon I took my old platoon, as Mohn was "hors de combat" (out of action). There are further indications that we go back into action before our scheduled rest period is up, probably some where in this general direction. Bill came back from school today, and we had a long talk after dinner. He has a keen mind. Nadine came out to play and fell asleep in my lap. I sang a little because I used to know and Madame said she thought it was a Frenchman singing. I nearly busted with pride.

Drill both morning and afternoon on August 27th. Had a letter from Happy Hatch in which he said Major Brewer told him he had recommended me for company commander confirming what Tucker had already told me. But now Jimmie isn't to go back to the States after all. Rode over to Battalion Headquarters at Domblain with Tucker this evening. Heard that we are to start an offensive extending from Belfort to Commercy, aiming particularly at St. Mihiel. It will engage from three to five American corps and some French. A fair sized push. We got back here at eleven.

Got up at 6:30 the next day, a bit stiff from the ride. A battalion problem took up the morning 7:30–12:30. I had one platoon in my charge to represent the enemy. All we had to do was sit on top of a hill and watch the others toil up in the boiling sun to capture us in the most approved manner. Have been sitting in the cool of the garden talking with Madame and Nadine. Just this minute word has come that we move tonight, very unexpected.

Saulxures, Vosges

Left Chaumont-la-Ville regretfully at nine o'clock last night on two hours notice. Shall have a most pleasant recollection of our stay there. Madame called us all in for a parting "goût" to speed us on. In several of the villages we passed through the people put out lanterns for us, as it was very dark, and many were along the path to wish us "Bonne chance." They all seem to know where we're headed for. Arrived here at 1:30 A.M. on the 29th and the whole regiment bivouacked in a field on the outskirts of town. Slept till nine and only got up because the breakfast that Happy was cooking smelled so good. Dor and I went into Saulxures on a tour of inspection and discovered nothing of note except large, pleasantly steaming manure piles. Kept to camp the rest of the day. Got some continental mail, letters from two of my men who have been wounded, Moon (Cpl. Woody C.) and Simerman, and one from Ned. Marshall (came back from the hospital a couple of days ago) and Brad had supper with us. Marshall has been attached to M Company, and Tucker remains as adjutant, which is a great blow to Marshall. Good news from the British front. They have taken Roye and Noyon.

Morelmaison, Vosges

Broke camp at 8:30 last night, very dark again, but cool. A tiring march. We bivouacked again although we had sent ahead billeting parties with the expectation of having everyone under cover. It turned out there was plenty of room for the officers in the village, not a hundred yards away, but the Major said if the men could sleep out of doors, the officers could too. It's all right if it doesn't rain, for the officers have no shelter and the men have their tents. I turned in at 4 A.M. and slept till 10:30. Had a good breakfast and then in town to look up our billets. Tuck, Dor and I are together in a large clean room that looks out on an attractive garden. We have two beds, so Dor is sleeping on my cot preferring that to doubling up. Our orderlies are in the "grenier a foin" (hayloft), and our cuisine and "salle a manger," downstairs, all very convenient. Billy Haply, the cook for L Company's officers entertained me for a full hour while I was waiting for Jimmy who lives over their kitchen. He is a choice type, ought to put us in a book. George Moyer came to shave us and cut our hair in the garden this afternoon. We sat out there till after dark, talking.

Got up at seven on the 31st, breakfasted at half past, and took over the guard at eight. Not much to do, only seven posts, and the sergeant is from K. Marshall shot himself through his foot with a 45 this morning. Opinion is divided as to whether or not it was accidental. John Currie and Wiener, who were in the room at the time, say it was. I saw him soon after, and am inclined to think so too. In the first place he wouldn't be such a fool to give himself such an ugly wound, right through the ankle. But in view of his previous conduct there are many who won't give him the benefit of the doubt. I feel very sorry for him. There have been times when I've really liked him. He is intelligent, has a delightful sense of humor, and can be as agreeable as anyone when so inclined. But he is selfish, lazy, and unquestionably a coward, and he has had the advantages of birth, breeding, wealth and education. Well with all that he had to wait till evening for the ambulance, and we shall probably never see him again. Band concert from 1:30 to 2:30, not very good. Major Brewer and I got to talking on the subject of our staff, we quite agree. The rest of the day, Dor, Tush and I whiled away at pinochle.

Sunday
Morelmaison

After walking the rounds of my posts last evening I dropped in the Major's room for some music. He occupies a gorgeously draped room once used by Marechal Joffre. Broke in my new Dunhill pipe. Madame then invited us, the Major, Tucker and me, down to her salon, which is also very gorgeous, for a "petite verre." We took the victrola down with us but they preferred to tell us of their two trips, for only pleasure to Africa, where they put up only at the very best hotels. We appeared properly impressed at such utter disregard of expense and bade them good night, to continue upstairs on a conversation ranging from law and politics to war and Catholicism. I left at two and made one more round before going to bed. Tex Pearsall who was to relieve me of the guard at eight didn't show up. So I left things in charge of a corporal and came back to breakfast. Went to church with Jimmy, and got something in my eye, not religion. Officers meeting followed that. Happy Hatch came over to have dinner with us, roast chicken and plum (Mirabelle) pie. Went to the infirmary to have my eye washed out, it bothered me so. Bill was notified of his promotion today and was slightly tight at dinner, supper, I mean, this evening. Tush is peeved because he has to sleep out with the men. It is cold and windy. He was supposed to do it last night and sneaked out of it. Have been in the room all evening writing letters. Dor's orderly brought up a washtub, and several pails of hot water, and he's taking a bath now. Had expected to leave tonight, but may be here some time.

Morelmaison

On September 2nd drilled the company from 7:30 to 10:30. Worked all afternoon on a battalion problem and didn't get back to town until nearly seven. Found a letter from Mrs. Knowles with the bridal pictures, and one from Cousin Alice who is in Haute Savoie. They left Paris on account of the long-range gun and the Gothas,[1] and haven't been back in some time. I had just sat down to answer them when Major Brewer sent for me to bring my pipe and spend the evening with him. We smoked, talked, and played the victrola until late. I wish I had known him well sooner, for he is o.k. It's my turn to sleep out with the company.

Turned very cold during the night, and having but one blanket, I got very little sleep. I got up the next day with a heavy cold and a heavier head. When I came home Dor heated some water in the kitchen and lugged it upstairs so I could have a hot bath. Then I popped into bed and didn't leave it until dinner time this evening. Happy Hatch stopped in to see me for half an hour. Feel fine now. Tush, Dor and I played cards till eleven. Return to the original drill schedule tomorrow.

Morelmaison

It's September 4th and I spent the morning on paper work while the rest drilled. At noon word came that we move tonight, so the afternoon drill was called off. Tush, Dor and I managed to get in our daily game in between times. Tucker told me that Tush is slated for the S.O.S (Squadron Officers School). I hate to hear that, for we've got along so well together. Went over to Gironcourt (Regimental HQ), and after chasing all over town to find out who had them, got our paychecks. Stopped in to see Col. Tinley for a few minutes. He is now commanding the regiment, Bennet having gone to the hospital. Col. Tinley intimated that he wouldn't return. He won't be missed. Also saw Happy Hatch who had a lot of dope to put out. Captain Casey (Major Charles J.), now operations officer, said he was going to take two officers from K and put them in companies that are short. But if Tush goes to S.O.S. that will leave us but three. We leave about eight tonight and will bivouac. Our destination is some where in the vicinity of Colombey-les-Belles.

Battigny, Meurthe-et-Moselle

Made about twenty kilometers last night. We bivouacked, and it rained. Ate my breakfast in bed, as that way only my head got wet. Got up at noon and have been trying to dry my bedding roll ever since.

Crezilles, Meurthe-et-Maison

We left Battigny about nine and arrived here shortly after three in the morning of September 6th, nearly twenty-three kilometers. The roads were muddy and it was hard going, but a surprisingly small number fell out. This pleased me particularly as I was detailed to the end of the column to pick up any stragglers, at best a disagreeable job. Luke (Lucas), with Sgt. Short (Walter S., L) and another detail were behind me with a helping hand for any that might have evaded the three-battalion details. Light marching has its advantages, but it's extremely difficult to keep awake after the first two or three hours. I fell sound asleep every time we halted last night. Fortunately we have billets, for it's raining again. Dor, Jimmy and I are together. We are about twelve kilometers south of Toul, back again where we have to be careful about lights and congregating in the open. The artillery fire must be lively in this sector, for throughout the hike last night, the sky was bright from flashes up front. None of us got up much before noon, and we ate at the company kitchen as Happy is not to be found, probably off on a spree. Jimmy and I had dinner with Brad and his F Company officers. I had no idea he could be so agreeable, He always seemed such a boor to me, but he put himself out, and I really had a pleasant time. A good meal and a congenial bunch of officers.

Went over the afternoon of the 7th to get some things from Happy Hatch. On the way back I met Dor who was coming over to tell me that Mrs. Knowles

8. *Away*

was looking for me. She came up from Colombey-les-Belles in a side car just to see me, but had left by the time I got back. We move tonight, supposed to be a great secret, but the villagers knew all about it before we did. Have only eleven kilometers to make. Jimmy got his captaincy today, so did Percy Lainson.

Sunday

The hike even shorter than we expected. Not over eight kilometers, but Bill led us up the wrong road. The wagon train was behind us and it was too narrow for them to turn around so we went without any bedding rolls or cover. It was a black night and many got separated from their companies in the confusion. Jimmy, Mohn and I spent the rest of the night propped up against a tree that offered little protection against the rain and cold wind. We got well soaked, and no sleep. Then instead of sleeping this morning when the sun came out and when we had a chance, Percy, Jimmy, and I went into Toul, though we had no passes. Had dinner at a good restaurant, did some shopping and sight seeing, and returned to camp at three. It has been a beautiful day, and this lovely country is at its best.

Marched from seven last evening till three this morning (September 9th). Pitch black, and muddy roads. However it was cool and we kept a steady cadence for the first two hours, at least. Came through Toul, Bruley and Lagney, ending up in a wood about eleven kilometers from the front. The mud here is frightful. It rained after we got in, but I rigged a poncho up over my cot so that not a drop got on me. Have been airing my possessions and cleaning equipment ever since I got up (eleven o'clock). Jimmy and the other company commanders have gone up to the front with the Major to make a reconnaissance. We hear that there never has been such a concentration of artillery as is on this front. We are to have plenty of tanks and strong airplane support, so with the huge number of troops to be engaged, our show ought to be a great success.

Foret de la Reine

While we were eating supper last night we were ordered to move immediately. Finally got the company together and plowed through mud a foot deep to a place about five kilometers further on in the forest. It poured all night, and hasn't let up ten minutes today. Have set up my cot on the leeward side of a woodpile, and with a poncho for cover, have a neat shelter. This morning over 75 Whippet tanks lumbered up the road towards the front, the most cheering sight in a long time. Due to the rain, no planes are up, so movements in the back area can be made in comparative safety. We had a long conference, went over the maps, studied the timetables, signals, etc., we move into the line tonight to relieve a company of the 89th Division. They have been holding this sector some time, and are to be in the attack, but will move over to our right. The First Division will be on our left, and the Third behind us as a Corps reserve. We jump off in a line between Seicheprey and Flirey. The first day's objective goes beyond Thiaucourt. From our previous experience we can know just what to expect. The French lost enormously trying to reduce this salient (St. Mihiel) in the past, but I doubt if they had our elaborate preparations. The attack order is a marvel of detail, explicit instructions, and everything is provided for. A depression seems to have settled down on us all. Maybe it's the miserable weather, and maybe it's premonition. This is Dor's first time in action, and he's made up his mind he's going to be killed, so I've tried to cheer him up.

Foret de la Reine

At the last moment last night when we were all packed up to move, word came that Alabama would relieve the 89th instead of Iowa, so we have one day more here. The attack comes off tomorrow at dawn. For the first time I feel a trifle uncertain. Anyhow it can't rain as hard tonight as it did last. The schedule and artillery timetables have been revised, and we had to study it all over again. Ours is to be the assault battalion, with the 2nd in support, and the 1st in reserve. Tush's platoon is to mop-up. The baggage is to be left here in the woods, and the men are to take reserve rations, and one blanket apiece. Have distributed rifle ammunition, 250 rounds for each man, and an ungodly load for the auto rifles.

9

Saint Mihiel Salient

September 12
Thursday

    We dragged out of the woods at 7:30 last night, inky black, mud up to the knees and rain. Only nine kilometers to the front, but it seemed like thirty. Ran into a terrific traffic jam at Beaumont, I think it was. To make the going more difficult the roadside was pitted with treacherous shell holes, up to the brim with water, and impossible to detect in the dark. Further on when the Boche started to shell the road we fell out into the fields for a while. So altogether we were an hour behind schedule. In the blackness the guide led us to the wrong trenches. It was getting so late we had to make time. Each one grabbed hold of the man in front of him (it was too dark to see that far) and we whipped back and forth, slipping and stumbling in the narrow trench. After an hour of that we got where we belonged, and worn out, sat down in the mud and water. After giving the final instructions, although our bombardment had been in progress over an hour, I actually fell asleep, but not for long. The say one million shells went over in four hours. We, of course, expected a return bombardment, but the enemy confined his rather feeble efforts to counter battery work. Left our trenches at five o'clock sharp. Had the greatest difficulty in forming up our men beyond our wire, through which we had to cut our way (engineers supposed to have made sufficient gaps). Mohn was unexpectedly transferred to M Company, and at the last moment I took over my old platoon, to find out that a large part of the recently acquired replacements had had little or no training. Of course they were terribly frightened. It was a crime to send them into action. Things happened so fast then that my mind is a bit hazy to details (I am writing on the 13th), but a thing that made a deep impression was the brilliant display

Kitchen following troops in the Saint Mihiel salient battle. Donovan Collection, United States Army Heritage and Education Center, Carlisle, Pennsylvania.

of rockets that went up from the Boche line the moment we appeared and the barrage that was immediately clapped down on us. Earl Draper, Swisher (Sgt. Claude D.) and Bud Rice (Pvt. Frank G.) were hit right off the bat. Dor, very much excited, came over to ask me his direction. I started him off right, but he crowded me out, so I veered off to the right and filled in a gap between us and the 89th division. The machine gun fire was terrific, and I saw many men drop. We were strung out so far we couldn't tell what was happening on our flanks. But as we came over the brow of the hill, I got a wonderful view of the plain, dotted with thousands of men and shell bursts, and Mont Sec to the extreme left looked like a volcano. Every one of the tanks that were supposed to cut a way through the Boche wire were stuck in the mud, and we had to go forward without them. I never saw such a maze of wire or complicated trench system. All the time we were getting through it, we were subjected to a deadly machine gun fire. Sgt. Simpson was wounded almost at the start and his section was lost from us. After we got over, we were temporarily held up by a nest of machine guns. I directed Woods with his half platoon to engage them from the front, while I took three men around to flank them. Put them out of business with grenades

9. Saint Mihiel Salient

and rifle fire, capturing three guns, and killing or wounding all the crew. The woods were very dense and matted with underbrush and wire, and that was the last I saw Sgt. Woods and his contingent for some time. Riflemen were taking pot shots at us and we had to keep moving. I soon picked up some men from the First Platoon, a few from the Third of L Company (who told me that Wally had been killed), a number of men from the Third Battalion of the 356th Infantry, and some engineers, altogether more men than I started out with. From then on we had little difficulty, the Boche we came across surrendering without resistance. Saw to it that they were disarmed and sent to the rear. As we were rounding up one frightened group, an officer named Nichols, from another outfit, asked if my name weren't Taber. He was at Columbia, and recognized me in spite of my tattered condition. Soon I met up with Jimmy Bonham, consolidated forces, and pushed ahead. Before we got separated, for it was impossible to maintain any liaison in the woods (Bois de la Sonnard) but rejoined him after we struck the open. Had some casualties, rather think it was from our own artillery. It ended by my getting up to the river (Rupt de Mad) before the main body of troops. So I withdrew behind a hill on the road about a kilometer south east of Essey, where the 2nd Battalion went through us, and ours reorganized. Major Brewer was wounded and Percy is in command. There we completed the disheartening task of checking up. Our battalion lost heavily, especially the officers, John Currie, Wally, Ed Wells (Lt. Edward D., L), Doocy and Wheeler (Lt. Karl H., L) have been killed; Major Brewer, Johnny Christopher, Dor, Tommy (his third), Wiener, McCann (Lt. James S., I) (seriously) and Gibbons (Lt. Charles A., I) wounded. K Company has but two sergeants left in the line, McHugh (Sgt. Leo P.) and Morgan, Powers (Cpl. Estill) and Nations (Pvt. James L.) are dead, and Sgts. Swisher, Nevins (Lee M.), Greenwalt (Clyde W.), Allen (Charles B.) and Simpson are wounded. It was first reported that Bill had been killed, in fact one of the men said he had taken a pistol from the body, but he put in an appearance shortly afterwards. At dusk we advanced several kilometers further. Spent a cold night with Jimmy on a hillside, a biting wind. Squadrons of Boche bombing planes flew over during the night, but left us alone.

Friday the Thirteenth
Bois de Dampvitoux

The advance was renewed at six this morning. The 2nd Battalion leading, the 1st in support, and ours in reserve. Ahead of us we could see great columns of smoke where the Boche were burning up their stores and ammunition dumps as they retreated. We had an easy time and got no shells, that is our battalion. Went beyond our objective and were ordered to withdraw about a kilometer. We are now in woods about two kilometers from Beney, not far from the Chateau of St. Benoit, which the Boche are shelling now. Nothing is happening here at all, and I've been writing for an hour comfortably propped up against a tree. Reconnoitered our position this afternoon up to Louisville Farm where the 1st Battalion is digging in. The Machine Gun Company must have walked into a barrage this morning judging from the number of dead bodies, mules, and blown up carts that we saw near there. We have captured a large number of guns, and throughout the attack maintained mastery of the air. But this afternoon the Boche brought down two of our observation planes while our chase squadrons were out of sight.

Bois de Dampvitoux

Spent the night in a ditch with Sgt. Woods and Tut Anderson. It was warm. This is a lovely forest, and a fine place to rest up in. Went over to the chateau the morning of the 14th. Our division has taken over the sector of the 1st Division in addition to our own. Can see the Hauts de Meuse, with Hattonchatel perched on top, from where I sit. Counted forty allied planes up at one time this morning. Splendid news from the British front. Pachek (Pvt. Peter) was slightly wounded in the back by a shell fragment while over in Beney with a water detail. He seemed to think it was a great joke and was grinning from ear to ear when he came to me to have it dressed.

Assigned to K Company a year ago today, September 15th. Happy Hatch came up yesterday with some chocolates, cakes and cigarettes that he got at the Y for the men. Also with the news that instead of being merely wounded, Dor was instantly killed Thursday morning. I had got to know him well in the constant association of these past six or seven weeks, and consider him one of the finest men I've ever known. Very much like Spence, endowed with many of the same rare qualities that made up his compelling personality. Slept twelve hours last night and would have been altogether comfortable, if it hadn't been for the cooties. The kitchen has moved up, and we're now getting hot meals. This wonderful weather keeps the sky busy with planes. Tut, Woods, and I have made a fine shelter with a sheet of corrugated iron which we policed further up the line. My men are dug in all around me. Got yesterday's paper this morning. The

9. Saint Mihiel Salient

Troops in the Saint Mihiel salient with Mont Sec in the background. Donovan Collection, United States Army Heritage and Education Center, Carlisle, Pennsylvania.

American First Army captured 13,300 Boches, and over 200 guns. We are consolidating our positions now, but it is likely that we'll make another advance soon. C Company lost a few out on combat patrol last night. Lots of artillery has been brought up, and this afternoon, twelve observation balloons are up behind our lines. Big issue of cakes, cigarettes, and cigars. Shaved off my four day growth and look almost civilized again.

Couldn't sleep at all last night on account of cooties. We got them from some German blankets we policed the first night of the advance. I got up and walked around a magnificent, moonlight night. False gas alarms about one A.M. and a heavy bombardment at four. The Boche attempted a coup de main on either side of us, both without success. Ever since we've been here we've been bothered by a 77 firing at close range. It appears that the 89th Division didn't advance as far as the 42nd and this particular gun was enfilading us from a position actually between our first and second lines. The 89th has come up even with us now, and captured the piece. Intermittent shelling all day decreases in aerial activity, though the fine weather continues. Happy gave us pancakes for breakfast. Rumors of mail.

A Rainbow Division Lieutenant in France

Bois de Beney

Wakened early on September 17th by some heavies dropping uncomfortably on our artillery. Rumors, which seem to be fairly substantial, that Austria is seeking peace. Rain this morning. Got twelve letters and had a visit from Happy Hatch. He was up front with a burial party and they all had to take refuge in the partly dug graves when the Boche started to shell them. No one safe up here. The line is being reorganized, greater strength in depth, and I've surrendered my comfortable shelter to Capt. Kelly of B Company (William A.). All the Third Battalion has come back a kilometer and a half to the northern edge of the Bois de Beney, near the Saint-Benoit Beney Road. Very smelly, formerly a picket line for horses. Tut, Woods and I set to work on a new home.

Rained during the night, and our own shelter wasn't waterproof. We made it so today, and widened and deepened it. Light mail, all from this side. A bunch from Dor that had been forwarded from his old outfit, the long waited for letters from his wife.

Heavy barrage fire during the night. Some stray shells came entirely too close. Rained again, but this time we kept dry. I let Woods shave me this morning (September 19th), and now my neck and face are sore. He is a bum barber. Cooties are frightful.

Wet cold, and it's still raining on the 20th. Shelling throughout the night. Had an alert at 6 o'clock this morning. The Boche attempted a raid against the 2nd Battalion. They took no prisoners, but left three of their own behind. Had my hair cut.

It was a brilliant night, clear, not a cloud in the sky, and a full moon. Bombing planes buzzed over us for several hours but favored us with no more direct attention. Shells fell around us, however a great many of them duds. The 1st Battalion relieved the 2nd last evening, but we are to remain here on the 21st, a slight advantage in having been hard hit. Had charge of an engineering detail constructing wire entanglements in the afternoon. Feel rotten and ate no lunch. Wish I could get some clean underclothes, for my corps of cooties in unnecessarily active. Shelling during the day. Good letter from GBN. He expects to be sent home on account of his wound. Alabama and Iowa are to go over on raids early tomorrow, 150 men and 4 officers from our regiment.

Slept soundly in spite of cooties until our barrage opened at 4 A.M., September 22nd. Raids were made simultaneously all along the line and the Boche evidently thought it was a general attack for they shelled the back areas wherever there were likely to be reserves. Our bunch, which raided Marinbois farm,

9. Saint Mihiel Salient

brought back nine prisoners and a machine gun besides inflicting heavy casualties. Johnson (Pvt. Ernest G.), of K Company, was the only American killed. Alabama raided Haumont and picked up sixteen prisoners. Happy Hatch came up for dinner with us, planning to hunt for Dor's grave tomorrow, he and I. Mrs. Knowles sent us a carton of cigarettes and chocolate as a pleasant surprise. She is back with the Division, at Boucq, wherever that may be.

Got a few gas shells here in the woods at midnight, and more interspersed with high explosives at three A.M., the 23rd. None fell directly on us but were close enough to keep us on the alert. At four our guns started a barrage. We thought perhaps the Boche were coming over, but it turned out to be in support of the 89th Division who were making a coup de main. A string of 88s plopped in front of us about fifty feet away this afternoon. They came with a rush and discombobulated us all. This is life.

Heavy shelling throughout the night. A battery of 75s to our left kept up a capacity fire for three hours. I couldn't sleep so I walked over, about an eighth of a mile to watch them. They kept slamming in one shell after another until at the end the gunners were about exhausted. Happy's orderly came for me at ten on the 24th and the three of us set out in search of Dor's grave. We stopped at the Y in Pannes, fortunately, for there I happened to see Mrs. Knowles. She stays during the day and leaves for a town further back before the Boche commence their nightly shelling. Mr. Hayden, a Y man (formerly a curate at St. Agnes in N.Y.) gave us a lift in his Ford beyond Essey. And from there we walked back over our battlefield of twelve days ago. It's a desolate region, torn up for miles, shell holes of all sizes, trenches, wire and debris, and every now and then a cross. We came across some Boche concrete trenches still in excellent condition. A road has been constructed, or rather the old one reconstructed, right across no-mans land. We found Dor's grave all alone out in the open beyond the tip of the Bois de la Sonnard, buried evidently right where he fell. His identification tag was nailed on the cross and his helmet hung on one of the arms. We heaped up stones around it and fixed the grave as well as we could. Then Happy recited the burial service. Found Doocy, McHugh and Powers, all buried together, but couldn't locate Wally or John Currie though we went all the way back to the jumping off line, and searched everywhere. Hailed an ambulance on the Flirey road and got a ride back to Essey. Got something to eat there (it was then three o'clock) and then caught a Red Cross truck to Pannes. Got our pay checks at the Supply Company and loaded up at the Y with supplies for the battalion, as much as we could pack. We walked into a mean bit of shelling on the way back here, and saw a plane brought down, that makes three today, all

Boches. They have at last set the chateau on fire. It's a shame, for it was a stately looking building and, I imagine, pretty old. Captain Johnson (Erney W., Supply Company) said we will be here at least ten days more.

A six-inch shell broke within a short distance of us in the night. So close that it drove my stomach right up into my mouth. I heard it coming and thought it was headed straight for us, but it missed us by fifteen feet. This promiscuous shelling, one here and one there, all near enough to be dangerous, gets on one's nerves. I'd much rather have a steady bombardment and get it over with. We piled rocks on our shelter to make it splinter proof the next day. Wrote two letters, one home, and one to Dor's mother.

Notified last evening of a six-hour bombardment to commence at midnight, and advised to dig down deep on account of retaliatory fire, but not a single shell came our way. It was an intense fire, and made it quite impossible for us to sleep. We are making a drive up near Verdun (September 26th), and the bombardment was to lead the Boche to think we were going to attack all along the line. They thought we were coming over all right, for a patrol reported them in combat formation in front of their own wire waiting for us. And they laid a barrage down on our front line. Today a deserter said our fire cut them up frightfully while out there. An enemy plane brought down from a great height this morning, didn't plunge, but came down slowly, turning over and over like a falling leaf. The kitchens were moved back several kilometers in anticipation of trouble, and we didn't have breakfast until eleven. Artillery to the north, at Verdun, I suppose, has been rumbling steadily all day. This evening a French crew brought up a 120-long mounted on a narrow gauge track. It ran off the track and we all helped to put it on again. They moved further up the line to fire, for which we were all thankful. They always pull out after they finish their job and the poor infantry gets the benefit of the shells intended for them.

I got four letters and some magazines today, September 27th. Night was comparatively quiet, but heavy firing to the left woke us at daybreak. The boys are amusing themselves coasting down the track. They're nothing but a bunch of kids. The 83rd Brigade is to relieve us this afternoon.

Bois de Pannes

Left the Bois de Beney at four on the 27th and got here at six thirty and we are midway between Heudicourt and Nonsard, a good supper was waiting for us. We officers have set up house keeping in a corrugated iron hut that was

9. Saint Mihiel Salient

partly filled with German 88 shells when we arrived. There is just room for four cots and the table, which Jack Dowling (Sgt. John C.), our company mechanic, made us today. Bill, who has been away several days with a detail to get replacements came back this afternoon. Last night we disrobed for the first time in three weeks and our cots were so soft, after so long an intimacy with Mother Earth that we couldn't sleep. We got to talking, of all subjects, on religion. Both Tush and Jimmy are Catholic, but liberal. I say the golden rule is the religion he tries to follow. Inventoried Dor's effects this morning, just the contents of his bedding roll. This afternoon our orderlies rigged up a clever contrivance under a tree and we took a hot shower. I changed clothes from head to foot and am clean once more. We are eating our meals under a natural arbor near the kitchen. This is a pacific spot, and I hope we stay some time.

Sunday

Stayed up till one o'clock writing letters and transferring the notes I made, chiefly on the back of envelopes, into my diary. Sent the letters that were on Dor where he fell to his wife. I sent his dairy and other papers to Cousin Alice, so that they can be forwarded by registered mail. Otherwise they would go to the Central Records Office and probably never reach his family. After lunch I went over to Pannes and found Mrs. Knowles frying doughnuts. I made myself useful for an hour, and then took her for a chat. The only secluded spot we could find was on the railroad track near a large manure pile. Caught a camion all the way back to camp. Here it is 2 A.M. and I'm not in bed yet. Sat down this evening to write letters, got one finished, and then played pinochle with Tush and Bill till after one. A shell has just exploded in the woods not far away. The first one that's come in this direction. Thought we were out of range.

September 30th is a disagreeable day. We move this afternoon. No one knows whether it is back to the front, or back to rest. The Belgians started an offensive near Ypres on September 28th. The Allies are now attacking at five different points on the western front. The Turks have been routed and Bulgaria has asked for peace. Things look promising now. If the war only ends before the rest of us are shot up.

10

On the Road

Apremont, Meuse

After waiting around hours, already to march, we left camp at eight last evening and had an easy hike of sixteen kilometers to Apremont. Spent the night in a cold damp cellar with only a slicker for cover. It's the first of the month and I woke up with a rotten headache and a mean cold. Cloudy and rain today, but went exploring with Tush in the former German trenches. They are so ploughed up as to be almost unrecognizable. The terrain about has been subject to four years of shelling. Apremont was in the Boche front line and is nothing but a shell. We move again this evening.

Deuxnouds Devant Beauzee

The entire regiment left Apremont at six last evening in over 250 camions. Briggs, Tush, Bill, Sefton, Happy, Luke and I had one to ourselves, so we weren't at all crowded. I was warm and had a comfortable ride. Passed the early evening in close harmony, but one by one we fell asleep, although we were bumping along at a great rate. At 2:30 the morning of October 2nd we "disembussed." It was very cold and clear, and ahead of us the gun flashes were particularly bright. A short hike brought us to Deuxnouds where we expected to find billets, but us, we were all dumped on the frozen ground on a rocky hillside. As our baggage hadn't come up, I crawled in with Tut and Woods, and all three of us were uncomfortable. There was a heavy frost, and as a result I've been much under the weather today, stiff, chills, and fever, and nausea.

October 3rd and I am now lodged in a place that were flattery to call a

Wounded being put in ambulance similar to the one used by the author. Donovan Collection, United States Army Heritage and Education Center, Carlisle, Pennsylvania.

barn, is just a glorified manure shed. However it is waterproof, and we shouldn't complain as our bedding rolls have come. Percy, Teddy, Jimmy Cotter, Jimmy Bonham, Briggs, and Bill are my fellow inmates. Still feeling like the devil. Must have the flu. Was horribly sick in the night. The American Corps in the last attack got themselves in a fine hole by getting ahead of their flanks where the Germans are making it hot for them. So the original First Army Corps (1st, 2nd, 26th and 42nd) have been reorganized and sent here to extricate them. All four divisions have been in the last two offensives. Half of our men are new, with little training, and we are short on non-coms, not to mention officers. Heard a heavy barrage this morning, they say it was the First Division going over. We don't know when we go up.

Brabant, Meuse

The fourth is a dreary day, but good for hiking twenty-two kilometers, and I've just about made it. A good supper and hot coffee heartened me up so that I played pinochle with Bill, Tush and Jimmy Bonham. All the officers of the regiment are billeted in this one shack, smug.

Bois de Montfaucon

We had hoped for at least a twenty-four hour halt in Brabant but we were routed out at five this morning, Saturday the 5th, and on our way by eight. We were on the road until 6:30 this evening. The roads were in terrible condition and so jammed with traffic, that half the time was taken up just waiting to move. Such desolate and hopeless country as we passed through, every village in ruins. Varennes and Cheppy were excellent examples of what war can do to peaceful communities. Our 18-kilometer trudge ended here in a place so completely pitted with shell holes that the men couldn't find a level place to pitch their tents. We're all in shell holes.

Sunday

Sick as the devil, fever, and no food will stay down.

Base Hospital 47, Beaune, Cote d'Or

I finally got so much worse that on the afternoon of the ninth, I went to the rear. I spent the night somewhere in the woods in a Field hospital. We were bombed twice by Boche planes. Everyone else fled to the dugout, but I was too weak to get out of my cot, which was perched up high with some apparatus underneath to keep me warm. Thought I was going to pass out anyhow. The next morning just as we got started in another ambulance, a Boche plane brought down an observation balloon directly overhead, and intentionally or unintentionally, sent a stream of bullets through the top of the car. Then farther on they started to shell the road where we got stuck in a traffic jam. So by the time we got to Evacuation No. 9. I didn't much care whether we blew up or not. I was put right to bed, and when I came to, I was already in the hospital train several hours underway. My fever broke during the night, and in the morning some hot soup pepped me up considerably. Arrived in Beaune that evening, the eleventh, and was assigned a cot in a tent where I've stayed until today. I got up for a while this afternoon, but am a bit shaky on my pins. But I've been improving so rapidly I've already put in for my discharge, as the nurse says it takes several days for them to go through. The doctor has diagnosed my case as a light attack of pneumonia. Vidal, a 1st Lieutenant, in the Tank Corps (ex–41st Division) whom I met at Gondrecourt has the cot next to me, beyond him is Butts, a garrulous engineer from the 26th Division.

It's October 16th and I am feeling much better. Walked around the hospital grounds a while. A convoy of wounded filled our ward up to capacity this after-

10. On the Road

Hospital receipt of 44 francs for meals for John.

noon. Such a shortage of nurses, that the few of us who are up helped them dress the wounds, a rather sickening job. One aviator had fourteen machine gun bullet holes in him. Two others died today.

Butts, Vidal and I went into Beaune the evening of the 17th and saw Irene Castle[1] in a terrible movie at the French cinema. We are all waiting for our discharges. Beaune is an ancient city and many of the old buildings have survived. The Hotel Dieu (which we peeked into and thought picturesque) was built in 1443, and the town hall and church of Notre Dame of the same period.

The next evening the three of us into town for a delicious dinner at a small restaurant, and then wandered around in the quaint alleys and narrow streets of Clair de Lune. The moon on the turrets and pinnacles and oddly shaped gables makes it all seem unreal, like a picture from a fairy book.

Hotel de la Cloche, Dijon, Cote d'Or

Our discharges arrived in time for us to catch the rapide from Marseille at 11:45 the morning of October 20th. Got here for lunch and then saw as much of the city as we could before dinnertime. I was not particularly impressed with the architectural treasures of Dijon. The most outstanding, the church of

St. Michel and Notre Dame and the facades of certain old buildings are all marked by a heaviness of style that is far from artistic. Butts and I saw a good movie in the evening. We three have a big room together with the luxury of a bath. The cuisine is excellent and we'd like to stay longer, but we're off on the American Express at 7:14 tomorrow.

Dijon

The next day we rushed through breakfast and tore to the station to find the train we had planned to take was sixteen hours late. So back we came to the hotel, shaved, and much to our waiter's astonishment, marched into the dining room for a second, and more ordered, breakfast. We now plan to leave at half past one this afternoon on the French train. We ought to be in Is-sur-Tille right now. Dijon was not on the itinerary provided by our travel orders, but we've enjoyed our little excursion tremendously. And I'm going to make Paris before the expedition is over or bust in the attempt. My orders direct me to St. Dizier.

11

Paris

Hotel Continental, Paris

On the 22nd we were not held at Is-sur-Tille as we feared, and as soon as the Regulating Officer stamped our orders we took a train for Langres. It is a scheduled journey of an hour and a half, but our "train omnibus" moseyed along so, that not until four and a half hours later, did we disembark at Langres. It was then eleven o'clock, and everything was shut up tight. But after an hour's search we located three beds at the Y.M.C.A. I was called at three o'clock, and leaving Butts and Vidal still asleep caught the four o'clock train down the hill, and left at 4:30 on the Paris Express. There were three agreeable artillery officers in the compartment, but I was so tired that I slept almost all the way. I had to watch my step at the Gare de l'Est for I had neither pass nor ticket. When I saw the Americans being herded into one group, I made straightway for the civilian "sortie," waved my orders at the guard, and before he had time to demand ticket or explanation, was out on the street. I hopped a taxi and came direct to the hotel. I am on the top floor facing the Rue Rivoli, and have a fine view of the Tuileries Garden. After a bath and breakfast in my room I called up Cousin Alice. She was out, but Lucy, who answered, promptly invited me for tea. Had to keep to my room while my suit was being pressed (all the baggage I have with me being what I could get into my kit bag) and then set out for a walk. Paris is wonderfully interesting right now, so many different armies represented. The Place de la Concorde is stacked with guns and airplanes captured from the Boche. All the principal monuments and statues are protected with sand bags and everywhere "affiches" (posters) and flags. Arrived at Cousin Alice's at four. Walked all the way. She and Lucy came back from Savoire only a day or so ago, and Ned is here en permission. They were all delightful. After tea Ned and I went out to get some theater tickets and then batted around a while before going back to dinner. The play wasn't very good and we had to walk back miles, for the metro wasn't running and we couldn't get a taxi. They run out of their daily supply of petrol before evening. There wasn't a ray of light anywhere, not even a moon, and we had quite a time finding our way.

Slept till nine on the 23rd and had breakfast in bed. Wasted the greater part of the morning chasing back and forth between the Hotel de Crillon and the Regina to settle about a note Dor had given the Red Cross. Then walked up the Champs Elysees to the Etoile. There are uniforms and "blesses" everywhere, and as much mourning as khaki and blue. So far I've seen no evidence of bombing or shelling except a slightly damaged building on the Place Vendome. Every thing is tranquil, almost gay, and the sidewalk cafés as crowded as in peace times. The general public is thoughtful of the wounded. Two men in crutches came in the metro. The woman guard called out "Places pour deux blesses" and the entire car got up to offer their seats. Cousin Alice, Lucy and I took a walk this afternoon ending up at Ixe where one can actually get ice cream soda. Dinner with them and then the four of us heard an excellent performance of *Louise*[1] at the Opera Comique. Cousin Alice seems to feel badly that she can't put me up, but they have taken a small apartment during the war, and just now Ned is occupying the only spare room. I'm perfectly comfortable here.

Up late on the 24th, and to Burberrys where I bought a trench coat (450 francs) and a pair of gloves. Had lunch at the hotel and met Ned afterward at the University Union. We whiled away the afternoon till five when we met Lucy at the Ixe for tea. Went home with them for dinner, and instead of going to the theater, for I was tired, we had a good game of bridge.

It's October 25th and my fourth day in Paris a.w.o.l. and so far nothing untoward has happened. I'm afraid however it won't be so easy to get out of the city as in, but I'm going to make a try tomorrow. From all I can learn the Division is in repos, but likely to move into the line again soon, so I must get back. Bought some presents for the family and shipped a small package to Mrs. Knowles. Lunch at Cousin Alice's. She, Lucy and I spent the afternoon at Versailles. It was a wonderful day. The leaves just are beginning to turn, so the parc was gorgeous, and the gardens lovely. Many of the more valuable treasures have been removed from the chateau for safekeeping, but nevertheless we went all through it. Got back to Paris just in time for dinner. We had tickets for the Folies Bergere, but again we decided to stay home and play bridge.

Got up too late the following day to catch the morning train, hurrah. And it's lucky too, for at the University Union I met Randolph Saville of my class

11. Paris

at Columbia, who has been wounded and is here waiting for a reservation to the Riviera. He told me of the performance one went through at the station before one can board a train. So I went to the Headquarters of the O.P.W. (Office of Public Works) in the Rue St. Anne and asked for a pass to stay 24 hours in Paris. The officer in charge wanted to know what time I had come in and why I hadn't got my permit at the station. I told him that I had arrived at eight o'clock and must have come out by the wrong exit. So he said I'd have to leave at two (it was then eleven) but as the next train didn't leave till 8:30 P.M. I was permitted to stay that long. Just as I was coming out of a shop where I had ordered some flowers for Cousin Alice, a French officer grabbed my arm. I turned around and there was Jack S. We had a joyful reunion and repaired around the corner to the Ritz for lunch, and then saw the show at the Folies Bergere. He was leaving to join his outfit at near Reims at six thirty. I rushed back to the hotel, threw my things together, had a hasty dinner, and to the Gare. Met Chaplain Robb as I was going up the "quais." He told me to get off at Bar-le-Duc instead of St. Dizier, as the outfit is nearer there. In return for the information I took from his charge, two enlisted men who were taking supplies back for the regiment. He himself suddenly deciding to remain in Paris overnight. So here I am in a stuffy compartment waiting for the train to move out. Hardly enough light to see to write. There goes the whistle, and here we go.

Sunday

Descended on Bar-le-Duc at three this morning, weary, chilled and creaky in the joints. Everything closed up and apparently no place to go, but after wandering around the streets, chanced on a Y where six or seven others who had come in early were huddled around a blazing fire. All but one were aviators. One of them was in a squadron with a number of Columbia men, and it seems many of them have met with hard luck. He told me that Hassinger was killed by a direct hit of an "archie" (anti-aircraft). I was unable to get any definite information as to the whereabouts of the Division, but the R.T.O. thought it was in the general direction of Auzeville. So at six A.M. I left on the "Meusieu," a funny rickety narrow gauge train jammed with French civilians and soldiers. I arrived some hours later at Auzeville, and found out that Division Headquarters was located at Recicourt, some ten kilometers away. I was fortunate enough to catch a truck going directly there. Jimmy Thomas (now a major) took me to the senior officers mess for lunch, and afterward in his limousine to the advanced

A Rainbow Division Lieutenant in France

Division P.C. some ten kilometers farther. I'm glad I was spared that hike, for I spent the next five hours hunting for the 168th. To begin with Ray Gannett (Pvt. Ray G., A) started me off in the wrong direction, and after that nobody could tell me where it was. I finally stumbled onto the Division M.P. Headquarters, now under command of Major Worthington. He saw that I was about all in, and insisted that I stay for supper and the night. The whole bunch of them have been mighty nice to me.

Shells popped in our vicinity last night, and I didn't like it a bit. It is a little more nerve wracking when one has been out of it for some time, and the bunch behind the lines are so panicky when any trouble starts that it makes it even more difficult. But I didn't leave my cot, as most others did. We were all together in a rambling shack. After breakfast October 28th Major Worthington gave me a horse, and sent a mounted orderly along to guide me up to the 168th. It was an eight-kilometer jog, and not a bit pleasant. Had a mean time when a bunch of shells broke on a cross road just as we were approaching. The horses bolted and we gave them full rein. They all seem glad to have me back here. The company was in the line while I was away, but lost very few. Motter (Pvt. Daniel P.) and Burks (Pvt. Thomas C.) of my old platoon were killed. The First and Second Battalions had a harder time. They lost three officers killed, and quite a number wounded, including Brad, who was shot through the lung. Haley, in our battalion, was wounded too. There have been some changes. Bill is Intelligence Officer, and Piggott (Lt. Albert T.), formerly of I, and two new second lieutenants, Peyton (Charles) and Robinson (Leo), have been assigned to K. We are in a shack in a valley north of Exermont, in a former German "Lager." News came on the wireless this afternoon that Austria had submitted to all of Wilson's demands, and that Ludendorff had resigned. One of our observation balloons was brought down a little while ago.

12

Back with the Company

There is little to do on the 29th other than try to keep warm. The weather has been miserable. During the night shells nearly got a bunch of our men just over the hill. The shrapnel rattled on our roof. It may be that the Boche are trying for a French anti-aircraft gun stationed in our midst in the daytime. It is mounted on a truck and pulls out at night. It barks away at a great rate whenever an enemy plane comes into range, but couldn't prevent one from bringing down another balloon this afternoon. While some German observation planes were up, a company of the 2nd Battalion tried a little close order drill. Before long a brace of shells exploded in their midst and got quite a number of men.

On the 30th I have been in the L Company hut most of the day for they have a little stove and manage to keep up a fairly decent temperature. L, K and Battalion Headquarters mess together in a lean-to behind our shack. We have a gay time, though a cold one. Played cards last night until the buzz of a bombing plane forced us to put out the candle.

The next day the Division Intelligence report states, "The enemy has complete and unchallenged mastery of the air." That is rather borne out by the fact there isn't a single balloon up behind our lines. The Boche have brought down every one, and they come and go as they wish. Not over half an hour ago one of our planes fell in flames. The 84th Brigade was commended by the corps commander for its fine work in this last action. It is rumored that we are to be relieved.

Last night we got orders to prepare to leave today, November 1st. I went up to Battalion Headquarters and found out that a big attack was scheduled for this morning and that we would move up in support of the 78th Division. About ten last night the guns to our right opened up a violent bombardment, which continued until three when I think everyone in the world, joined in. There was an unbroken roar all along the line. Our shack rattled continuously.

But we were safe and I went sound to sleep. This is an excellent day for an attack, very misty. Our artillery has been rumbling all day. Bill, Tush and I played pinochle all morning. Now we are ready to move. Bill and Piggott have gone ahead to look for billets.

An American observation balloon, several of which John wrote of being shot down. Donovan Collection, United States Army Heritage and Education Center, Carlisle, Pennsylvania.

12. Back with the Company

After all our preparation we didn't move, but stayed over-night in the same place. Today on the 2nd we hiked to an abandoned German camp between Fleville and Sommerance. Our artillery created frightful havoc in St. Georges, through which we passed. The village is in utter ruins and the countryside a mass of huge craters. The roads are in bad condition, and to add to the general discomfort, it has begun to rain. Our wagon train got mired, and it was late before we had anything to eat.

Sunday

Advanced as far as Imecourt where we are camped on a hillside. Below us are quite a number of guns, judging from the amount of personal belongings strewn about, hastily abandoned. Above on the plateau are numerous bodies, American marines and Boche, and machine guns still in position. The fighting though must have been bitter. In the middle of the afternoon rumors of an armistice began to float about. Some one had actually seen the communique posted on a Headquarters bulletin board in Imecourt. A bunch of us had already been in the town, or what was left of it, but a couple volunteered to go back to verify the information. Our high hopes were almost immediately shattered by the arrival of orders for tomorrow's advance. The roads were so jammed and in such bad condition that we advanced "cross lots" today. The fields were muddy and the going difficult. Met with four disgusted ten-inch howitzer crews on the outskirts of (Sivry-les) Buzancy. They had just emplaced their battery, after much difficulty, to find the Boche had retreated so rapidly that they were out of range before our men had a chance to fire a round. We are in the open again, on a hillside just beyond Bar (les–Buzancy), on the site of a German aviation camp. A little while ago an American bombing expedition of at least 150 planes went over us, each squadron in a wedge formation. The largest number any of us have seen in the air at one time.

Shortly after dark last evening when we were about asleep, some Boche bombing planes buzzed over and dropped several cartloads of big bombs in our vicinity. The first one raised me right off my cot. They were flying very low and we could hear the swish of the bombs as they came down. There was nothing to do but be quiet and try to remember that we were fatalists. To me there is nothing so terrifying, for one absolutely helpless, no way of hitting back or determining whether it's best to move or stay put. After dumping their cargo they departed, and I had just fallen asleep when I heard that ominous buzz again, and then more excitement. November 5th and the road ahead of us was jammed with traffic for the Boche were raining shells on it about a quarter mile further on, so that attracted the attention of the planes. They must have done a lot of damage for I heard both men and mules screaming. The last one fell directly ahead of us, uncomfortably close. Not content with that, they made a third trip, this time over Bar, where they dropped bombs promiscuously. After that I slept soundly until five. We moved forward at seven and advanced to a line with Verrieres where we were supposed to relieve the 78th Division. There were no troops of any description in sight, so we just went ahead anyway. About this time "John the Baptist" took time out to pray. He is a religious fanatic of recent acquisition who wears a full beard in imitation of the apostles, I suppose, and the men have dubbed him J.B. Gene Cruise and I went ahead on a scouting expedition of our own. Ran into rather heavy shelling near Grandes-Armoises, and as we were a considerable distance ahead of the troops, decided to wait in a ditch along the road. While we were sitting there a closed car went over the road above us towards Grandes-Armoises but had to turn back as it had been mined. We of course thought it was a French staff car, but after it had speeded off towards Stonne, we realized no French car would be rushing so far ahead of the advancing line, and as we came to think of it, it was grey and not horizon blue. We missed the opportunity of a lifetime, for we were in a concealed position and could easily have stopped it with a grenade and perhaps have captured a general or two. The battalion soon came up and advanced a few kilometers further and halted for the night on the reverse slope of a steep hill. The 2nd Battalion is on a ridge behind us, and the 1st on still another. Here a sergeant from the 77th Division, on the right, came over to see where we connected up. He thought he was having a terrible time. Said he had a family and ought not to have been drafted. Gene threatened to knock him, and that ended his whine.

Haraucourt, Ardennes

We had a horrible night, black as pitch, a pouring rain, cold, and the wind blowing a gale. We tried to dig in the bank along the road, but it was like granite. So I wrapped myself in a wet blanket and awaited developments. Jimmie brought in some corned willy that Frankie and Rust had managed to heat up under their shelter halves. Instead of warming me up, it made me sick. The Boche shelled us steadily, but that was the least of our worries for they all broke in the ravine below us. I got up after a while and walked around in an attempt

12. Back with the Company

to stir up my circulation. I finally settled down next to a man who was sleeping upright against the bank, and edged up close for warmth. I actually got a little sleep, but in less than an hour, just before dawn, we were routed out. When I tried to wake up my neighbor the morning of the 6th, I found out that I had been sleeping next to a dead man. He had been shot through the head, a member of the 77th, and his body had been propped up against the bank. In the darkness, I took him for one of our own men. During the night Percy Lainson went to the hospital, and Jimmy Bonham is now commanding L. We were a haggard looking outfit as we pushed ahead at seven this morning. A heavy fog screened our movements at first, but it soon cleared off and we encountered light machine gun fire, no artillery. Jimmy and I with Co. Hdqs. got caught in advance of the others on the crest of a hill by a burst of well-directed bullets. We dropped to the ground, which was boggy after the rain, and they came close enough to us to spatter water in our faces. We got out of that by running one at a time to a woods on the side. Sievers (Pvt. Oren M.) and Bob Drake, who were hit about this time, were our only casualties during the day. Oren had a slight flesh wound in the neck, but he was making a great row. I told him I had some morphine with me that would instantly stop his pain, and gave him two aspirin tablets. His relief was instantaneous. I left the company and struck out with Joe Napier (Pvt. Joseph B.). The people at the first farm we hit went nearly wild when they found out we were Americans. They had been under German rule for four years and were kept in absolute ignorance as to outside events. Further on we joined up with Sgt. Langan (Thomas E., L) and the battalion scouts. Our combined force made for Le Lavoir Ferme, which was deserted, and then we divided into two parties and cautiously entered Haraucourt. Three women whom we met on the outskirts told us the last of the Boches had left only ten minutes before. A very demonstrative reception followed. Found a dozen new camouflaged machine guns in a building used as a storehouse. About that time Captain Means' Company of the 151 M.G. rolled into town, and before long French flags were flying from every house. When the main body of troops arrived an hour later there was a reception. Our battalion advanced to the further edge of town and dug in for the night. Major Yates, Bill, Tucker, Jimmy and I are in the chateau on the outskirts. Had a wonderful dinner, at least it tasted so to us. I have been sitting here in comfort for at least an hour writing up my diary. A few big ones that shake the house and rattle the windows are dropping on the road ahead of us.

Jimmy and I shared a big soft bed last night, and nothing but a direct hit could have made us abandon it. We were on the top floor, and in spite of the frequent explosions that jarred the chateau, I was soon asleep. The owners spent the night in the cellar. At eleven o'clock I Company was routed out and sent over to take position at Le Lavoir Ferme. About one this morning (the 7th), a battalion of the 16th Infantry, 1st Division, disregarding the outpost's warning, passed through them and got themselves into a fine hole further on at Pont Mangis. Without sending scouts ahead to investigate they walked into a town full of Germans, and were badly shot up, a brilliant stunt. All day long survivors have been straggling back through our lines. A number of them were trapped in a hollow and unable to move on account of machine guns until we moved up and drew the fire on ourselves. We formed up at seven o'clock and advanced to the heights south of the Meuse where we can see the spires of Sedan. At the last we ran into intense machine gun fire, and a lively artillery fire has developed. Our guns have not yet come up. I and M Companies have taken over the front line and L and K have retired to the reverse slope of the hill. I spent most of the day on the crest with Luke (he has been in command of I since Bill Haley was wounded) and was his guest at a sumptuous lunch of hardtack, corned willy, and jelly. It was most exasperating to watch a Boche battery on the other side of the river fire on us, and not be able to do anything. With field glasses we could actually see the gunners pull the string. They rained shells on the road from Thelonne to the river all day long and showered us on the hill with trench mortar bombs (small ones shot from "granatenwerfer"). When none of them exploded we thought they must have delayed-action fuses, but later came to the conclusion that they were all defective. Our few casualties in the morning were practically all from machine guns. Tucker stewed up a mess of turnips and cabbage this afternoon. I sampled it and wished I hadn't for it was anything but palatable, and turned my stomach. It got very disagreeable towards evening, wind and heavy rain. Sloshed through the mud and the blackness with Major Yates back several kilometers to Regimental Headquarters at Beau Meuil Ferme. Colonel Tinley gave us a bit to eat, which I almost immediately lost. So Captain Bunch (Major Henry) trotted out some White Mule, which he slightly diluted with coffee to fix me up. If it hadn't been for an occasional gun flash or shell burst, we two would never have found our way back to the Battalion P.C. It was so dark, and the mud about a foot thick.

Major Yates and I had a mattress on the floor of L Company's shack for the night. I was frightfully sick this morning (November 8th) and didn't get up till noon when we were all driven out by shelling. I found out that we were to be relieved in the evening, so I got permission to come straight back to Haraucourt. Palmer (Lt. Newell, L) came with me and got a room chez Carlier. I got

12. Back with the Company

into bed right away and feel better now. Madame dosed me up on an "infusion."

Le Vivier, Ardennes

Had a fine night. The Boche promised not to shell Haraucourt for forty-eight hours and the few shells that came over broke well out of town. But Madame Carlier was apprehensive and asked us, in case anything did happen, to carry her aged mother, who recently broke her hip, down to the cellar. We had a hike the next day of about eleven kilometers back to Le Vivier. Jimmy and I are spending the night in the orderly room, for after we got the men all stowed away and went to look for our own billet found Billy Witherell and another B Company officer in possession and all ready for bed. It was a mix-up on the part of the billeting officer. Gene Cruise was notified of his promotion to a second lieutenancy this evening, the first direct promotion from the ranks and a well deserved one.

Sunday
Verrieres, Ardennes

Made ten kilometers today. Hear that we are on our own way to join in an attack against Longuyon and Montmedy, Mon Dieu. This is a filthy town, and we K officers drew a room unfit for a drove of hogs, but an hour's cleaning and scrubbing has made it fairly habitable. We rigged up a stove and had our dinner here. Opposite is a large German army bakery where the Boche in their precipitate retreat have left a large quantity of flour. The civilians and doughboys have been carting it away. It makes excellent pancakes.

13

The End

Briquenay, Ardennes

We set out at eight o'clock the morning of November 11th, and while we were marching along, a staff officer in a passing motor called out that an armistice was to go into effect at eleven o'clock. It was then about a quarter of. We had learned to fortify ourselves against rumors and none of us took him seriously as we could still hear the guns rumbling up front, and two planes were peppering away at each other not so far away. However word soon came down the line that the report had been confirmed, and we strained our ears to hear the last gun shot. It was quite different from what I had anticipated. There was no demonstration at all, and we continued to march on in unbroken ranks, the whole regiment in a column of squads. For the first time since I've been in the war zone, I'm writing by an unshaded candle, but even now I'm afraid I'll wake up to find that it's only another dream. For a while I gave up hope of ever seeing the end of the war, and now that we've actually lived to see it finished, it's difficult to accustom our ideas to the change. Hiked about twenty kilometers and pulled in here around one o'clock in the afternoon. Had trouble finding cover for the outfit as there isn't much left of the town. A short while ago we got newspapers telling of the Kaiser's flight into Holland, and of the revolution in Germany and declaration of a republic. Events are tumbling over each other. Likewise rumors, but we hear on good authority that the 1st, 2nd, 42nd, and 89th Divisions are to guard certain bridgeheads on the Rhine. We have built a roaring fire, and our morale is pretty high.

The next day we are still at Briquenay enjoying ourselves as best we can. We officers of K Company have taken over the second floor of a dilapidated house, minus windows, doors, and portions of wall, floors and roof. The shat-

13. The End

tered bits of furniture and some window sashes have gone into the fire, and our bed-dining-living room is not so forlorn as it sounds, for in spite of the many apertures we are quite warm. We also have an excellent view of the melancholy ruins of Briquenay through a gaping shell hole in the front wall. Have annexed a new orderly in the person of "Aunt Jane" (Blake). He is a character, has false teeth, and chews tobacco. That makes the sixth I've had since I joined the outfit. Kit Lane, Skip Johnson, George Woodard, George Kalles, Eddie Bray all having preceded him. A detachment of replacements for the 77th Division passed through town this afternoon and is camped just outside. Most of them are non-coms from the old 1st and 2nd Iowa regiments. All of them have friends, and many of them, relatives in the 168th.

Landreville, Ardennes

We depart from Briquenay on the 13th with augmented personnel, for many of the aforementioned non-coms took French leave of their detachment commanders and have attached themselves to us. We're going to keep them if we can for they appear to be a fine bunch. Wayne Simerman's and Bill Drake's (Cpl. Will A.) brothers are among the ten or twelve that have come with K. A mean hike of some twelve kilometers through country completely devastated all the way to Landreville, which is as triste as its surroundings. We were at first assigned to a wind swept hillside, but later to a barn, which, though forbidding, is preferable to the other, for it is cold and cheerless outside. Today's papers (that is yesterday's that have arrived today) announce the terms of the armistice. It amounts to an unconditional surrender, for Foch has demanded everything he wants, and it leaves Germany practically helpless. Some think it a shame that we didn't carry the war into Germany and give them a good taste of it, but I'm glad that we don't have to see any more of our own killed or wounded. I never could overcome the shock of seeing someone who had been living the same life, sharing the same views, hardships, and associations, suddenly struck down, although it was the thing to expect. It's reported that the Crown Prince has been assassinated.

Landres-et-St. Georges, Ardennes

Had a short hike of three kilometers the morning of the 14th, which brought us within stones throw of the place where the regiment saw such fierce fighting just a month ago. The fields are pitted with shell holes, and the village, of course is in utter ruins. The last word in desolation. We officers are in a mangled shack on the edge of town, but the men are stuck on a bleak hillside with only their pup tents for shelter. We built a fire, and Bill, Tush, and I passed the evening at pinochle. General MacArthur, much to everyone's satisfaction, is now commanding the Division. General Menoher has been promoted to command A Corps. A year ago today we sailed from New York on the *Celtic*, and with many who won't go back with us. The sensations of a lifetime have been crammed into this one year, and I'm glad it's behind, and not before us.

It is frightfully cold the next day, and we've spent the day huddled around a smoky fire. The men are having a hard time of it. Their food gets stone cold in their mess kits before they can eat it and the only way for them to keep warm is to wrap up in their blankets and keep to their tents, but in spite of it all there is remarkably little complaint.

Murvaux, Meuse

Below freezing all day, and a stinging wind that made marching a misery, but we put twenty-two kilometers behind us on the 16th. As we were coming into Dun-sur-Meuse we were greeted by a contingent of newly liberated prisoners of war, French, Russian, and Italian, all oddly clothed, unkempt and haggard, but happy. A French corporal told me they had been walking for three days. Dun is picturesquely situated on and around an eminence above the river, and in spite of debris and filth is a really artistic ruin. Murvaux, though shattered, is anything but artistic, already crowded with Pioneer troops, and poor accommodations. We had to take what we could find.

It's November 19th and what a hopeless place this is. We have the alternative of freezing outside, or suffocating inside from the smoke of the stove in our billet. There are twelve of us in one room with bunks formerly occupied by German soldiers. For once the enlisted men are more comfortably located than the officers. However our mess is quite cozy, so small that when we all squeeze around the table there isn't room for any cold air, and our hot cakes are still holding out. I think the Boche made a special effort to dirty Murvaux before withdrawing, and their methods of scattering hate are illustrated on the building across the way. On it in large black letters a foot high is painted "Gott Strafe England."

13. The End

Ire-le-Sec, Meuse

We were on the road all the next day but made only twenty kilometers as there was such congestion that we were held up for hours at a time. Came through Brandeville and Louppy, arriving here after dark. But have been repaid by drawing a warm clean billet with mighty nice people. Marichel Foch and President Poincaré were here in the afternoon, and it was the daughter of our home who presented the bouquets. She is very much set up about it. From all we hear, there was a great celebration. This is the first intact place we've struck, for it was behind the German lines when the armistice was signed. But the Boche have stripped it clean of livestock, food, copper, linen, and everything else of any value. Since they left, and I imagine for a long time previous to that, these people have been living on black bread and a vile coffee substitute made of roasted barley, and that is absolutely all. This evening we shared our rations with our hosts, the first white bread and the first butter they've tasted since the German occupation in 1914. The women were all forced to work either in the fields or on the roads, rain or shine the year round, and even the children had to make their contribution. All the grain raised was commandeered by the German army. Madame, who is between 70 and 75 years old, told us that she was imprisoned for 15 days for having in her possession a small quantity of wheat which she had gleaned from the fields after the harvest. Our Division is now in the newly organized Third Army, composed of the 1st, 2nd, 3rd, 4th, 5th, 26th, 32nd, 42nd, 89th, and 90th Divisions.

Lamorteau, Province de Luxembourg, Belgium

We are just over the Belgian border within sight of Montmedy, which we passed the afternoon of the 21st. Fine weather and good roads, so our jaunt of twenty kilometers seemed like nothing, and we got in at half past one. Saw any number of long-range guns, which the Boche have abandoned along the road. None of the bridges or highways is blown up back here and we are well into the region of good billets. Jimmy, Tush, and I are together. Our mess is below, and in the kitchen is a real porcelain bathtub. Our hostess, a semi-invalid, is a genial, rotund old soul, and from what she has told us of her encounters with German officers billeted on her, is not entirely lacking in independence. The Belgians, after the first fury of the Boches was spent, suffered less than the French in the "pays envahis" (invaded countries). There are tales of harsh treatment and unending requisitions, but the women were not forced to manual labor, at least in this section. In each of the villages around here are from 40 to 45 evacuees. Before the last offensive was well under way the Boche compelled the inhabitants of the threatened villages to leave at a moments notice, and distributed them among the places beyond the zone of operations. A woman from Brandeville (through which we passed yesterday) told us this afternoon that on October 2nd the civilians of that village were given less than an hour's notice to pack up and get out, so they had to leave most of their possessions behind. She did roadwork practically every day of the four years occupation, and said they probably would have starved if it hadn't been for the American and Spanish relief commissions. We can buy here, at fabulous prices, milk, chickens, rabbit, and meat, for the Boche went through here in such a hurry they didn't have time to gather it all up. Eggs are 15 francs a dozen.

Rachecourt, Province of Luxembourg, Belgium

November 22nd has been a day of triumphal progress. The civilians have had time to recover from the bewilderment at the sudden change in affairs, and have made great preparations to properly receive us. We have met with one tumultuous demonstration after the other at Harnoncourt, Saint-Mard, Chenois, Latour, Vire, Signeulx, Baranzy and Musson. Each village has its triumphal arch, and many flags and banners. We were most wildly acclaimed at Musson. The entire population augmented by a number of Italian prisoners met us on the outskirts with flowers and cheers, and escorted us not only through their own village but halfway to Rachecourt where we were received by the assembled Rachecourtois. We made our entries with the band gaily playing and flags flying, and a good time was had by all. Billets are scarce, for Rachecourt is a small place, and the entire regiment is here, but Jimmy and I were lucky, and drew a good room with a big bed whose comfort I shall soon test, and solicitous hosts with whom I've spent the evening talking. The things they told me, of atrocities in this very neighborhood in 1914, are no hearsay fabulations. Three hundred civilians were shot at Ethe, about six miles from here, and at Latour (on today's march) 45 men were lined up and shot down in cold blood by a machine gun after first being made to dig their own graves. The offense being, that after an engagement outside the village they cared for the wounded Belgians left on the field, and were thus condemned for "rendering assistance to the enemy." And similar outrages at St. Leger and neighboring villages. It will take more than one generation

13. The End

for the hatred for the Germans to die out. We hiked steadily from nine to three today, and covered twenty-five kilometers.

Eischen, Grand Duche de Luxembourg

November 23rd was a continuance of yesterday's celebration, an ovation all along the route of march. Crowds were even more vociferous, bouquets and arcs de triomphe in profusion. Painted banners with "Homage a nos Saveurs," "Homage a Wilson," Homage aux Americains," "Homage a nos Liberateurs" greeted us on every hand. But what took my fancy was the hastily improvised American flags, some with five stripes and four stars, others all stripes and no stars, many weird combinations that might approximate our colors. But we recognized the effort to show their gratitude and were properly appreciated. Our last reception was at Arlon, and then we crossed into Luxembourg, and what a change, sullen looks from the few on the streets, and furtive glances behind curtained windows, rather dampening after the wonderful spirit in Belgium. We made, in all, twenty kilometers and are just four from Arlon. It has been a magnificent day. These people all understand German, but speak among themselves an unintelligible Landblatt. Jimmy and I have a tiny room without a stove, but there's one downstairs where we have our "popote."

Sunday
Eischen, Luxembourg

Everyone resting and cleaning up. We are to be here four or five days. A decided change has come over the villagers. Their disobliging attitude yesterday was chiefly due to fear, for the withdrawing Boche told them we would probably make a second Belgium of Luxembourg for having been friendly with Germany during the war. And now since they see we're quite civilized, they've become much more obliging. Our landlady speaks fair French as she worked for a number of years in Reims. She tells me that even before the war Germany had a stranglehold on Luxembourg. It was a member of the German Zollverein (tariff union), and German capital controlled all the mines and railroads in the country. But popular sympathy was with the Allies in the war, though they didn't dare express it, as the Boche army overran the duchy at the very beginning and were in occupation until a few days ago. It was very galling to them as they are

Ihre königl. Hoheit Marie Adelheid
Grossherzogin von Luxemburg.

13. The End

particularly jealous of their independence, and were afraid of being annexed to Germany. Their national motto is "Mir wolle bleiwe wat mir sin" (we want to remain what we are). Eischen is a neat little village, guiltless of manure piles, and surrounded by beautiful pine forests, reminiscent of the bosqes. Wrote a lot of letters this evening.

November 25th was a disagreeable day. Paid the company in the morning and attended regimental officers meeting in the afternoon. Colonel Tinley read an order just sent down from GHQ to the effect that if we officers do not toe the mark and strictly follow regulations we will be superseded by "anxious and willing" officers from the S.O.S. Now that we've done all the dirty work, they are going to hold us in place by threats. The spirit of the order has created general dissatisfaction.

Went to bed at six o'clock last night. Had the 26th to ourselves. I took a long walk and read some. Met the Burgomeister, who invited me in to have a glass of wine and to discourse on the political situation. The present Grand Duchess, Marie Adelaide,[1] is unpopular because of her pro–German inclinations, and has been asked to abdicate. So far she has refused to. There is a strong movement for the establishment of a republic, but the Herr Burgomeister is opposed to that. He prefers the monarchy with one of Marie Adelaide's sisters as head of state.

Spent the following day in the city of Luxembourg. It can't be more than twenty kilometers from here, but we went by such a roundabout way that it took nearly three hours, including a fifty minute wait at Petange, where we changed cars. The dinky trains are in keeping with everything else in this comic opera country. Hope must have visited here before he wrote *The Prisoner of Zenda*. It is less than 1,000 square miles in area, and has only 300,000 inhabitants. Luxembourg with 25,000 is the largest city in the duchy. It is built on both sides of the deep valley, almost a gorge, of the Alzette, and the two parts of the town are connected by a graceful bridge. I thought it very quaint in spots and would like to have had more time to wander about in the out-of-way places, but it was raining and I confined my sight seeing to the main thoroughfares. I saw the modest grand ducal palace, inside and out. Met Jimmy Bonham and Teddy Jones (more or less pie-eyed) about one o'clock at the Staar Hotel and had lunch with them. They steered me to the municipal bathhouse where I had

Opposite: Marie Adelaide, the Duchess of Luxembourg, who was forced to abdicate and went into a convent. One of her sisters was later sent to concentration camps by the Nazis.

a "Luxusbad" in an individual marble lined Roman bath. Then we repaired to a confectioner to consume many portions of real ice cream at three francs a dab. Things are atrociously high, and as they give us only even exchange, we made very few purchases. The streets were gay with flags, and a court of honor had been erected for the reception of General Pershing with the first detachment of Americans. Just caught the 5:24, and had seats all the way home. Yesterday Firth (Lt. Robert M., M), Piggott, and another officer missed it and had to walk back to Eischen, some thirty kilometers by road. They got in at four this morning.

Thanksgiving, November 28th

A late breakfast and a light lunch in preparation for tonight's feast, which had been three days in the making. Luke was put in charge of arrangements, and scoured the country to set before us the most prodigal and lavish display of food we've seen since leaving home. He reserved a café especially for the officers of the Third Battalion, and at five thirty we sat down to a banquet of roast turkey with stuffing, chicken, duck, mashed potatoes and gravy, pie, cake, and many other delicacies, all washed down with generous quantities of well chosen wines and champagne. Until overcome, Bill acted as toastmaster when Tucker ably substituted. Luke gave a clever dance, and had engaged a good tenor, while between speeches (to which nobody listened) the ten-piece orchestra played. Major Brewer, who has just returned after ten weeks in the hospital, was the guest of honor. We didn't leave the table until ten o'clock.

The day after the Regiment went off somewhere to be reviewed by the new Divisional Commander, General Flagler. I stayed home to inspect billets, write letters, and be lazy.

I went over to Arlon the afternoon of the 30th with Tush and Piggott. They stayed over for the evening, but I found nothing of interest, and came back to Eischen for dinner. Nothing else to report.

Sunday
Walferdange, Luxembourg

On the road again. Set out with a cloudy day and a discouraging hill before us, but by the time we got to the top it cleared off beautifully, and we struck

13. The End

the loveliest pine forest yet. Our path lay through Steinfort, a surprisingly up-to-date town, and just skirted the northern edge of Luxembourg, arriving at Walferdange, just five kilometers beyond, at three o'clock, making twenty-seven or eight kilometers altogether. Billets are scarce, so Madame Bofferding has opened up her whole house to K Company. The halls, kitchen, dining room, living room and attic are carpeted in khaki. Jimmy and I have a sumptuous apartment, stove, electric light, and embroidered linen sheets.

Biwer, Luxembourg

December 2nd saw a hard hike of 24 kilometers, mostly uphill. The family on whom Jimmy and I are billeted entertained us this evening in the dining room, the only warm spot in the house, and put out some excellent wine.

14

Germany

Edniger, Germany

At 1:30 the afternoon of the 3rd we crossed the Sauer River, at Rosport, into Germany. No triumphal arches here, but no display either of ill feeling. This is a dirty village, and we have a filthy billet. All the K officers in the same room, and all on cots, as no one wants to take a chance on the beds. Twenty monotonous kilometers today.

Eisenach

Short hike of six kilometers on the 4th, but uphill practically all the way. Have a clean room. Charley, Jimmy, and I. A relief after the dirty hole at Edniger. The people are very friendly, although we hold aloof. The woman of the house asked at bedtime if we found things satisfactory, and brought us a jugful of cider. We are due for a days rest tomorrow, but hear that we're going ahead Just the same.

Ordorf

A stiff march on December 5th, up hill and down dale, more up than down, and wretched roads. A dismal day too, foggy and a penetrating drizzle. But the Third Battalion has a good village all to itself, and Tush, Jimmy and I are snugly ensconced in a warm, clean billet where we also have our own mess. I got busy, as soon as we arrived, and bought apples, eggs, and milk, which Happy converted into tasty pies. The Germans are so obliging and amiable that I'm beginning to believe it is all part of an organized movement to win us over, and it certainly is having its effect on the men. Surely no people with the least spirit could so ingratiate themselves with the invading troops. But there's no denying it. It is pleasant to find the bed warmed up at night, with a glass of cider nearby, and one's boots cleaned in the morning. In our house live two 75-year-old twins with bushy white hair and beards, the spittin image of Santa Claus.

Manderscheid

Our wanderings over twenty-six perpendicular kilometers in a heavy mist brought us to Manderscheid on the 6th, which, in peace times is a popular "Luftkurort" (health resort). Hence numerous hotels, and the luxurious (comparative) apartment that Jimmy and I drew. Not only have we a stove (no fuel however), twin beds, and electric light, but gorgeous sofas, chairs, and any amount of impediments all violently upholstered in bright red plush. No meals are served here so we have located our mess in a tidy cottage nearby. The natives are cordial and accommodating as can be.

Neunkirchen

We were sanguine enough to hope for a day or two's rest at Manderscheid, but no such luck. Out on December 7th we marched at eight o'clock into the mud and the mist for the hills that lead to this place. Surely there never was a dirtier, smellier, gloomier excuse for a village. We had only 18 kilometers to make. During the rare intervals when the sun broke through the fog we got glimpses of lovely forest but most of the time it was impossible to see across the road. However I had a huge beefsteak sandwich to cheer me up at lunchtime. We hike steadily with no halt for the mid-day meal, so we eat what we can take with us. We hope to reach our destination in four days.

Sunday

This, of all places, is the one chosen for a stopover. A murky day, and equally disagreeable indoors, though this billet is a slight improvement over the one we were dumped into yesterday. Jimmy and I are somewhat cramped in our dark, damp room, Gott Strafe Deutschland.

Neichen

Actually had an hour and a half of sunshine Monday morning, and that made our etape of eighteen kilometers seem much less. K has a tiny village all to itself, not even Battalion HQ to rank us out of the best billets, and we are comfortably lodged. Al and I have rooms in the same house. Our mess is "bei der schulmeister" (in the school house), just across the street where we have a comfortable living room with a piano, stove, and brilliant red wallpaper. Neichen hasn't more than 25 houses, most of them so old that the moss on the roofs is a foot thick. We are to stay here for two or three days.

Neichen

Tuesday is another dreary day, with less diversion than yesterday. This is the quietest place I've ever been in, some distance off the main road, and practically isolated. Not a single vehicle has passed through the streets since we arrived. The civilians have little contact with the outside world, and seem content to live in this little universe of their own. I stayed in bed until eleven, and feel quite fit now. But this sitting around twiddling our thumbs is getting on everyone's nerves. Rumors of mail.

Neichen

Miserable weather continues on the 12th, gloomy, foggy and rain. Doesn't get light until 7:30 and by 3:30 in the afternoon it is too dark to read. But I escaped our funeral surroundings long enough to make a trip to Regimental HQ at Kelberg (8 kilometers). I borrowed Al's charger. Stopped on the way at Boxberg (Battalion Headquarters) to have an ambulance sent over to evacuate three or four men, Tommy Reese (Cook) is very sick. The roads were muddy, and badly cut up by the numerous trucks that crowd one off to the side and spray mud all over at the same time. I got our paychecks from Captain Davis and exchanged francs for marks at the rate of 130 for 100. The civilians give us only 80, the pre-war rate of exchange. Also picked up some old mail at the P.O.

14. Germany

where I met Captain Bunch. I rode back to Boxberg with him. He is a very good sort, and everybody likes him. Devoted most of the afternoon to paper work, straightened out the mess account with Happy, wrote a letter and now it's dinnertime.

Later the Herr Schulmeister, accompanied by two lovely "lehrerinnen" (teachers) from Boxberg, appeared in our midst this evening. Their mission being to entertain us, the females supposedly being able to speak English, and sing. They did both, very badly. They had the nerve to start in on "Heil Dir Im Siegerkrauz".[1] I nipped that in the bud and suggested that if they must indulge in patriotic airs they might try the Marseillaise. Now to bed.

Neichen

This place has a monopoly on rotten weather. I had some thing to occupy my mind all day, December 13th, so I didn't get the blues like the others. Anyhow our mess keeps up to standard, though the menu is somewhat restricted. Eggs, when obtainable, now bring 15 marks a dozen, and to the Germans a mark still represents 25 cents. We did manage to corner some chickens which Happy served fried for the past two evening meals, and to avoid repeating last night's dessert (rice-pudding) we did without any tonight. Have had all my laundry done and am all ready to leave tomorrow. Hurrah. The mail just came in.

Luxem

Up at five the next morning in order to have breakfast, Pack up the kitchen and get over to Boxberg in time to march out at seven with the rest of the battalion. Bad roads, and I'm beginning to think the entire surface of Germany must be corrugated. Drizzled all day long. We made twenty-eight kilometers and landed here at Luxem about two o'clock. Jimmy and I are in a good billet, two small beds, electric light, and holy pictures. Our dining salon is next to us.

Sunday
Glees

Things more cheerful today, sunlight and good roads. We got up early and were well on our way at sunrise, which was gorgeous. The country we passed through just missed being mountainous, and we had several hard pulls. Wound our way through Monreal, a delightfully picturesque old town with the ruins of a feudal castle perched on a hill high above. En route we met a battalion of the 47th Infantry coming from the other direction. Saw De Graff of my class at Columbia but didn't recognize him till after he had gone by. He was on horseback at the head of a column. Came through Mayen, a larger city, and judging from the architecture, quite as old. I noticed a heroic stature of the Kaiser, which was diplomatically shrouded in burlap. Clicked off the thirtieth kilometer at half past two, and halted at Glees where we are happily settled for the night.

Niederzissen, Brohltal

At last our trip is ended, for we hear this is to be our permanent station. Last night after Jimmy and I had dropped off to sleep Runt came in with a bunch of mail that had just arrived, so we switched on the light, and read letters till early in the morning. Having heard the plaint of a woman whose hives had been robbed during the night, we set out, in a drizzle again, at half past eleven and got here on December 16th via Burgbrohl in two hours. Niederzissen is a large village with plenty of rooms for us all. The Gasthaus Schleich where Jimmy and I live is a cross between a country inn and a modern roadhouse. I have a large refrigerated "schlafzimmer" (bedroom), hung with battle pictures. Jimmy's is smaller, has a stove and holy pictures. Below, our dining room boasts of a good piano and a warm fire. Had some unpleasantness with our waspish hostess who has not yet reconciled herself to the American occupation. She objected to furnishing us with dining and table linen, but saw the force of our arguments.

Did little other than inspect billets on December 17th. This evening I had a fine hot bath at the convent. It is the only place in town with a tub, but said tub is large enough to make up for the deficiency. I am really clean this time. A wonderful night.

Drilled a short while the morning of the 18th. It was called off on account of the rain. I have made a great find, two rooms, and a well-appointed bedroom with a pleasant living room adjoining, at the Balushof, so I promptly moved. My suite is all by itself on the second floor and I am the best-situated officer in the battalion. My new hosts have kept up the fire in my living room all evening. I am surrounded by holy pictures, bleeding hearts, etc., and in one corner is a shrine to which I can repair in case of necessity. Al (Piggott) and Robbie

14. Germany

The Rainbow Division was the Army of Occupation on the Rhine after the armistice. Donovan Collection, United States Army Heritage and Education Center, Carlisle, Pennsylvania.

(Mohn) spent the evening with me. I got a lot of magazines in the mail and had a good time reading.

Such a sleep, between embroidered linen sheets, and a feather bed surrounding. If the Major sees this he'll surely rank me out of it. From where I'm sitting I can see the ruins of Raubritter castle picturesquely sprouting from a hilltop several miles away.

From the other window I get a view of a wide meadow cut through by the Brohl, which gives this valley its name. The railroad is quite close, but it is a tiny narrow gauge affair with but four trains a day, there is little noise, and the place is scrupulously clean. Another advantage is that Herr Holthausen gets all the briquettes he wants from the Brohltalbahn, so warmth for winter is ensured. A short drill the next morning, followed by a stupid meeting. Wrote letters all afternoon. Later, after dinner, a pianist, native, but good, came in to entertain us with Chopin.

A Rainbow Division Lieutenant in France

Herr Holthausen had my fire burning briskly when I got up on December 20th, and brought me hot water for shaving. Although there wasn't a speck of dirt anywhere, the whole place has been carefully gone over by Frau Holthausen and her young daughter, Trautsche. I shall be horribly spoiled. Happy served notice that if we want a real Christmas dinner, he'd have to have many things that can't be purchased here, among them eggs, apples and chickens. So I started out with John Tanner (Pvt.) to see what luck we'd have in the neighboring unoccupied villages. We had a fine walk, several miles, mostly through forest to Konigsfeld. The peasants weren't so docile there, and refused to part with a thing, even at a price of their own making. So I announced that if they wouldn't sell, we'd just requisition what we wanted. We came away with as much as we could carry, five chickens, a basket of apples, and 39 eggs, collected and paid for, piece by piece at fifteen different places. Happy, though drunk, gave us a fine lunch, but had succumbed to the effects of too much vin blanc by dinnertime, so Fraulein Schleich, who has experienced a complete change of heart, prepared the evening meal for us. Aunt Jane came in a little while ago banged up from a fight in which, among other casualties, his false teeth were demolished. So he is utterly forlorn, and whistles when he talks. Jimmy and Charley came up for a quiet evening, we read and wrote letters.

After inspection in morning of the 21st we had the day to ourselves. I got ten letters at breakfast and have already answered most of them. I thought of walking to Niederbreisig, ten kilometers to the east, on the Rhein, where Regimental Headquarters and the 1st Battalion are stationed, but it is to mean outside, and too comfortable in. The second Battalion is at Burgbrohl halfway between the river and us. I Company and the Machine Gun Company are at Oberbreisig, just a little way up the valley (Oberzissen).

Didn't get up till ten on the 22nd, and when I walked into my living room there was Frau Holthausen bringing in my breakfast on her best china. I ate at ease in the streaming sunlight. This evening the entire family came in to invite me to take Christmas dinner with them, and stayed two hours. Their landblatt is almost unintelligible, and I hope they understood more of my conversation than I did of theirs. They are typical Germans in that they stand in great awe of the officer class. I am treated with the greatest respect and deference, and am addressed as Guadiger Herr Lieutenant. I gave Herr Holthausen twenty-five marks to buy a "weihnachts geschenk" (Christmas gift) for Trautsche. He was quite overcome.

The next day everything is running smoothly. Frau Holthausen just brought me a big plate of freshly baked "weihnachtskuchen" (Christmas cake).

14. Germany

Aunt Jane, too, is being well looked after and he thinks this is a very "Bon" place.

The morning of December 24th I climbed the Bausenberg to get a wonderful view of the Brohltal, the Eifel Mountains in the distance, and a glimpse of the Rhein and the Siebengebirge. Once upon a time the Bausenberg was a volcano, and the volcanic formation is still plainly evident, though it is well grown over. Teddy and Dick Lombard (Lt. Richard, L) made me a long visit this afternoon, during which mein Frau appeared with a plate of waffles and a bowl of apples. The Holthausens are such souls that one can't help liking them, though they probably hurrahed as loud as any when the *Lusitania* went down. I found out today that Trautsche is their adopted daughter. She doesn't know it yet. Therese had prepared a great surprise for us when we walked into the dining room this evening. She had trimmed up and lit a big Christmas tree in the corner, and in the center of the table, which was decorated in style, reposed a huge cake, her handiwork too. While we ate, the two-piece orchestra (piano and violin), which she had engaged, played for us. She and her brother Eduard (who was rather ill at ease) ate with us, and we had a merry time. Then when I came home to bed, here was another beautiful tree all lit up for me, and a bottle of champagne ("schaumwein") and some cigars as a Christmas present from the Holthausens.

Christmas Day
Niederzissen

After a late and hearty breakfast I turned up here to find one place set for dinner. I was to dine in solitary state, as the family did not think it would be fitting for me, an officer, to eat with them. But after much protest on their part I induced them to draw up three more chairs and attack the scrumptious (from the German viewpoint) meal steaming before us. We had some of everything on the Rheinish culinary list, including four different kinds of meat. Spent the afternoon talking with my hosts between sips of "Apfelwein" (cider), and at four we partook of coffee and a delicious "Bauer Kuchen" (farm cake). So I wasn't exactly ravenous when I arrived at the Gasthaus Schleich for our own celebration. Therese and Eduard were our guests. Gene became so demonstrative that he had to be led away to bed. Happy did himself proud, and gave us a wonderful treat. I am prepared to review a long line of ancestors in my dreams. We had a heavy fall of snow last night, and the moon on it tonight is lovely.

A Rainbow Division Lieutenant in France

Gene left early December 26th for the Officers School at Chatillon-sur-Seine. Some continental mail today, and among other things I got a peach of an amber pipe that Mrs. Knowles bought for me in Belgium. Charley, Tush, Al and Jimmy came up this evening after officers meeting to see my tree and drink my excellent champagne. Frau Holthausen brought in apples, cakes and a jug of cider, so we had quite a party. But nobody would take a chance on the cigars.

Set out bright and early December 27th for Neuenahr. I had intended to ride over but the roads were too icy for the horse, so I hoofed it. Went through Waldorf to Franken where I met a native, recently ushered out of the army, who offered to show me the way. He took me through Sinzig, six kilometers out of the way, but pointed out the objects of interest en route, among them the "schloss" (castle) of Graf Von Spee[2] who gave the English so much concern in South American waters. My friend hadn't much to say about the war except that he was glad it was over. He wasn't very enthusiastic about the new republic. I left him at Lohndorf and walked on through Heimersheim to Neuenahr, about twenty-four kilometers in all. Found Mrs. Knowles at home in Telegrafen Strasse, and had lunch with her and Major Conkling, who had been invited previously. While we were waiting she made us both Rainbows for our sleeves. Later went over to the hospital (formerly the "kurhaus" casino) and there met Captain Neetz whom I last saw with Hilbert in Hempstead. Neuenahr is a fine little town, the house of Apollinaris water, and being a popular "kurort" (spa) is well equipped with shops and hotels. I left at four in a mean drizzle thinking I could hop a truck or ambulance, but not a thing came my way. I left the main road at Lohndorf, and took the short cut through the woods for Franken. By that time it had got so dark I couldn't see my hand before my face, and a heavy wind and drenching rain made the going more difficult. In the middle of the forest I missed the trail altogether and thought I was lost for sure. The walking was frightful, a foot of good rich mud glazed over by a thin coating of ice, so that I went through at every step. But I finally came out at the right place and got here about nine, soaked to the skin, cold, hungry, and a trifle weary from my forty-kilometer jaunt. I got into my pajamas and in front of the fire where I ate the hot dinner Happy had saved for me. I was put on guard during my absence, but Al generously mounted guard for me at two o'clock, so there's nothing to be done but look wise. A goodly batch of letters for me in tonight's mail. Rumor that we leave on the ninth of January.

Got up somewhere near nine o'clock Saturday morning. Frau Holthausen served me breakfast in my living room. Jane has got my clothes dried and

14. Germany

pressed, so I'd better dress and inspect the guard. Just notified that I have been delegated to write up the trench period of our battalion for the Regimental History. It is supposed to be in tomorrow and I haven't even seen the four company representatives who have been selected to help me.

Sunday

Busy all day collecting and consolidating the material for the history. The assistants aren't much use. This afternoon Tucker came over and persuaded me to write up the St. Mihiel show. I'm letting myself in for a lot of work, but I'm glad to have something to occupy my mind. Tucker, Ball (Lt. John W., Rgt. HQ), and Witherell have been relieved from all other duty so they can devote all their time to the history.

The whole battalion hiked over Monday to Brohl to see the river. Tucker met us there and took Major Yates, Jimmy Cotter, Pritchard (Lt. Herbert, I) and me home to lunch with him at Niederbreisig. He has a wonderful billet, the Villa Carlsheim, overlooking the Rhein, with three servants, the products of a good-sized hothouse, and a wine cellar at his disposal. He could have had Schloss Rheineck but found it too inconvenient. The Major left early to preside at a court martial. The rest of us caught the evening train to Brohl and hiked up the valley to Niederzissen.

Tuesday is a wonderful, crisp day. I walked down to Brohl and climbed the hill to get a look at Schloss Rheineck. The present Schloss is an ugly modern affair owned by the ex–Reichskanzler, von Bethmann-Hollweg, but the view is superb. The ruins of the original castle are further back. There are numerous legends connected with the place.

Stayed the old year out, the six of us, and Therese. High time and Rhein wine. Tush, Al, and Charley came up to my room to wake me at eleven, and to look for hats, coats, and other articles of clothing reported missing during the jubilating. Therese had hidden them. We had a delicious venison roast for dinner. This evening Frau Holthausen brought me a "brotchen" (bread roll). Have been in Europe parts of three years now.

Jimmy has been at Niederbreisig since yesterday morning, January 1st, but the responsibility of commanding the company hasn't weighed on me heavily. Relieved Teddy Jones of the guard at two o'clock and went up afterward with him to his house where I stayed for dinner.

Thursday, January 3rd I put in the morning on the history. Relieved of the guard by Robinson. Went up to Battalion Headquarters with Tush after dinner to hear Chaplain Strickland (Lt. Henry W.) play on the piano. Then Bill, Tush and I played pinochle till after midnight. Rumor that we leave on the 15th. Raining.

Sunday

Spent last evening with L Company and got to bed at one o'clock this morning. Tush and I climbed the Bausenberg in the afternoon. It was clear and windy. I got a few pictures with a roll of film Jimmy gave me. I doubt if any of them come out for he bought them in Baccarat eight or nine months ago and they have been in his trunk ever since. We went from there up to Battalion Headquarters to have a game of pinochle with Bill. Robb came in. Said we were to be here for three months more. Chaplain Strickland gave us a concert on the piano. He was born in Danville (Pennsylvania, where the author is buried). My Christmas box from home was in my room when I got back. It was crammed with all sorts of things I wanted. Al spent the evening here. I worked on the history and wrote some letters. Frau Holtenhausen brought in some cake.

January 6th being "Heilige Drei Konige" (holy three kings), a high feast day with the Catholic people of the Rheinland, I wasn't called in time for breakfast, as the family thought we had a holiday, too. So I had mine served to myself in my room. Laura's Christmas box from London arrived today. Venison again for dinner tonight. Took a walk through Oberzissen where the guard held me up for not wearing side arms, and wouldn't let me in till I got word to Haley. I intended to get to bed early but my host brought in his father to make a formal call, also some cake and apfelwein. They started in to extol the virtues of the German army and got an earful on the subject from me. They were surprised later on in the conversation to find out that I knew something about German history and politics, too.

January 7th is a beautiful day. After lunch walked over to Burg Olbruck with Aunt Jane for company. He entertains me extraordinarily. He firmly believes in ghosts. He says he has actually seen them and didn't want to go into the tower because it was so dark and spooky. Several of the rooms and the staircase have been restored (by the Kaiser I am told). A magnificent view from the top of the tower for miles in every direction. The top of the mountain is honey combed with underground passages and dungeons. Stopped at a quaint inn at

14. Germany

Hain for refreshment on the way back. This evening the officers of the Third Battalion met at the Gasthaus Schleich for the purpose of organizing a club. Jimmy Bonham was elected president, and Strickland "general manager." No, Strickland was elected treasurer, and Gibbons, vice president and general manager. Bill became tight as usual, and made a long speech. Strickland played the piano till 11:30 when we adjourned.

Made myself unpopular with the kitchen force at inspection the next day by giving them a well merited bawling out. Had a run in with Murphy, the Knights of Columbus man, who messes with us now, at noon. He is bigoted and uneducated, who aired his views on the English, Republicans, and the war, the very first meal he had with us, which was yesterday. At lunch he lit into Roosevelt who has just died, and I left him in no doubt as to where I stood.

He also had a slam for the YMCA. I didn't answer that, though I could have told him that they served us faithfully all through the war, and that we never even saw the Knights of Columbus until after we got to Germany, and then all they've done is to hand out moldy cigarettes. The battalion was paraded this afternoon as a mark of respect to Roosevelt's memory. Argument over the relative merits of the various organizations for the platoon at a meeting this evening. Then the bunch came down to the Gasthaus Schleich, consumed a certain amount of wine, and gassed much.

It's January 9th and nothing is particularly interesting today. Six letters from the states. Baker says we will be here at least until the conclusion of peace. Major Yates intimated that K would go to Waldorf. Aunt Jane has a cold and lays it to a jinx at the castle and won't be convinced otherwise. This afternoon he asked me just where Persia was. I asked why he wanted to know, and he said, "Well I've heard so much about this here Persian guard (Prussian) we were all the time running up against." First meeting in the new club rooms at the Hotel Mertens. I left early and came home to bed.

It was a pleasant evening on the tenth at club. After the others left, Bill, Gibbons, Strickland and I had a long discussion. The chaplain is opposed to prohibition because, among other things, the laws of Oklahoma forbid the use even of sacramental wine.

January 11th was an uneventful day. Bad weather that put an end to a contemplated trip to Burg Olbruck. Party at the club tonight, very stupid. The conversation was chiefly anti–British and anti–French. Bill, Bonham, and Chaplain Strickland had the most to say. Strickland being a Roman Catholic hates the English as part of his religion. Made me tired.

A Rainbow Division Lieutenant in France

Gibbons spent the night here. We talked till one thirty. I slept on the couch in the living room, and not very well. The next afternoon Al and I rode over to Burg Olbruck. I had the Major's horse. It snowed and was cold, but we had a good ride just the same. Bud Patton (Sgt. Paul K.) came in pie-eyed while we were at the dinner table tonight. Brought with him two Russians to play the piano for us. I had to take him to his billet and put him to bed. Listened to a lengthy gabble at the club this evening.

Walked alone through the woods on the 13th to Konigsfeld. Officers meeting tonight. I had an interesting copy of the *Atlantic Monthly*, so I didn't mind it. Had a good letter from GBN. He has gotten on the Peace Mission and is stationed in Paris.

A battalion maneuver the morning of the 14th, which consisted in climbing up and down all the hills between here and Gonnersdorf where we sat around until we got orders to come back. The First and Second Battalions are theoretically fighting a bloody battle at Rheineck, and we were the reserve. Thursday we hike over to Brohl to take over the line from there. Some more mail.

Went to bed at seven thirty last night. About ready to pass out from sheer ennui, but today an order has come down actually granting leaves. I want to put in a few days in Paris and spend the rest of the time in Lorraine, Luneville, Baccarat, Neufmaison and Badonviller. Tonight Bill, Gibbons and I formed a new club. We are the sole members. Gib has been trying to introduce a Bohemian atmosphere into the other one, so instead of paying for the wine as it was served, we were each to put in a box, provided for the purpose, enough money to cover what we had drunk in the course of the evening. It turns out that one or two have bad memories, and Gib is a hundred or so marks out of pocket. So the system has to be discontinued.

Stayed in bed till late. Had lunch alone on the 16th as the rest had gone to Brohl on maneuver. Went up to Strickland's room for an hour and then mounted guard. Bill and Gib dropped in for dinner, and so did Happy Hatch. A very enjoyable meal for me, but uncomfortable for another. Then we all went to a clever show at the Y put on by the Divisional troupe.

There was an animated discussion at the club the next evening on the restriction of immigration. Only Major Yates was opposed to it as he says Iowa needs farm labor. Some people don't ever look beyond their own noses. Luke has asked me to go on hunting and fishing expedition at Maria Laach with him tomorrow. The forester of the district, an ex-lieutenant of the German army, is to act as guide.

14. Germany

Hotel Disch
Cologne

We gave up the hunting trip as we had a chance to come to Bonn on January 18th to witness a field meet between the enlisted men of the Rainbow and the Second Canadian division, which is occupying the city. The delegation consisting of Charley, Tush, Bill, Gib, Teddy, Hagerty (Lt. Sheward, Jr., I), Tittsworth (Lt. William D., L), Pritchard, Firth and I left in a truck at 7:30, and after bumping for two hours through Brohl, Niederbresig, Sinzig, and Remagen, were dumped out on the "Platz" in front of the university. Two truckloads of enlisted men came up with us. We weren't particularly anxious to hang around the field so we set out to see the town. Tush and I broke away from the crowd, but rejoined them later at the Continental for lunch. Gib suggested that in as much we had got that far we might as well go up to Cologne, which we decided to do, though we were supposed to return to the regiment tonight. We watched a soccer game until a quarter of two when we had planned to meet in order to catch the two o'clock train. Teddy, Tittsworth, and Pritchard were missing so I volunteered to wait over a train to look them up, Gib promising to meet me at Cologne. I couldn't find a trace of the three, so left Bonn at half past two. It was just an hour's trip. Gib wasn't on hand to meet me. So I set out to hunt for the crowd and after three quarters of an hour of fruitless search, being held up once by an M.P., I returned very much out of humor to the station and was for taking the next train back.

They all arrived as I was about to pull out, but I cooled off and decided after all to stay. They had been misinformed about the trains. We applied to several hotels for rooms and found them all taken over by the British, so we went boldly up to the British Town Major's offices and asked for billets. The man who happened to be in charge at the time was a German civil servant who speaks English. He confided to me that he always gave American officers precedence over the English, and sure enough gave us rooms at the Disch, which is the chic hotel. We were too late to get in any of the theaters as they all commence at five. All the civilians have to be off the streets at nine. Missed *Rigoletto* at the opera, too. But we landed at the Café Bauer, a gorgeous establishment with a first rate orchestra, where the elite of Cologne gather to guzzle. No signs of starvation here, cakes, pastry and candy in quantities. At seven thirty we went to the Hotel Dom for dinner. Wandered around a while, and then we all turned in early.

A Rainbow Division Lieutenant in France

Sunday

Bill, Gib and I got up later than the others, and when we found the rest breakfasting on many sausages and sewereish looking chocolate (all they could get) we made up our minds not to eat. But a most amiable British officer, overhearing the conversation, volunteered to steer us to an officers' club at the "Evige Lampe" where we had a real English breakfast. Thus fortified we attended High Mass at the cathedral, fine choir and organ, but it was very cold, no heat at all. I think the exterior is magnificent, and the interior proportions admirable, but I was a bit disappointed with the interior. Then we walked around for some time.

The city is occupied by the Grenadier Guards and some other picked troops, a fine looking, well disciplined lot. We met with courteous treatment, and punctilious salutes everywhere. We decided to go back to Bonn for dinner but at the last minute Tush and Charley thought they'd stay over in Cologne till evening, and Firth and Hagerty, getting a trifle nervous, decided to go on straight to Niederzissen. Bill, Gib, and I had a good meal at the Continental, and after seeing a terrible movie, gave Bonn one last look and departed on the 3:58.

Had no trouble in getting seats, as a certain number of compartments on each train are reserved for allied officers. Reached Niederbreisig about five, eluded the guards at the station, and dropped in on Tucker for dinner. At ten we got a car from Regimental Headquarters to bring us home. In our absence Major Yates had been transferred to another outfit as he was anxious to get home, and Major Brewer is in command. Now we'll probably have some system to things. Major Yates is an easy-going, well-intentioned individual whom every one liked, but he lacked executive ability and push. Bill practically ran the Battalion by tactful suggestion.

Jimmy has gone off to Bonn on the 21st. Drilled the company in the afternoon. This evening at the club Major Brewer, Chaplain Strickland, Bill, and I got on the topic of religion, an amicable discussion of course, but I must say the Catholics have no elasticity of viewpoint. Brewer rather leans towards the Episcopalians, and what Bill's religion is, I don't know. After covering and settling every thing in Protestantism, Catholicism, spiritualism and theosophy we broke up for the night. Outside my billet I came upon three drivers whose truck had broken down and who had no place to sleep. So I've given them blankets from my bedding roll and put them in the living room where they'd at least be warm. A grateful lot.

14. Germany

Neuenahr

The Major gave me permission to come over here on the 22nd to have my new uniform made up from the material I bought from Robb while we were in Luxembourg. Tush walked over to Burgbrohl with me. Stopped in a few minutes at Battalion Headquarters. Major Casey said he, Colonel Tinley, Colonel Stanley, Major Ross and several others may be transferred to the First Division, and they're more or less up in the air, as none of them want to leave the outfit. Caught an ambulance and arrived here about eleven. Mrs. Knowles had tried skating down a flight of stone steps, and wasn't feeling very chipper, but recovered in time for lunch. The other guests were a Miss Wilson, of the Red Cross, and Lieutenant Clarke of the 151st. Interviewed the tailor who has agreed to make my uniform for 190 marks, me furnishing all the material. Captain Murray, Miss Wilson's fiancé, got me a fine room in the Kurhaus, steam heat, electric light and bath. Lieutenant Clarke was in for dinner and the three of us went to the movies, and tried making fudge when we got back. Major Conkling, who has the room next to mine, called me in to sample some of his private stock. He is expecting his promotion to Lt. Colonel before long.

I overslept on the 23rd and missed breakfast. Just had time to rush over to Telegrafen Strasse to say goodbye before catching the ambulance. I had a long, cold ride back. It has been snowing all afternoon. This evening I went up to the convent for a bath. While I was waiting for the water to heat, a very good-looking sister entertained me in the kitchen on a bowl of hot milk and cake. The nuns aren't guarded so closely here as at home, and they talk quite freely with us. They are very much interested in the happenings of the outer world.

Breakfasted in my room the next morning. Had two agreeable officers, one from the 149th and the other from the 150th in for lunch with us. Relieved Tittsworth of the guard. Long drawn out meeting this evening.

Sunday

Had a "cafard" (depression) all morning. I walked down to Burgbrohl to spend a couple of hours with Happy Hatch. The cold air and the wind brought me to, and I feel fine now.

Monday I walked to Burgbrohl again with Charley. Brisk and a light snow. Played football in the afternoon. Held non-coms school after dinner, then an officers meeting at the club. Major Brewer spoke on discipline and Bill on morale. M Company furnished the refreshments.

Went over to Neuenahr for a fitting on January 28th. I rode in an ambulance from Burgbrohl to Niederbreisig and the transferred to a truck, which landed me at Neuenahr about noon. Had lunch with Mrs. Knowles, and then to the tailors. The ambulance I had hoped to catch back was crowded, but I fortunately met Major Spealman who sent me home in a touring car. I dropped off at Tucker's to go over with him some of the work I had done. He has tea every afternoon and at four Witherell and Ball dropped in. We had dinner a little early, as I wanted to catch the 7:50 train from Brohl. Amchen said the train for Brohl left Niederbreisig at 7:21. I got to the station to find the next train south was at nine o'clock, so rather than walk the twelve or fifteen kilometers to Niederzissen, I ran all the way to Brohl and just caught the Brohltalbahn. Had an agreeable Lieutenant from the 39th Infantry, 4th Division, for company. They are stationed at Kempenich at the head of the valley. Got some letters in the mail. Rumor that we leave on the sixth of February is quite persistent. Hope it's true.

Wednesday I breakfasted alone and inspected billets. This afternoon we had a great game of football. The officers and some non-coms against a team picked from the rest of the company. I was completely knocked out for a while. Jimmy was kicked in the nose, and Tush, elsewhere. Satisfactory N.C.O.S. school in the evening followed by a lengthy officers meeting.

Last night Happy Roberts got tight and hit Ben Monroe over the head with a bottle. Gave him a nasty gash, where for it has been decreed that Happy be reduced, but not until after tomorrow night when we've invited Battalion Headquarters to have dinner with us. Teddy and I tramped around the country the afternoon of the 30th ending up at Oberzissen. There is great rejoicing with the Schleich family, for the younger brother, Ludwig, has just returned from the Russian front. Jimmy and Luke start tomorrow on a fourteen-day leave to Nice.

On January 31st Jimmy left early. This morning an order came down transferring Robinson to L Company and Charley to F, also assigning a 2nd Lieutenant H.W. Wages to K. I'm glad to lose Robinson, as I find him offensive, but not so with Charley. He is a good officer and well liked. I came in early from drill to see the Major about keeping him and he thinks it can be arranged. Leaves discussed at company commanders' meeting after lunch. I can have mine now, and think I'll put in for the Riviera, too.

Bust all afternoon. We entertained Battalion Headquarters at dinner this

14. Germany

evening. Major Brewer, Strickland, Bill, Doc Van Zandt (Lt. George T.), and Tucker who dropped in unexpectedly. Happy gave us an excellent meal. I Company entertained at the club.

The Major seemed pleased with things at inspection the morning of the 1st, and had no criticisms to make. My pass for Nice has been put in. Charley is to be kept with K Company, temporarily, at least, but Robinson has already gone to L Company. L Company put on the entertainment at the club tonight.

Sunday

My pass came back approved today and I can leave as soon as I want, but I have to wait to get my suit from Neuenahr, and I haven't a cent to my name, as I lent all I had to Jimmy. Also my check hasn't come in. Later, Teddy, Bill and Gib left tonight and wanted me to go with them. My check arrived in the afternoon, but I couldn't get off as Charley has been ordered to school. Al is acting as Adjutant in Bill's absence, and with Gene still away, it would leave Tush alone with the company, and there must be at least two officers on duty. I can leave as soon as Gene gets back, he's already overdue. The Frau Burgermeister got up a concert this evening. She yowled some Wagner at us, terrible, but the cellist was very good.

This week of February 3rd is my week for standing reveille, so I was up early, made a hasty inspection after breakfast and beat it for Weiler to catch the Neuenahr ambulance but it went only as far as Niederbreisig. I hopped a steel tired Boche truck, which had three breakdowns in as many miles, and fortunately a signal truck came along to take me as far as the Ahr. I ended my journey on an American truck. Had lunch with Mrs. Knowles. I garnered some sugar at the cantine for Cousin Alice, some soap for Frau Holthausen, and newspapers for myself. Then we drove over to Ahrweiler with Captain Murray, cashed my check and got the information that we'd be sailing for home in a month from Rotterdam. Captain Murray lent me a car to come back in, first going up the river to Rolandseck to deposit a captain. It was dark and bitingly cold. I stopped at Rheineck to see Witherell about some work. He wasn't in. Tittsworth was there waiting till train time (he had been ordered off to school) and hearing that Percy had just returned from the hospital. I wanted to see him before leaving, so I brought him back to Niederzissen in the car. K Company was in charge at the club, and put out some good food. Charley left this morning, but his order has been countermanded and I expect him back tomorrow. Gene got back this evening, but I haven't seen him yet. Among other arrivals are Woods and Bud Patton who went on an a.w.o.l. trip to Cologne. They got on a spree and stayed longer than they intended. The Major found out they were absent and asked what disciplinary action I'd taken. He thinks I should prefer charges against them. I hate to do it, for all through the war they've both been good soldiers, and Woods and I have been through some mighty tight places together. They've just left my room, a contrite pair. Told them I'd have to reduce them. They said they expected at least that.

Hotel Kaiserhof, Coblenz

No drill this Tuesday morning. The company had its bedding and clothing deloused, instead. Gene had a disagreeable time at Chatillon, and coming back, the officers were shipped in boxcars with the men, a three days trip. Somewhere on the road they broke into a train loaded with champagne and the whole outfit got drunk. The new Lieutenant Wages (Hal W.) reported this afternoon and appears to be quiet and inoffensive. When I found out I was leaving so soon, I decided not to do anything about Woods and Patton, though I have already signed the recommendation breaking them. If they have to be punished, some one else can do it. Left Niederzissen on the 6:21 with a package of cookies, Frau Holthausen especially cooked for me, in my kit bag. Rode down to Brohl with a 4th Division officer who is also headed to Nice. I didn't like him particularly and left him there to go up to Niederbreisig to check out. Waited at Tucker's until train time. He had expected me for dinner, but I had already had mine. Left Niederbreisig at 8:45 and got to Coblenz about ten. Bumped into the aforementioned lieutenant (4th Division) at the billeting window, and was assigned a room here at the Kaiserhof with him.

15

En Route to Paris

I barely caught my train at eight this morning, February 5th, for instead of calling me at seven as I asked, the stupid maid waited until 7:40. I didn't have time to shave or eat. I was in a compartment with a Lieutenant Colonel from GHQ and a staff captain, both of whom turned out to be agreeable and interesting. I got out at Treves (Germany) to hunt for food, and retrieved a couple of sandwiches from the Red Cross and shared them with the other two. Then a lieutenant from Captain Means' company of the 149th Machine Gun Battalion joined us. He was a peach of a chap named Johnson from Lewisburg. We two passed a couple of hours playing cards. The train was wretched, just crawled along, and was unheated. It snowed heavily after we left Treves. We came though Luxembourg and arrived at Metz at half past four. Our train went only as far as Toul, and when I found the Paris train was on the next track, I hopped over in no time and grabbed a seat in a first class compartment. I was just in time, for though we didn't pull out until 5:45, the train soon filled up and the corridors were jammed all the way. My friend the Lt. Colonel shipped me some sandwiches just before we left, or I should have starved, for I haven't been able to get anything else. I got off at Toul to see if there wasn't something to be found at the buffet, but had no luck. I had a hard time crawling over the people and the bundles in the "couloir" (corridor) in order to get back to the compartment. In it with me are two Italian officers en route to Rome from Berlin, a greasy, boorish French Lieutenant, and an American lieutenant named Smith, from Cincinnati, who is on his way to join the 26th Division. He hasn't had anything to eat in twenty-four hours. The Italians brought a well-filled hamper with them and ate loud and long, but kept it all to themselves. We arrived at Nancy at 9:30, four hours late, and stuck there in the yards until 10:45.

A Rainbow Division Lieutenant in France

Paris

Hardly slept at all last night. It got frightfully stuffy so I opened the window a trifle to let in some fresh air and the capitaine of the cabin immediately slammed it down, so we took turns opening and slamming it throughout the night. He got furious at me. Passed through Bar-le-Duc, Chalons, Epernay, Chateau Thierry and arrived in Paris at ten the morning of the 6th. Had to wait half an hour in line to sign up with the M.P.s. I saw Kenneth Todd, who is on his way to see his brother in England. Then I tried to get a room at a hotel. Everything appears to be taken for two weeks in advance. So I called Saxe 17.05 and announced to Lucy, who answered the phone, that I was coming to lunch. As soon as I got there I took a bath and shaved. Both Cousin Paul and Ned were there, Ned, en permission, and Cousin Paul on his way to Nice to visit his mother. He is very distinguished looking. Looked up Hupp at his office, but found only Peckam (Lt. Harold D., 2nd Battalion H.Q.), who told me that he had gone to Bordeaux and also told me where I could find GBN. On my way there I stopped at the O.P.W.'s office to stay over a couple of days in Paris. I expected to be turned down, but there was a kind-hearted officer in charge, who told me to come around five, and he'd see what he could do. I found GBN at the Crillon just about to escort a young lady to the Louvre. So I took them up with me, and went, at Bernard's (GBN) suggestion, to the commandant of the troops in Paris who flatly refused to permit me to stay in Paris. Then I did a lot of shopping, and as I was coming out "Old England," Teddy Jones spotted me, and led me to the taxi where Bill and Gib were reclining. We decided to go to the "Olympia" but I left early to make a last stab at the O.P.W.s, and I actually got permission to stay until 8:15 Sunday morning. I rejoined the bunch at the Grand Hotel where we had dinner and then went to the Folies Bergere. It was the same show I saw in October. Teddy and I left before it was over and came here to the hotel where they've had rooms for several days. Teddy is sharing his bed with me.

Hotel de Crillon, Paris

We had breakfast in bed the next morning just to be lazy. The three of them had overstayed their leave in Paris by two days and knew if they left by railroad they'd be picked up by the M.P.s. So we hunted up a car at the opera and arranged with the chauffeur to drive them to Fontainebleau where they can

15. En Route to Paris

catch a through Express. The chauffeur demanded five hundred francs but I beat him down to 350, an atrocious price. When I came up here to see GBN, he invited me to stay with him as long as I'm in town. He has two rooms and a bath, so I joyfully accepted. I had lunch at Cousin Alice's, and then brought my things over here, and did some shopping. I met them later at the Ritz for tea (Cousin Alice and Lucy). Dinner here with Bernard. All sorts of celebrities

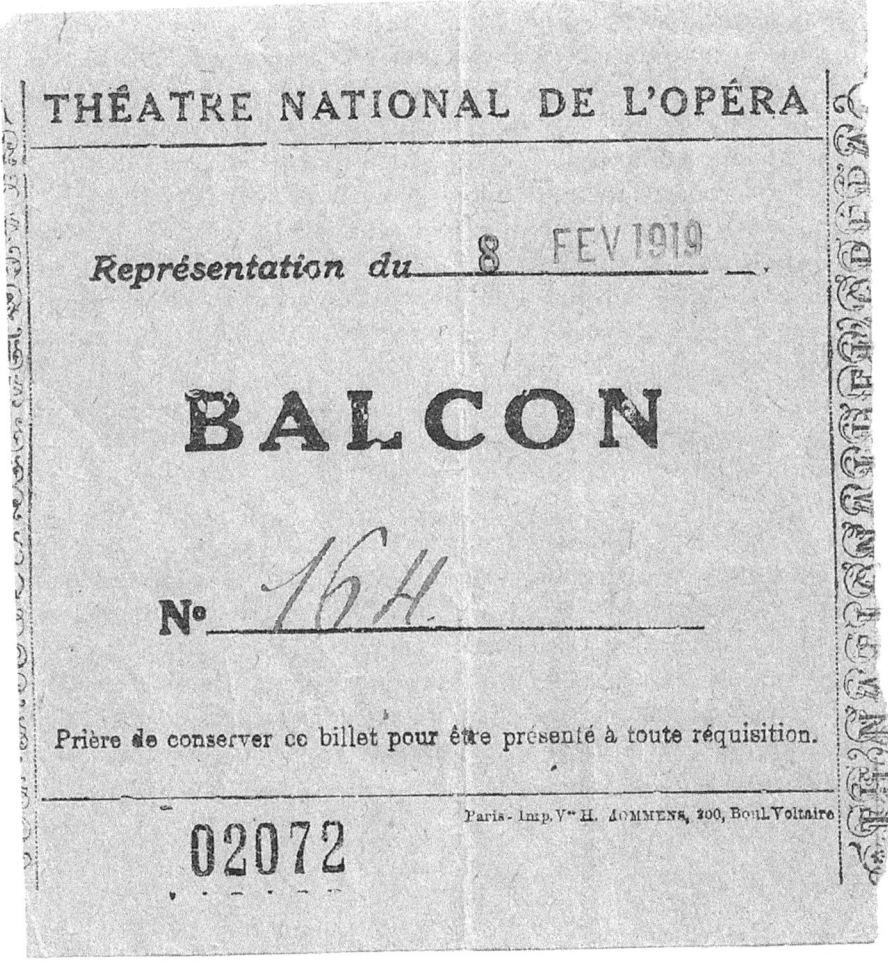

John's opera ticket while on leave in Paris. The Serbian Prince Regent went to the same performance.

sitting all around us. Everyone of importance on the Peace Commission, with the exception of Wilson, is quartered here. Saw General Bliss, Secretary Lansing, and Ambassador White who had a table next to ours. Took a good hot bath and am ready for bed.

GBN got up at six on the eighth, but didn't call me until 8:30 when we had petit dejeuner in the room. It has been a beautiful day, cold and invigorating. Had an interesting time just walking around this morning. Stopped at the Opera for tickets to tonight's performance of *Otello*. In a shop on the Rue de la Paix I spotted a charming baby dress, which I bought and sent to Mary. Lunched at the Crillon with GBN. Got a good view of Wilson as he came out of the elevator with Mr. White and Hoover. We walked to the Louvre and spent a half hour inside, all Bernard could spare, as he is awfully busy. Went over to Cousin Alice's for tea. A delightful woman, the wife of some government official, there too. Captain Hupp came in from Bordeaux today and rushed over here to have dinner with us. We three had a really good time, and talked so much that Bernard and I were quite late for the opera. It wasn't particularly fine, and Bernard left at the end of the third act to come home and work. The Prince-Regent of Serbia, Alexandre, was there, and created a great stir. Had to fight my way home.

Sunday

Captain Hupp told me to stay in Paris as long as I wanted and he would sneak me on to any train through the mail entrance. So I'm staying over on the strength of that. Went to High Mass at Notre Dame this morning. Singing very good. Had dinner here with Bernard. This afternoon as I was starting for a walk I came down in the elevator with President Wilson. He noticed the Rainbow on my shoulder and made some complimentary remark on the work of the Division. I was so flustered at suddenly looking up and seeing him there that I can't remember just what he said.

Hotel de Crillon

Monday is another magnificent day. Walked up the Champs Elysee and out towards the Bois de Boulogne, and then back to the commissary to buy some things for Cousin Alice. Met Major Casey and Riley (Cpt. Chales J., Rgt.

15. En Route to Paris

H.Q.) there. Casey told me that Tush was in town, and when I got back to the hotel I found out that he had already been there and was coming back for lunch. I saw him for a few minutes but had to rush off as I had promised to go to Cousin Alice's. After lunch she and I went to see a remarkable picture at the Pantheon de la Guerre. A panorama with thousands of individuals, leaders of the allied countries and armies, accurately drawn. Bernard had a French friend, Madamemoiselle Dimont here under the patronage of Mrs. Sabin-Pasley, one of his secretaries. He was up to his ears in work, so I took her home, and met her family. We got through dinner so late that we decided not to go out, so we came up, took a bath and are going to bed early.

Was wakened on the 11th by Bernard ordering breakfast. I had slept for ten solid hours. Went out alone this morning and covered about thirty miles of Paris partly in taxi, and partly afoot. Had tea with Cousin Alice and Lucy. There was an oddly dressed and fierce looking individual parading up and down the hotel lobby when I came back. On inquiry I learned that he was the bodyguard of Mr. Venizelos,[1] who was upstairs in conference with House (Edward Mandell)[2] and Wilson. And in a moment a shower of celebrities stepped out of the elevator, Wilson, Lloyd-George, Clemenceau and Venizelos. Went this evening to see a very rotten movie, *Hearts of the World*.[3]

I was out all Wednesday morning. Peeked in the church of St. Gervais, which was struck by a shell from "Big Bertha" last Good Friday. There are scarcely any signs of the shelling and bombing in the city. Captain Hupp had lunch with us and we laughed all through the meal. He is just like he used to be. I've stayed here so long that I'll have to give up my trip to Badonviller. Hupp is to get me a ticket and reservation on the Nice Express for tomorrow night, at least he says he can. He walked around to the Place de la Madeleine while GBN and I had our pictures taken. The photographer said one of the big shells had exploded right on the corner but the only damage it did to the church was to decapitate a statue. Mlle. Dimont came around again for tea, but I missed her as I had already arranged to meet Cousin Alice at Rumpelmayers. Went home with her for dinner and spent a pleasant evening there. Walked home via the Quai d'Orsay. A beautiful misty night and a bright moon overhead.

Thursday and I made most of my last morning in Paris, and scurried around till lunchtime. Captain Pettit, one of Bernard's friends who has charge of the division dealing with Russia, had lunch with us. He had many interesting things to tell. GBN, being one himself, has made friends with a number of brainy men, and has come into contact with many influential people. Captain

Hupp phoned that although the train was running in three sections, it was impossible to get a reservation for tonight, so I'll probably have to stand all the way. If I get too tired I'll get off in Dijon and run up to Baccarat after all. GBN and I met Lucy at Ixe for tea, and she behaved like a stick the entire time. I took her home and said goodbye to the family. All packed up and ready to go. We're going to have an early dinner, for I'm to meet Captain Hupp at the Mediterranee at half past seven.

Hotel Regina, Nice (Cimiez)

Evaded the M.P.s by going through the mail entrance at the Gare de Lyon with Hupp and for a substantial "pourboire" (tip) (50 francs), I managed to get the last reservation from Cook's pirate. Rather an amiable crowd in the compartment, all French but me. It was pretty cold, but I got a bit of sleep. We left Paris at 8:15, Dijon 2 A.M., Avignon at 10 and arrived at Marseille at 12:30. There was snow and ice way south of Lyon. At Marseille the coach I was in was taken off and I had to stand up in the corridor all the way to Nice. But it was so lovely coming along the Mediterranean I didn't mind it much. Arrived at Nice just about six o'clock on the 14th. I got a room and bath for forty francs. Hopped into the tub and had dinner in my room. Walked down to Nice and got a note Gib had left for me at the O.P.W. He said they were staying at the Ruhl, but of course weren't in when I got there. It was so lovely out that I walked all the way home. The moonlight was beautiful and the flowers so fragrant. I had no sooner got into bed then Teddy called up. There is no direct connection with the rooms, so I sent word for him to call up in the morning.

On the morning of the 15th he timed his call well, just as I had finished dressing. Walked down to the Ruhl to meet them. Bill and Gib were under arrest and ordered to leave on the one o'clock train. While the other two kept an appointment at the O.P.W.s, Teddy and I walked up the beach and I heard the story of their escapade, very funny. Had an early lunch and saw them off. I have engaged a room at the Ruhl. It is so much more convenient and lively, though not so chic as the Regina. I hate to give up this marvelous view. Called on the Baroness de Heeckeren to whom Cousin Alice had given me a letter of introduction. She has a suite here at the Regina. I found a charming old lady with a delightful accent.

The next couple of days were too much fun to bother putting it down. Caught the train the 18th.

15. En Route to Paris

On February 19th on the train we're now north of Pout-a-Mousson, and have just passed over what for four years was no-mans land. It was dark when we came through here before. The destroyed towns and factories a vivid reminder of the war.

16

Back to the Rhine

Metz

Got here at 1:30 P.M. four hours late, and now that I've missed the 11 A.M. train for Coblenz, won't be able to get back to Regimental HQ in time. It took us 17 ¼ hours from Paris. In the station I met Graham, the Third Division Lieutenant, who came up in the same compartment from Nice. We had lunch at the Kaiserhof and then walked around the city. The Kaiser's statue which is in a group of saints on the west porch of the cathedral now holds a painted sign "Sic transit Gloria Mundi" and another wag has added a pair of chains to his hands. And in one of the various "Platz" a heroic statue of a Poilu stands on the pedestal formerly occupied by an equally heroic likeness of Wilhem I, now lying face downward at its foot. All signs on shops, public buildings and streets have been changed from German to French, and one hears nothing but French spoken. Metz is a drab city and we soon tired of sightseeing, and went to the movies. A mediocre American picture, *Civilization*. The audience was composed chiefly of French poilus, and I wish the movie director could have heard them laugh at his ideas of battle. *Lelotte, Reine de Cirque* however, was without exception, the funniest bit of slap stick comedy I've ever seen. We had dinner at the station and are now in the train waiting to pull out.

Some difference between the French and German railway service. We left Metz at 6:54 and skimmed along, arriving at Coblenz at midnight. Graham left to rejoin his outfit across the river. Major Brooks (16th Infantry, 1st Division) who traveled with us, got a billet de luxe for the two of us. I got up just in time to shave and catch the 9:28 for Niederbreisig. Riley was unpleasant as possible on my returning late. Said I should have allowed for the Metz train

16. Back to the Rhine

being behind schedule. So I made myself equally disagreeable, and I've no doubt he'll get back at me by shoving some unenviable detail in my direction. I found out later that he got back a day late himself for the very same reason. Met Gene on the train coming up from Brohl. The family gave me a hearty welcome, and after I finished my lunch (that Frau Holtshausen prepared) in walked Louis Savy, the French kid who disappeared so mysteriously just a year ago at Mordor. He says that the French police took him away and put him back in the Orphans Home. He escaped again and started after us, but by that time we were hopping from one front to another, so he got with an American ammunition train and was wounded near Chateau Thierry. Then he spent several months in an American hospital. At Dijon he heard the Rainbow was in the Army of Occupation, and some how or other managed to get up to us. He has learned to speak English well.

Inspected billets (for three companies) the morning of the 21st. I am to be sent to a Liaison school near Coblenz the day after tomorrow for a week. Riley's doing, of course, damn petty of him, I think. Gib is to be a companion in misery.

I got Percy (he is commanding the battalion while Major Brewer is on leave) to call up Regiment HQ on February 22nd to see if he could get me off the school detail, and as a result I'm not to go (I thumb my nose at Riley). Jimmy is sick in bed and we are really short on officers. Inspection of company and muster in the morning. Company commanders meeting this afternoon, and showers all day. The Schleichs' brother-in-law died this morning in Cologne, and I made ineffectual efforts to get their passes issued so they could leave this evening, but they have to go to Division Headquarters for permission to leave the area. I spent the evening at Battalion Headquarters with Bill and Gib, who between drinks wrote up their diaries or read aloud from *Omar Khayyam*. They are a pair. I read a book of Emerson's essays. I'm afraid we're going to lose Louis, for this evening I received a copy of an order from Division Headquarters calling attention to General Order 189, which prohibits French minors from attaching themselves to units of the AEF. And I also got a letter dealing specifically with Louis' case. He begged me to let him stay. Gene leaves tomorrow for Rolampont with a detail to hunt up our lost baggage.

Sunday

Last night Simerman and Umbarger (Cpl. Hiter B.) (both of German descent) got on a toot and carelessly stabbed a Dutchman, not seriously, however. He turns out to be Frau Holthausen's brother. They are now under arrest. John Christopher had dinner with us today. Either I've misjudged him all along, or he has changed considerably, for he was most agreeable. Jimmy is still in bed with bronchitis. Spent the afternoon initialing property records. My package from Hupp arrived tonight. Things of mine that have been in his trunk since last March, and an overcoat of Bill's.

Tush and Piggott are back from Nice on the 24th. Entertainment by the "Alabama Bound" (167th) troupe at the YMCA this evening. Afterwards we went to Battalion Headquarters for a feed, real ice cream that Bill Hoply (Cook William) made. Spent the day on service records and other company papers.

The inspectors arrived on February 25th and found all Company K records in satisfactory condition, which is a relief. I've been the only officer on duty today. Jimmy is in bed. Tush on civil affairs. Al is acting adjutant. Wages on guard, Gene in Rolampont and Charley on leave, so I've had plenty to do. Had dinner with Percy, Teddy, and Dick Lombard. Company L had a quartet and a nimble pianist as entertainment for the club this evening. The "speisen" (dinner) was K's offering, and good. All the former members of the 27th Division, which is to sail in a week, have been recalled to the outfit. Firth is one of the fortunate, and I suppose Gibbons will go to. We are not to leave until the latter part of April.

All alone again on the 26th, for Wages has gone to Coblenz. Stood reveille, was present at the mess line, drilled the company, attended the official correspondence, worked on service records, on hand at noon mess, supervised athletics, held non-coms school, stood retreat and evening mess and put in two hours on the new I.D.R. (Infantry Drill Regulation) in preparation for the officers' examination tomorrow. Between times managed to shave and get in three meals. I am quite ready for bed.

Two full days, yesterday and today, the 28th. Got up at 5:45 and didn't have a chance to come back to my room until 8 this evening. Wages returned this evening, and Piggott is back with the company. We had the exam this afternoon instead of yesterday. It was a farce. The non-coms had theirs afterwards and I have some fifty papers to grade. Two guests for dinner tonight, Luke, and a friend of Lieutenant Sutton's, the dentist, who has been messing with us for some time. Pershing is to review the Division in a week or so, and we are scheduled to leave here by the middle of April, and sail on the twenty seventh.

Tush and I took a long walk this afternoon of March 1st, over the hills through Glees to the Laacher See. It's a lovely place, a sort of bowl surrounded by forest. At the upper end is the famous old monastery, the Maria Laach Abbey.

16. Back to the Rhine

We went into chapel as the brothers were having vespers. The atmosphere of it all carries one back centuries. There was some beautiful music on a fine organ, but I can't say as much for the vocal accomplishments of the monks. The "Kloster" is very old, I believe, of Romanesque architecture. A King Henry (which one I don't know, other than he built the church) is buried there. Came back with a good appetite for it was a trifle cold when we started and quite sharp by the time we got home, and I suppose we walked at least sixteen kilometers. Didn't know I was to be the officer of the guard, and wasn't here to either mount guard or to take the repost at retreat. Time is to be set ahead one hour at midnight.

Got up late on Sunday and had breakfast in my room. Then read Stephen Leacock's *Sunshine Sketches*[1] which Teddy lent me. After guard mount took a walk, all by myself to Wehr and through the woods on a sunshiny, spring day. Gene came back from Rolampont. He couldn't find a trace of my trunk, so I imagine it's lost for good. Bill Drake leaves for Badonviller tonight, so I've spent an hour composing a letter in French to Mathilde for him to take along.

On Monday I took the company out to drill this morning and held non-coms school as usual in the afternoon. Jimmy has recovered, but is over at Battalion Headquarters on Court Martial. Rotten weather. I felt punk and stayed in my room for dinner but feel fine now.

On March 4th Al has been permanently, and Wages temporarily, transferred to M Company. Neither of them will be missed. I stayed at the orderly room to attend to paperwork while Gene took the company out to drill. Jimmy is still on court martial. Tucker and his brother dropped in at Battalion HQ while I was there. He is leaving the day after tomorrow to take a four-month course at the Sorbonne, and wants me to write up the advance to Sedan. I most certainly don't want the job but promised to go over to Niederbreisig for dinner tomorrow and talk it over. I'd like to go to the Sorbonne myself, but that would mean not going home with the outfit. The chaplain played a bit for us after Tucker left. He says we are booked to go home this month instead of next. I don't know where he gets this perfectly good rumor. We all went to a minstrel show given by members of the 310th Signal Battalion in the Y this evening, very good.

Have a cold and stayed home on the 5th until dinnertime. Teddy, Gib and Luke spent most of the afternoon with me. This evening some members of our regiment put on a show at the Y. Parts of it were very clever, especially the drill of the awkward squad from F Company. Today is the anniversary of our first battle losses.

A Rainbow Division Lieutenant in France

March 6th and the Battalion is going to change places with the First. Major Brewer being the Senior Battalion Commander thought we ought to have a chance at a good town. We've been so comfortable here that none of the men and few of the officers want to go, but we're going to just the same. K won't be at Niederbreisig but at Oderbreisig where A Company is now. It isn't anything like as nice as Niederzissen. Luke (for Battalion HQ), Dick, Pritchard, Wages and I went over in the Colonel's car to look over our respective billets. It is certainly a come down for us. I've been spoiled by the Holthausens and do hate to leave them. I walked back here in the wind and rain. Got in at eight and had dinner with Charley who has just returned from his leave.

Oberbreisig

After sad farewells all around I set out cross-country at nine o'clock on March 7th with Frankie, Cap Zig, Jane, and a squad to relieve the A Company guard. Had a muddy but otherwise pleasant hike over the hills through Gonnersdorf and made it in an hour and a half. The company, which came the long way via Niederbreisig, took four hours and a half. Now that we are settled, things don't look so bad. The men are grumbling a bit about their billets, but that's to be expected, and they'll be all right in a day or so. Jimmy is in the priest's house, and Tush with the schoolmaster. The rest of us are at "Marienstatter Hof" an old, quaint place on the edge of town. Gene has christened it our "country place" because we're so far from the others. I have a big sunny room in the front wing with windows on three sides. Charley is the next, then the orderlies, and Gene's rooms. The most attractive feature of the place is the bathroom, and Aunt Jane is this minute heating the water for me. As far as I can find out our estate is owned by two very old women. I saw one of them looking out the window but the moment she saw me, in went her head. They must be noble, for our bed linen is embroidered with coronets. Downstairs there are some interesting old pieces of furniture. That in our room is quite simple. There are ample grounds about the house, and outside my front windows, two magnificent pines. There is no electricity in the village, and as oil is a non-essential, we have to use candles. Have a good fire going and am sitting by it in my pajamas on a chaise lounge waiting for my bath. I don't think I shall mind staying here in the least, especially as we are away from both Regimental and Battalion Headquarters, and the last bunch said no inspectors ever got out here.

Weekly inspection the morning of the 8th. Doc Wayland (Lt. Clyde, San-

16. Back to the Rhine

itary Detachment) is out here and is messing with us. He thinks he ought to have my room because the medic with A Company had it. We miss the cheerful dining room at Therese's. The present one in the schoolmaster's house is gloomy and dirty. We went to Niederbreisig at five for an officers' meeting. Battalion Headquarters has a wonderful billet, a beautiful modern house with grounds running down right to the Rhein. No wonder Major Brewer wanted to move. Jimmy stayed there for dinner. Teddy invited me to have dinner with them but I thought I'd better come back to keep Gene and Charley company. Jane got homesick tonight and has skipped over to Niederzissen.

George Blake came up from Mayer Sunday morning in a flivver to see Les, so Charley and I impressed his car and went over to Niederzissen with them. The Holthausens greeted me as if I'd been away for a year, and gave Jane and me a delicious meal (they were expecting us). Dropped in to see Billy Witherell who occupies my old suite, and read part of the history. Called on the Schleichs with Charley. Therese and Marie-Luise very much on the job, and then back to the Holthausens for coffee. Gene brought us back here at six. Found I'd been appointed counsel for a man to be court-martialed tomorrow morning. So I beat down to Major Brewer's to inquire from Bill as to the duties and responsibilities of a counsel, being absolutely ignorant of anything pertaining to courts martial. I got in on the tail end of a dinner Major Brewer was hosting for the two Y girls, Colonel Conkling and Van Order the other guests. We took up the rug in the drawing room, and the Major, Luke, Doc Van Zandt, and I took turns dancing with the ladies to the accompaniment of the three piece orchestra that plays for them every evening at dinner. Bill brought forth from the cellar a couple of bottles of fifty year old wine, and after consuming a certain amount proceeded to initiate in the great hall, the two girls into the "High and Infamous Order of the Knights of Omar Khayyam" and ended by decorating Miss Potts with the D.S.C. (Dispatcher of Steero Cubes), the decoration being a "Steero" sign attached to her person with a large safety pin, and Miss Johnston with the D.H.C. (Dispenser of Hot Chocolate), a hot chocolate sign appended in like manner. After the guests left we sat around and talked till midnight. I am spending the night with Luke in a large room on the top floor, overlooking the Rhein.

After Monday breakfast with the Major and Luke I hurried over to the brig to interview my client. He was charged with having gone a.w.o.l. during the Argonne attack, and admitted to me he was guilty. I personally think he's a bit unbalanced, but I think I got him off in the trial, which took place at nine o'clock. I nearly botched the case in the beginning because I didn't understand the pleading. Prince (Lt. Harold A., H.Q. Co.), the Judge Advocate, handled his side very unskillfully. Louis returned to France today under the escort of Rennie Moore, but he's a resourceful kid, and I wouldn't be surprised to have him pop up again. Les, Cap Zig and I indulged in a game of poker before retiring, and I won some five thousand imaginary marks.

Company went to Niederbreisig Tuesday morning to bathe. In the afternoon two non-coms and I represented K Company at a preliminary meeting of the 168th Society at Colonel Tinley's quarters. A constitution and by-laws were adopted. Jimmy came out to the chateau for a bath this evening and stayed late playing poker with Les, Cap Zig and me. I won all the money again.

March 12th has been a regular spring day, sunny, warm, and fresh. The first fine weather we've had here. Took the company about a mile up the valley to the drill field (the only level spot near us). Spent but twenty minutes in drill, and the rest of the time in games. Now if we were where "high ranking" officers were roaming about, we couldn't do that, but it was too lovely out for work. This evening we all went down to Niederbreisig to see the 166th show, but stopped so long at the officers club in the Rhein Hotel, that the Y was jammed to the doors when we got there. So we came on home, beautiful moonlight. Latest rumor is that we embark between the first and tenth of April at Antwerp instead of Rotterdam.

Cloudy and chilly the morning of the 13th, and we had to keep moving to keep warm. Tried a lot of new games, some physical exercise and a little drill. In the afternoon, Pace, Woods, Allen, Stinson and I were the K delegates at the meeting of the 168th Infantry Society held at Burgbrohl. We went over in trucks. Colonel Tinley was elected president, Colonel Stanley, vice president, and Sergeants Royce (Rgt. Sgt. Major Willis G.) and Risse (Rgt. Supply Sgt. John E.), members of the executive committee. The most important office that of permanent historian will be filled at a later meeting.

Took the company out to the rifle range March 14th. The ground was still white from last night's heavy frost but after the sun got over the hill, it warmed up considerably. We stayed out until one o'clock and finished the two and three hundred ranges. Between shifts we got on some physical exercise and snappy drill. Luke and Pace shot a deer in the woods nearby. This afternoon I climbed the steep hill opposite us, and got all the exercise I wanted. Ball has asked me to come over and help him on the advance to Sedan. It probably means writing the entire chapter, but he has so much to do, or says he has, that I can't very well refuse. Pershing is to review the Division on Sunday, and maybe I can get out of it by being busy with history.

16. Back to the Rhine

After inspection on the 15th I went down to Villa Carlsheim to see Ball and he was out, but Amchen and Cutchen were home and gave me something to eat. I went down again in the evening with Charley. Saw the 4th Corps show at the Y first. Ball has the information that our first train leaves Remagen on the morning of the first of April for Antwerp. The 165th and the 167th are to load first. Major Brewer has been promoted to Lieutenant Colonel, Captain Haynes to Major, and Luke to Captain.

The Division has at last been inspected and reviewed by Pershing. Unfortunately for us, Sunday, March 16th, was a windy day, cloudy and cold. We hiked to Niederbreisig where we embussed with the rest of the regiment and rode to Sinzig. Then another hike to a plain near the river between Kripp and Remagen. By noon we were drawn up in mass formation in this order: 166, 165, 167, 168, 117 Engineers, 149, 150 and 151 7.A. We had the best position, the right center, with the General's tent directly ahead of us on the hill. Our Battalion was in front, then the First and the Second. M, at the head followed by L, K, and I. I had the first platoon, Tush, the second, Charley the third, and Gene, the runts. After we had eaten the lunch we brought along with us, we stood for two hours shivering in the cold wind that was blowing up from the river. As Pershing arrived, bayonets were fixed and Division Headquarters mounted, took position ahead of the Brigade Headquarters, which in turn were ahead of the regimental groups. I should like to have been up on the hill with the Commander in Chief when Flagler presented the Division to him, and all those thousands of bayonets came up at once. Joined then by Division Headquarters, Pershing and his staff circled the outfit. He appears well on horseback, soldierly and commanding. That finished, we prepared for the inspection by opening ranks and about-facing the front one, so that each platoon formed a lane through which the inspecting party passed. He started on the right with the 166th and their band played until he moved to the next regiment when the 165th band took it up, and so on. I got a good look at him while he was inspecting Alabama. He impresses one as favorably a foot as on horseback, well built, straight, and rather fine looking. He wore several rows of ribbons, but no medals. Each company commander fell in on his left and answered his questions as they walked through the ranks. I heard him ask Jimmy if he had ever eaten with the men, and if the food were good. Behind him came Lt. General Dickman, the Commanding Officer of the Third Army, Flagler, and numerous other generals, colonels, majors, captains and lieutenants. After it had been expected the colors of each regiment took post in the interval between us and the Engineers, directly behind the line of decorations, which had been formed there at

Black Jack Pershing (front), Commander of the American Expeditionary Force. The author had two distant encounters with him. Donovan Collection, United States Army Heritage and Education Center, Carlisle, Pennsylvania

the beginning of the ceremony. This all took about two hours. Then, at the command of Flagler, the decorees and colors advanced to be presented to Pershing. The Division Adjutant read the orders, the band played the "Star Spangled Banner," the colors rejoined their outfits, and Pershing came forward, and addressed the decorees, a poor, stereotyped speech, of which I could hear every

16. Back to the Rhine

word. Then he proceeded with the decorating. A private from the 167th who received the Medal of Honor was at the right of the line, then General MacArthur and a Colonel who got the Distinguished Service Medal, followed by Colonel Brewer and forty other recipients of the Distinguished Service Cross. Next the entire party, including those just decorated moved to the reviewing stand at the extreme right. At the command "Pass in Review" each regiment, still in mass formation, executed "squads right," and "eyes left" as we came abreast the reviewing party. We thought we'd had about enough by that time, but no, we were crowded up to the end of the field to hear Pershing make another stupid speech. And what he said was most general, it could have been said to any division. There was not a word about anything the Rainbow had done in the war, but he did make reference to the "glorious victory of Cantigny," by his own First Division. He also urged us not to knock the AEF when we got home. At the conclusion General Flagler jumped up beside him, and called for "three cheers for our beloved commander in chief." The response wouldn't have done credit to as many hundred as there were thousand there. We extricated ourselves from the jumble, made good time back to Sinzig and caught the same trucks for home.

Today, March 17th, we leave the Fourth Army Corps, and enter the Third Army Reserve, our first step towards embarkation. We hear that no troops are to replace us in this area. No drill today to make up for yesterday's loss of rest. Cold and dreary with occasional snow flurries. I had an encounter with Baroness Von Wetten Kampf, who owns the chateau. She arrived from Berlin just the other day and until this evening had not adjusted her ideas to the conditions of occupation. She took the opportunity while we were away yesterday to remove our embroidered linen sheets, certain rugs, and other things from our rooms. When I requested an interview and demanded their return, she said "Why, I can't let you have them, they are my best," so I had to issue an ultimatum. I also told her that if we were German officers and she a French woman, her house would have been burned down by that time. She then got very haughty and said, "Sir, I am a Prussian noble woman," and I, "Madame, I am an American officer." After these amazing revelations, and some further passages at arms, I took my leave, first requiring all the things restored to our rooms by five o'clock, and after that forbidding her or any of her servants to enter our apartments. I was a courteous as I could be to her until she flatly refused to return the above mentioned articles, and started on a tirade against the French, Belgians, English and Allies in general. Well, anyhow they're all back in place now. Pace shot another deer this morning and donated a hindquarter to the officers' mess. Gene took a shot at one on the hill from my window this afternoon. It was about a thousand yards away, and he missed though the bullet kicked up dust right under it. Charley, Zig, Les and I whiled away the evening at cards.

Neuenahr

Suddenly decided to come over here the next morning and arrived in an ambulance at noon. Had lunch with Mrs. Knowles, Gertrude Bray and a man from the 168th named Kocher. By the time lunch was over I had an invitation for dinner and to spend the night, Schwester Ella having a room vacant. We went out to the Kur Theater to see what we thought was going to be *Seven Keys to Baldpate* but which turned out to be a pretty poor vaudeville performance. The others left early, but I stayed on till the bitter end. I met Mrs. Knowles at the cantine and went for a walk with her. Two Y men were here for dinner. Stayed till ten o'clock. We then discoursed until midnight on varied and diverse subjects.

Had breakfast together at 8:30 the morning of March 20th. Being a clear, cold day I walked home via Heimersheim, Lohndorf and Franken, a fair jaunt. A lot of mail waiting for me. Again our sailing plans have been altered. We leave, not from Antwerp, but from a French port presumably Brest. But our schedule will not be affected by the change. Has been snowing hard for an hour.

Sunday

Feeling a little bit off from the shot in the arm we all had to take the day before yesterday. Woke up to find the ground white in snow. The sun has since come out and everything is green again. Rumor that we leave on the fifth.

I have two very ribald guests this evening, Cap Zig and Aunt Jane, who have just come, as they inform me, from the Old Soldiers and Sailors reunion. The O.S. and S have been running all evening, this having been pay day, at the principal cafe, and, from the lack of sounds issuing there from, I take it that the honorable members have at least been led to their respective billets. On March 24th we started out for target practice this morning but by the time we got out to the range it was raining so hard that we about faced.

Snowing today on the 25th. Took a long walk though the woods over towards Waldorf. The trees are all white and heavy. Saw two deer. All the rolling equipment, with the exception of the kitchens, was turned in today.

16. Back to the Rhine

Spent March 26th in town, as the rain didn't let up till afternoon. Captain Hout, who commanded Company K of the old First Iowa, had lunch with us. Marie-Luise and Ludwig drove over from Niederzissen in an equipage closely resembling the old one hoss shay, and stayed for dinner.

I got rather bored with things around Oberzissen, and took a Mainz bound train early in the morning of the 27th. No difficulty at all as the French guards let me by without question. I saw a lot of the city, had lunch at the hotel with a French Lieutenant, Maurice, who being off duty, suggested a trip to Wiesbaden. He got hold of his Captain, Deronet, and his military car, and off we went. We drove to the limit of the French lines, all over Wiesbaden, and stopped at the casino long enough for a "gout." I had to come back then, as I wanted to catch a five o'clock train. Considering the casual way in which I met them, they certainly were hospitable. They offered to put me up for the night in case I missed the train, which I very nearly did. So my pleasant little excursion ended without mishap. As there was no drill today, or anything else to require my presence, I don't think I've even been missed.

Tush, Doc Wayland and I went over to Neuenahr after lunch, the 28th, under the pretext of having pictures taken for our identity books. A Y truck took us all the way. I stayed over for dinner with Mrs. Knowles, the other two having to refuse on account of an important engagement here. Everyone at the Y is getting ready to leave. Mrs. Knowles plans to go to Brussels next Wednesday and join us at Brest. The boxcars are already on the sidings being fitted out with bunks and stoves, so the men will be as comfortable as possible. Each train is to have two cars fitted up as kitchens. I left on the 8:29 expecting to make connections for Niederbreisig at Remagen, but found all the night trains had been discontinued, and as there was no traffic at all, I had to walk home, numerous kilometers. It was dark but clear and I rather enjoyed it.

Got up late the 29th and when I got out of the tub found out Aunt Jane had brought up my breakfast. I drew up the table by the fire and ate in comfort. Our militant baroness has been quite subdued of late and our family life has been very quiet. But she honored me with a smile and wished me good evening when I met her in the hall a little while ago.

Sunday

Colonel Brewer asked me to come down and see him last evening. He was alone when I arrived and we talked together for several hours. Bill and Luke came in about half past eleven and we all had a bite to eat before going to bed. I slept in Luke's room. Had breakfast at half past nine and stayed on for lunch. Soon after all the officers met there to board trucks for Neuenahr, where, in the Kur Theater, we heard a most illuminating lecture by a Colonel from General HQ. He said, among other things, that the staff believed if the initial attack in the Argonne had been made by the same tried troops who took part in the St. Mihiel offensive, that what actually took over a month could have been accomplished in two days. He also gave our division full credit for all we did, and said we ranked ace high at GHQ. We were surprised to hear that we had more troops than the British on the front at the signing of the armistice, and four fifths as many as the French. He followed his lecture with moving pictures of troops in action, war official, and splendid. Our departure has been postponed for three days. It will not delay our sailing. It merely means less time spent at Brest.

It is unusually cold March 31st. Took the company out for a short hike toward Waldorf and gave them a half hour's physical drill in the woods. Came home, took a bath, shaved and went down to Niederbreisig for the afternoon. Had coffee with Cutchen. Cap Zig and Les are both in a hilarious mood again. Cap admits of being intoxicated, but swears he is not drunk.

On April 1st I took the company down to the Rhein Hotel for their final physical exam. No one turned down.

Went to a dinner party last night at Colonel Brewer's. There were eleven Red Cross nurses, Colonel Tinley, Colonel Stanley, Colonel Brewer, Major Haynes, Major Bunch, Major Thomas, Captain Riley, Luke, Bill, Doc van Zant, and I. Really quite a party. Elaborate decorations, extensive menu, and divertissements. A ten-piece orchestra played throughout the meal, and between courses we danced out in the great hall. I took in Miss Castle, the best dancer of them all. She lives at 28 Telegrafen Strasse in Neuenahr where five of them came from (all had to sneak away) and the other six came up from Coblenz. The Battalion quartet sang for our entertainment, as well as a first class baritone from the First Battalion. We danced until half past eleven when the ladies had to leave, but the officers continued the party for some time afterward. Teddy Jones came in for dessert and I went home with him for the night. It was nearly daybreak when we got to sleep and we intended to stay in bed late on the 2nd, but Bill Tittsworth and Dick Lombard pulled us out on the floor at breakfast time. Percy put them up to it as he says we disturbed his sleep last night. The officers of the Third Battalion had their pictures taken at the Villa Lucia this afternoon. Of the thirty officers who left the states with the Battalion, only

16. Back to the Rhine

nine are with it now. At last we have our moving orders. Two companies of the Third Battalion leave on the eighth and two on the ninth. The Division will embark at Brest between the eleventh and seventeenth. Gene is celebrating by having a "King George's" time.

The Battalion went down to Niederbreisig the afternoon of the 3rd to hear a talk on the consequences of Bolshevism by a YMCA man who also took our pictures and recited for us "The Doughboy of the Rainbow Division" which he wrote himself. Marie Luise and Therese were here to see us when we got back. I happened to have a couple of rolls of film, so we took a lot of snaps out at the castle. They stayed for dinner and Jimmy and I took them home. It was pretty dark and I wasn't altogether sure of the way. Nearly got mired in the forest just before we got to Niederzissen. I stopped in to see the Holthausens and they asked me to come over Sunday for dinner. Jimmy and I left after twelve and got back here at two.

Good Friday

I didn't get up till late. Nothing to do, as we aren't drilling any more. Just marking time. Colonel Stanley came out for lunch and spent part of the afternoon. Les and I took a walk over the hill. We met Tush, Marie, Charley and Henriette on the way back. We leave on the eighth.

Regular weekly inspection April 5th. It has been a lovely day, and I spent all of it out of doors. Took a walk and slept a while "au soleil." Took a lot of pictures, Gene, Frankie, Tush, Cap Zig and Les. I wanted to get my old non-coms together for a picture but some of them were out on pass. We are to leave Monday night instead of Tuesday as expected. After all the false rumors and changes of plan it is hard to believe the time is so near. We ought to be home in three weeks and a half, at the most. Wages came back to us this evening. He's harmless, but the most stupid mortal I've ever known. He has gone over to Niederzissen for the night.

Sunday
Coblenz

At breakfast this morning the regimental Sergeant Major called up to tell me that my request to go to Brest via Paris had been approved, and as they were making out my orders then I could leave as soon as I got down to Regiment Headquarters. I didn't tell him that I had never put in such a request, but rushed back to the chateau to get my things together, hoping that I could get away before the mistake was discovered. Les being at Niederzissen, Cap Zig helped me to pack up, and with one last look at Oberbreisig, set out. I got word as soon as I arrived that Colonel Tinley wanted to see me. I thought I was found out, but he heard that I was going to Paris on a three-day leave and asked me to attend to some business for him at the bank. Colonel Brewer also had some commissions for me and Billy Hopply gave me some lunch to take along. It might come in handy, he said. Having twenty-five minutes to spare I went down to Villa Carlsheim to say goodbye. Left at noon and rode down to Coblenz with a D Company officer. I think his name is Fraser (Lt. Charles A.). I found the next train didn't leave till nine tonight, this being Sunday. We had a cup of coffee at the Red Cross room, and there we parted, he to meet a friend, and I to find diversion. There wasn't much to do as all the places of amusement were closed, but fortunately it was a fine day, and there wasn't much of the city that escaped me. Coblenz is an attractive place, and prides itself on being, or having been a "Residenzstadt" (residence city). I crossed over the river on the pontoon bridge, and explored as much of Ehrenbreitstein as was permitted. When I got tired I went to the officers club, a very fine one, and read till dinnertime. Ate at the Monopol with Major Francis of G1, who proved interesting. I took a final walk in the moonlight up to "Deutsches Eck" where the Moselle flows into the Rhein.

17

⚞ Leaving Germany ⚟

Grand Hotel
Metz, 4 A.M.

 The train last night not at all crowded, and after Treves, a 1st Division lieutenant and I had the compartment to ourselves. Dumped out here at two this morning, April 7th, this being all the further the train went. Couldn't get a room anywhere, but the night porter said two other American officers were in the salon and that he could fix me up there if I wanted to stay. I have a comfortable arrangement of two lounge chairs but can't sleep. I had a bite to eat and talked till three with the two officers. They wanted to catch a 4:30 train to Conflans so they'll be in time for reveille. I've just tried to wake them up but they've had too much straight cognac and I can't budge them. My train leaves at 6:30. Can't make through connections.

Excelsior Hotel
Nancy, 11:30 A.M.

 The train from Metz was wretched and didn't get into Nancy till after nine. If it weren't for the fact I'm so tired for lack of sleep I'd be on my way to Badonviller now for I could have made excellent connections. I went to the Credit Lyonnais to cash a check so I'd have enough money, but when I got a glimpse of myself in a glass decided I needed a shave and a little sleep more than the trip. So after walking around for an hour came here and got a room. The square on which my window faces is all in ruins from bombing. They are at work reconstructing the buildings now.

Hotel de Crillon
Paris

Had lunch yesterday at the Excelsior with a lieutenant of Chasseurs who was wearing five wound stripes. I got the "rapide" that came from Strasbourg at one o'clock. It was a fine day and the country looked so inviting. Several planes followed us from Toul to Chalons doing stunts all the while. I had an American lieutenant from Texas, a French colonel, a sous-lieutenant, and two women, mother and daughter, from St. Die, as companions. They were coming to Paris to buy the daughter's trousseau. Got in the Gare de l'Est at ten and was here soon after. Bernard wasn't here so I took a bath and hopped into bed. He was somewhat startled to find some one in it when he came in two hours later. We talked till late, and the poor fellow had to get up at five, but mercifully let me sleep till nine when we had breakfast up here. He had just got a note from Mrs. Knowles saying she was in town, and without letting her know I was here, invited her for dinner. I put in a full day.

I had quite a time at the American Express Company about Colonel Tinley's check. They couldn't give me the money but arranged to transfer the account to their Brest office. As I was so near, I stopped in the University Union. I met Francis Henderson, who is now an "aspirant" (officer cadet) in the French artillery. He has acquired such a British accent that I could scarcely understand him. Personally I think he's an ass. Had lunch with Bernard at the Crillon, and in the afternoon started for Tucker's to leave a package. I met Robb en route and delivered the letter to him and bumped into Miss Potts on the Rue St. Honoré. I didn't see Tucker as he was out. I got a reservation for the night of the tenth to Brest at the Gare de Montparnasse. I got to Fullers, where I was to meet Cousin Alice at 5:30, twenty minutes late. Lucy and Cousin Kate Hegeman, a very distinguished looking woman, were with her. I took her home, up in the Etoile district, and rushed back home for dinner. Such a jamboree as we had.

Mrs. Knowles had no idea that I was in Paris. After dinner we three went to the Casino de Paris, but left long before it was over, it was so putrid. Planning a great day tomorrow.

17. *Leaving Germany*

Hotel de Crillon, Paris

Bernard couldn't get the car, so we had to give up the trip of April 9th to Fontainbleau. I tore around all morning and took Bernard over to Cousin Alice's for lunch. We rushed from the table to Gare des Invalides where we met Mrs. Knowles and Gertude Bray and went out to Versailles. We sauntered around the parc and took some pictures of the chateau before it started to rain. Had tea at the pavilion. Bernard had to leave early to attend an official dinner. We took our time getting back, and had a most delicious meal at Premiers, sweet breads and lobster, and Sandemans Port. We got through too late for the theater, so we went instead to the Pathé and saw Mary Garden in *Thais*.[1]

Hotel de Crillon Paris

Shopped all morning the tenth with Edith Knowles. I lunched here with Bernard and then went for a walk with him. I saw Captain Hupp at the Mediterranee. He got in late last night. I had a fine talk with him. He wants to come home too. Nobody home at Cousin Alice's when I went to say goodbye, except the parlour maid who seems to think all Americans susceptible. Mrs. Knowles and Gertrude coming for dinner. My train leaves at eight.

18

On the Way Home

Camp Pontanezen, Brest

We had a merry meal last night, but I had to leave before we finished. There is no one so hospitable as Bernard. Fred had already got me a taxi, and as I rushed out of the door (a revolving one), I ran plump into President Wilson. Captain Nash of the 308th Infantry who was in my training company at Plattsburgh had the seat opposite me. Many of our old company have been killed, and I was sorry to hear from him that Tommy Hastings, who had gone through the war as a captain in the 308th, shot and killed himself last week.[1] We made excellent time and I slept all night. Had a stop of ten minutes at seven o'clock at St. Brieuc for a breakfast of coffee and sandwiches. Arrived at Brest at a quarter of ten, April 11th. As I was on my way out to camp in a motor I saw the company marching along the road and joined them. They had got in at eight after a three-day journey. It is now raining, but the camp is in much better condition than we expected, so we can't complain. We officers are in a tent at the head of the company street. We have our bedding rolls, but our boxes are down at the "quai." No one knows I over stayed my leave. Route from Paris: Chartres, Le Mans, Laval, Rennes, and Saint-Brieuc.

April 12th I went in a car down to Brest with Colonel Tinley and Colonel Brewer. There wasn't any mistake about going to Paris after all. Colonel Tinley sent me purposely to see about that check. It rained most of the day, but the drainage system is so good that after a few minutes of sunshine in the afternoon everything dried up. The officers all mess together and not a very good fare. I have charge of policing of this plot, a snap.

18. On the Way Home

Sunday

Rained hard all night, but cleared up and has been fine all morning. Saw Gertrude Bray last evening. She brought my famous blue pajamas with her. I had left them at Bernard's. It is rumored that we embark tomorrow or the next day, probably on the *Leviathan*.

Brest has a most variable climate. It rains twenty out of twenty four hours

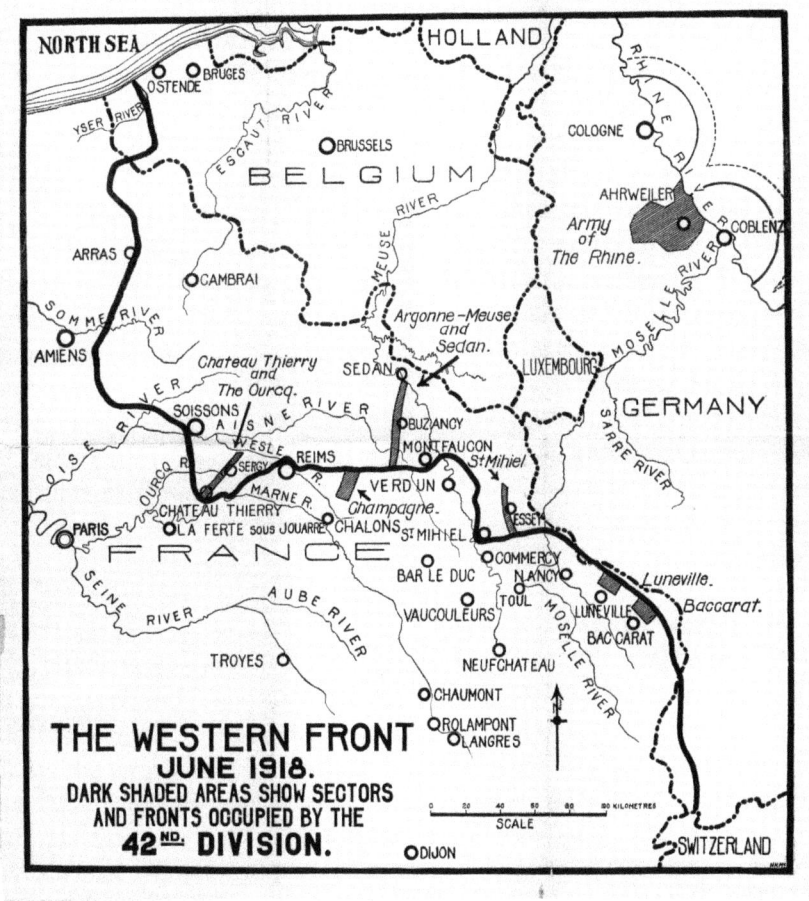

Map showing the places occupied by the Rainbow Division during the war and occupation.

but between storms it is as clear as a fine June day. Our tents stand up well under the heavy wind that hasn't let up since we arrived. Last night our company had their equipment inspected, a mere formality. They also got paid. Colonel Brewer sailed yesterday in charge of a detachment of nurses, but will rejoin us at New York. He received the Legion of Honor the day before. Thirty some officers of the regiment have been temporarily detached and will go home on the *Pretorian* because there is not room for all on the *Leviathan*. We hope to load tomorrow, the 15th. The high wind has made embarking out in the harbor difficult, and the *Leviathan* is too large to come up to the "quai." I went down to Brest with Luke this evening and had dinner at the Moderne, the first meal that was fit to eat since we arrived here. We happened to mention Bernard's name, and another man perked up his ears and said he knew him well. He was Captain Ferebee who was also on the Peace Mission and who had just arrived from Paris. Coming out of the dining room I met Lieutenant Johnson of the 149th Machine Gun Battalion, whom I traveled with on my leave in February.

Visited in the middle of the night by Teddy, Dick and Clark (Lt. James R.) of L Company, all very tight. Clark had recently been commissioned, and got a medaille militaire and croix de guerre at the same time. I got up late on the 16th to make up for the lost sleep. We may or may not load today. It's blowing pretty hard. We have been ordered not to leave the regimental area. Later, Jimmy and I went down to Brest anyhow for lunch at the Moderne. Happy joined us at the table and told us his tale of woe. It seems to me that he's had a rotten deal. I had dinner with Bill, Luke and Gib at the Field Officers mess. Two good meals in one day. We had our bedding rolls done up preparatory to leaving but were informed we would spend the night at Pontanezen after all.

Aboard S.S. *Leviathan*

Eighteen months ago today we set sail on the *Grant*, and today we put on our third service stripe to commemorate that occasion. Got up early April 17th to report to Major Haynes who is in charge of my section. He was still incapacitated for duty. Had breakfast, a good one too, at eight. Had the rest of the day to myself. The *Aquitania* came in this morning, and is anchored near us. The troops were all loaded by last evening and the only thing that held up our sailing was the delay in coaling. Some volunteer doughboys replaced the stevedores, and did as much in six hours as the stevedores had done in two days. So we expect to sail at five o'clock, and it's a quarter of now. The *Aquitania* pulled

18. On the Way Home

out a minute before the *Leviathan*. We left France in sunshine, and it was so beautiful, that instead of going to an entertainment in the dining salon, I stayed out on deck until after nine. It was then still light. The sea is calm and the ship so steady that down here one can't tell we're moving.

April 19th is a delightful day. I have been out on deck most of the time. The weather has been fine. It is growing warmer. Just now the sea is a bit rough (I've just come in from a walk before going to bed) and the ship is rolling slightly, but not enough to be unpleasant. We have on board, in addition to the navy personnel, eleven thousand soldiers, between five and six hundred officers and a small number of "distinguished civilians," congressmen (typical), a few nurses and some French. There are over 14,000 in all. Johnston, one of my companions in stateroom 145, is a fraternity brother from the University of Illinois, besides he is a fine chap. He and O'Neale (who is affable) are both Kentuckians. I walked around the deck with Gib all morning. He is tiresome and uninteresting at times, chiefly when not lit. Abandon ship drill in the afternoon. Saw some porpoises, and passed a tramp. Shot craps with Dick, Doc Wayland, Tush and Johnston, and won all their money. Funny Charlie Chaplin movie after dinner. Mess continues to be excellent. In fact everything is going just right. There are five bands on board.

Easter, April 20th was an uneventful, but pleasant day. Officers meeting in the morning, boat drill in the afternoon, and movies in the evening. Nazinova[2] as a nurse running all over a battlefield for her wounded lover. It was supposed to be tragic, but to those of us who have been on battlefields, mirth provoking. Came out even in a crap game with Doc Wayland and Tush. Stayed out on deck till midnight. It was very black and a rough sea. Passed three ships, two westward bound.

On the 21st we were 1,312 miles from Brest, and 1,827 from New York at noon. Game with Luke, Doc Van Zandt, Teddy, Dick, Tush and Haley all morning. Doc cleaned up. Percy told me that Teddy and I had again been recommended for captaincies, but I doubt if anything will come of it this late. I heard about it back in Niederbreisig.

There was a band concert in the afternoon. I learned a lot about fuses, etc., from Taussig (who was an instructor at the Artillery School) while we walked around the deck. A fine show by the Rainbow Troupe this evening in the mess hall. Johnston and I did a couple of turns before coming into bed. He introduced to Connor, a Purdue SAE, who is a corporal in his battery. It has got much warmer. I believe we are in the Gulf Stream.

Not even a boat drill to break into a very pleasant day on the 22nd. Nothing to do but read and shoot craps. I took a lot of pictures and walked about ten miles. We passed several ships, among them the *Pretoria*, which has a lot of our officers aboard. We are due in New York on Friday.

We are 907 miles from New York at noon on April 23rd. A fine windy day with the sea running high. Some few are seasick. Out on deck seven hours. I played bridge in the lounge in the afternoon with Jimmy, Taussig and another officer from the 150th 7 Army named Thorpe. After dinner with Taussig, Gilbert (another SAE) and Haley, there was a concert and dance in the lounge that broke up our game. I met two more brothers before going to bed. Grant, an ensign, and another naval officer from Harvard, whose name I've forgotten.

The next day we are 469 miles from New York at noon. It's cloudy and cold outside, but warm and comfortable in the lounge where I played with Johnnie, Tausig and Thorpe and won. This evening, Gilbert took Thorpe's place and we played till one o'clock.

On Board the U.S.S. *Leviathan* Off Ambrose Lightship

It is cold and blustery again this morning of April 25th. Had another game in the lounge. Snow flurries after breakfast. Met by several destroyers at noon, and anchored off the light ship about two o'clock. We will stay here till four. All the organizations with the exception of the 168th will disembark this evening. We stay aboard till tomorrow morning. Everybody happy, but I can't help regretting that the trip is over, for I certainly had a good time.

Finis

I was demobilized at Camp Upton on the 12th of May, exactly two years from the day I entered the army, and having been nineteen months with the 168th and Company K.

18. *On the Way Home*

Blow out, your bugles, over the rich Dead!
There's none of those so lonely and poor of old,
But, dying, has made us rarer gifts than gold,
These laid the world away; poured out the red
Sweet wine of youth: gave up the years to be
Of work and joy, and that unhoped serene
That men call age; and those who would have been,
Their sons, they gave, their immortality.

—Rupert Brooke

Chapter Notes

Preface

1. Leonard P. Ayres, "The War with Germany, a Statistical Summary" (Washington, D.C.: Government Printing Office, 1919).

Chapter 1

1. The following month, December 6, saw the largest explosion before the atomic bomb, the result of a collision between a munitions ship and another ship in Halifax harbor.
2. *Brittanic* was an Olympic-class ocean liner that sank off a Greek island on November 21, 1916.

Chapter 2

1. Battle of Cambrai, November 20–December 7, 1917.
2. Tirailleurs were French colonial units.
3. "Sambre et Meuse" is a French song and military march.
4. *Ruggles of Red Gap*, Henry Leon Wilson, 1915, later a 1935 comedy film.

Chapter 3

1. Daisy Polk, San Francisco society figure, married a French army general and became a countess.
2. Princess Troubetzkoy was an American novelist who married Prince Pierre Troubetzkoy.
3. Stanislas, deposed King of Poland.

Chapter 4

1. Prince Eitel Friedrich, second son of Emperor Wilhelm II.
2. Rex Beach *The Barrier* 1908.
3. *The Winning of Barbara Worth* Harold Bell Wright, 1911.
4. Madelon was a popular French song of Word War 1.

Chapter 5

1. Novel by the American writer Winston Churchill, published in 1915.

Chapter 6

1. "Café de la Femme a Barbe," Clementine Delait (1865–1939).

Chapter Notes

2. Names of an American singer and actress who entertained troops during the war.
3. Popular French weekly magazine.

Chapter 8

1. German heavy bombers.

Chapter 10

1. American actress and dancer.

Chapter 11

1. French opera by Gustave Charpentier.

Chapter 13

1. Marie Adelaide (1894–1924) abdicated in 1919 and became a nun in Italy. She was succeeded by her sister, Charlotte. The Nazis sent another sister, Antonia, married to Rupprecht, Crown Prince of Bavaria, to Dachau and Flossenburg.

Chapter 14

1. Unofficial national anthem of Germany.

2. Chancellor of the German empire, 1909–1917.

Chapter 15

1. Eleftherios Venizelos, Greek Prime Minister.
2. Presidential advisor to Wilson.
3. World War I propaganda film by D.W. Griffith.

Chapter 16

1. *Sunshine Sketches of a Little Town*, a classic of Canadian humorous literature.

Chapter 17

1. A Scottish-American operatic soprano.

Chapter 18

1. Of the 307th. Date of Death listed as February 19, 1919.
2. Silent film star.

Index

A Company 1, 61, 176, 177
A Corps 138
ABC Restaurant 8
Abri 53, 75
Adrian barrack 18
AEF (American Expeditionary Force) 173, 181
Africa 106
Ahr 163
Ahrweiler 163
Alabama 1, 69, 70, 82, 83, 87, 110, 116, 117, 179
Alabama Bound troupe 174
Alexandre, Prince Regent (Serbia) 167, 168
Algerian Tiralleurs 12
Alice (cousin) 2, 14, 107, 119, 125, 126, 127, 163, 166, 168–170, 188, 189
Allen, Sgt. Charles B. 113, 178
Allies 41, 119, 141, 181
Alpha Delta Phi 8
Alsatians 54
Alzette 143
Ambrose Lightship 194
ambulance 16, 24, 61, 101, 106, 117, 121, 122, 161, 162, 182
Amchen 162, 179
American Corps 121
American Express 124, 188
American First Army Corps 115, 121
American relief commission 140
Amiens 41
Amons, Cpl. Archie K. 47
Andelot 13, 14, 15
Anderson, Sgt. Otto F. (Tut) 47, 48, 49, 50, 65, 66, 114, 116, 120
Anichino, Pvt. Belardi 48

anti-aircraft guns 28, 86, 88, 91, 100, 127, 129
Antwerp 178, 179
Anverville 30
"Apfelwein" 153, 156
Apollinaris 154
Apremont, Meuse 120
April 44, 45, 49, 50–52, 174, 178, 179, 185, 187, 190, 192–194
Aquitania 192
Arabs 77
Archangel 10
"Archie" 127
Argonne 177, 184
Arlon 141, 144
Armistice 131, 136, 137, 139
Army of Occupation 173
Artillery School 193
aspirin 75, 133
Assis 63
Atlantic Monthly 158
August 96–98, 102, 104
Aulnay-l'Aitre, Marne 74, 75, 77
Aurania 4, 5
Austria 10, 11, 116, 128
auto-rifle (A.R.) 22, 38, 48
Auzeville 127
Aviation camp 131
Avignon 170
A.W.O.L. (Absent Without Official Leave) 126, 164, 177
Azerailles 31

B Company 1, 116, 135
B Scout officers 46
Baccarat 28, 31, 32, 38, 40–42, 55, 61, 62, 71–74, 156, 158, 170

Index

Badmenil, Meurthe-et-Moselle 31
Badonviller 30, 35–40, 43, 47, 51, 53, 55, 63, 66, 67, 70, 72, 77, 158, 169, 175, 187
Baker, Secretary of War Newton 69, 157
Balkans 11, 68
Ball, Lt. John W. 155, 162, 178, 179
Balloon company 101
Balushof 150
Bar-le-Duc 75, 166
Bar-les-Buzancy 131
Baranzy 140
Barr, Pvt. Carl H. 93
Barr, Pvt. Chauncey W. 91
The Barrier 44
Base Hospital 25, 47, 122
Bates, Lt. Francis 34
Battigny, Meurthe-et-Moselle 108
Bauer Kuchen 153
Bausenberg 153, 156
Beam, Pvt. Earl 50
Beatty, Pvt. Leon M. 48, 84
Beau Meuil Ferme 134
Beaumont 111
Beaune, Côte d'Or 122, 123
Bedford Basin 4
Belfast Harbor, Ireland 6
Belfort 104
Belgium 10–12, 14, 15, 45, 119, 139–141, 154, 180
Beney 114
Bennet, Colonel Matthew A. 8, 13, 14, 17, 50, 62, 63, 77, 97, 104, 108
Bentley, Pvt. James A. 93
Bentz, Lt. Leon 17, 18, 63, 77
Berlin 165, 181
Bertrichamps 38, 43
Beuvardes 99
Bidons 79
Big Bertha 169
billets 11, 12, 14, 16, 32, 42, 75, 77, 88, 99, 100, 102, 105, 108, 120, 130, 135, 139, 140, 144, 145, 147–149, 155, 158–160, 162, 164, 172, 173, 176, 177
Birmingham 7
birthday 77
Biwer 145
Blake, George 177
Blake, Lt. Gerald O. (Jerry) 3, 16, 24, 27, 28, 31, 32, 37, 42, 44, 46, 47, 56, 58, 59, 64, 75, 76, 96, 98
Blake, Pvt. Leslie C. (Aunt Jane, Les) 49, 137, 152–154, 156, 157, 176–178, 182–186
"blesse" 9, 97, 126

Blevaincourt 103, 104
Bliss, General 168
"Boche" 12, 24, 28, 30–33, 35, 38, 40, 48–50, 52–54, 56, 57, 59, 61–63, 65–68, 70, 72, 77–82, 84–88, 90, 93–96, 98, 103, 111–18, 120, 122, 125, 129, 131–133, 135, 138–141, 163
Bofferding, Madame 145
Bois de Beney 116, 118
Bois de Boulogne 168
Bois de Dampvitoux 113, 114
Bois de la Cote 80
Bois de la Sonnard 113, 117
Bois de Montfaucon 121
Bois des Pannes 118
Bolivia 59
Bolshevism 58, 185
Bonham, Cpt. James C. (Jimmy) 86, 109, 113, 121, 133, 143, 157, 178
Bonn 159, 160
Bordeaux 58, 78, 166, 168
Boston 42
Boucq 117
Bourdet, Lieutenant 72
Bouresches 99
Box barrage 63
Boxberg 148, 149
Boyau Central 35, 45, 49
Brabant, Meuse 121
Bradley, Cpt. Glade T. (Brad) 8, 11, 13, 16, 17, 26, 27, 31–33, 37, 43, 44, 46, 47, 55, 56, 64, 74, 75, 77, 81, 84, 93, 98, 105, 108, 128
Bradshaw, Cpl. Vinton 5, 46, 48, 92
Brandeville 139, 140
Bray, Pvt. Arthur E. (Art) 93
Bray, Pvt. Edward C. (Eddie) 99, 137
Bray, Gertrude 182, 189, 191
Bremen 72
Bremenil 67
Brest 182, 183, 184, 184, 185, 188, 190, 192, 193
Breuvannes 102
Brewer, Colonel Guy S. 5, 11, 13, 15, 16, 27, 31, 32, 37, 40, 42, 43, 46–48, 52, 53, 62, 66–69, 78, 83, 87, 88, 93, 95, 98, 101–107, 109, 113, 144, 151, 155, 157, 160–164, 173, 175, 177, 179, 181, 183, 184, 186, 190, 192
bridge (card game) 5, 8, 76, 94, 126, 139, 143, 194
Briggs, Lt. Howard B. 102, 120, 121
Briquenay, Ardennes 136, 137
Britannic 5

Index

Brohl 151, 155, 158, 159, 162, 164, 173
Brohltalbahn 151, 162
Bronchitis 174
Brooke, Rupert 195
Brooks, Major 172
Brotchen 155
Brown, Lt. Dan W. 23, 57
Brown, Pvt. Leigh A. 53, 93
Brown, Gen. Robert A. 63, 93
Bru 40, 43
Bruce, Pvt. Elmer B. 50, 51, 101
Bruley 109
Brussels 183
Bulgaria 119
Bunch, Cpt. Henry E. 134, 149
Burberrys 126
Burg Olbruck 156–158
Burgbrohl 150, 152, 161, 162, 178
Burks, Pvt. Thomas C. 128
Butler, Lt. Charles W. 5, 17
Butts (engineer) 122–125

C Company 1, 13, 53, 95, 115
C7 22, 59
"Cafard" 161
Café Americain 21
Café Bauer 159
Café de la Femme a Barbe 74
Café de la Vendurette 33
Café du Pont 43
Cahill, Pvt. Joseph J. 68
Cambrai 10
Camion 25, 73, 90, 119, 120
Camp de Ker Arvor 43, 44, 46, 51, 53, 59
Camp de la Noblette 87, 99
Camp de Vautivet 79
Camp Mills 1, 13, 16, 42, 53
Camp Pontanezen 190, 192
Camp Upton 194
Cantigny 181
Carlier, Madame 134, 135
Carlisle, Pennsylvania 2
Casey, Major Charles J. 108, 164, 168, 169
Casino de Paris 188
Castle, Miss 184
cathedral 8, 160
Catholics 45, 76, 100, 106, 119, 156, 157, 160
S.S. *Celtic* 1, 4, 25, 138
Central Records Office 119
Century magazine 104
Chalons-sur-Marne 76–78, 79, 86, 87, 88, 104, 166, 188
Chamigney 101

Champagne 46, 58, 101, 104, 144, 153, 154
Champs Elysées 126, 168
Le Chanson des Saisons 47
Chatillon-sur-Seine 154, 164
Chartres 190
Chasseurs 55, 67, 70, 188
Chateau of St. Benoit 114
Chateau Thierry 75, 78, 85, 90, 93, 99, 102, 166, 173
Chattanooga 14
Chauchat automatic rifle 18, 32
Chaumont 25, 101, 102
Chaumont-la-Ville, Haut Marne 102, 105
La Chaussee 76
Chaussee Romaine 82
Chef de gare 28, 29
Chemin de Fer de l'Est 26
Chenois 140
La Cheppe 86, 87
Cheppy 121
Chopin 151
Chris, Intelligence Officer 46
Christmas 14, 15, 16, 24, 26, 27, 75, 152, 153, 156
Christopher, Cpt. John C. (Johnny) 13, 33, 72, 113, 174
Churchill, Winston: *A Far Country* 67
C.I.A. 1
Cierges 95
Cimiez 170
Cincinnati 165
Cirey 64
civilians 31, 37, 51, 57, 63, 72, 99, 125, 127, 135, 140, 148, 159, 193
Civilization 172
Clair de Lune 123
Clark, Lt. James R. 192
Clarke, Lieutenant 161
Clemenceau, Georges 169
Coblenz 164, 172–174, 184–186
Cognac 187
Collecteur Trench (C.T.) 37, 39, 55, 66, 70, 83, 85
Cologne 159, 160, 164, 173
Colombey-les-Belles 108, 109
Columbia University 1, 8, 24, 113, 127, 150
Commercy 104
Conflans 187
Conkling, Colonel William S. 62, 154, 161, 177
Connor 193
The Continental Hotel 125, 159, 160
Convent 150, 161

201

Index

Coolus 89
Coons, Pvt. Earl E. 6
cooties 97, 104, 114, 115, 116
corned Willy 132, 134
Corning 57
Cosby, Sergeant 33
Coss, Pvt. Floyd E. 48
Cotter, Cpt. James F. (Jimmy) 7, 8, 11, 13, 16, 21, 23, 26, 31, 33, 35, 38–43, 53, 64, 74, 75, 77, 78, 80, 81, 91, 94, 100–104, 106, 108, 109, 119, 121, 132, 133, 135, 139–141, 145–150, 152, 154–156, 160, 162, 163, 173–177, 179, 185, 192, 194
Coulvagney 75, 76
Coup de main 83, 115, 117
Coupru 99, 100
court martial 155, 175, 177
Courtisols Ouest, Marne 77, 78, 87, 88
C.R. Chamois 47, 54
Craps 193, 194
Credit Lyonnais 187
Crezilles, Meurthe-et-Moselle 108
Crocker, Mrs. 29
Croix de Guerre 192
Croix Rouge Farm 91
Cruise, Lt. Eugene B. (Gene) 95, 132, 135, 153, 154, 163, 164, 172, 174–177, 181, 185
Crystallerie 73
Cuperly 87
Curé 26, 27
Currie, Lt. John M (Currie) 13, 15, 17, 33, 46, 75, 85, 103, 106, 113, 117
Curry, Pvt. Trimble C. 85
Cütchen 179, 184

D Company 1, 186
Danville, Pennsylvania 156
Davis, Cpt. Homer 14, 63, 148
December 11, 12, 146, 147, 149, 150, 153, 154
De Champigney, Lt. 85
deer 178, 181, 182
De Graff, Lt. B.R. 150
Dejeuner 72, 83
Deneuvre, Meurthe-et-Moselle 40, 43
Denver 41
Deronet, Captain 183
deserter 54, 118
detention camp 8
Deutsches Eck 186
Deutschland 148
Deuxnouds Devant Beauzée 120
D.H.C. (Dispatcher of Hot Chocolate) 177
Dickman, Lt. General 179

Dickson, Cpl. Walter D. 47, 48
Dijon, Cote D'Or 123, 124, 170, 173
Dimont, Madamemoiselle 169
Distinguished Service Cross 181
Distinguished Service Medal 181
Division Intelligence 129
Doan, Pvt. Donald A. 38
Dolan, Lt. James H. 72
Domblain 104
Donovan, William 1, 92
Doocy, Lt. Elmer T. 103, 113, 117
Dostoevsky, Fyodor: *The Brothers Karamazov* 68, 75, 76
Doty, Lt. William D' Orviller, III (Dor) 2, 97, 99–108, 110, 112–114, 117–119, 126
The Doughboy of the Rainbow Division 185
Douglas, Sgt. Grover C. 84
Douglass, Lt. Ercell B. 53, 58
Dowling, Sgt. John C. (Jack) 119
Drachens 70
Drake, Cpl. Will A. (Bill) 137, 175
Drake, Pvt. Robert E. (Bob) 48, 133
Draper, Pvt. Earl E. 48, 112
D.S.C. (Dispatcher of Steero Cubes) 177
Duck-on-the-Rock 42
Ducs Decrees 15
Dun-sur-Meuse 138
Dunhill 106
Dunn, Cpt. James F. 13, 38, 56, 98
Dutchman 173

E Company 1, 31
Easter 193
Edniger 146
Ehrenbreistein 186
88s 94, 95, 96, 117, 119
84th Brigade 129
89th Division 110, 112, 115, 117, 136, 139
83rd Brigade 118
Eischen, Grand Duché de Luxembourg 141, 143, 144
Eisenach 146
Eitel Fiedrich, Prince 40
Ellison, Pvt. Percey A. 65
"Elsie Janis" 75
Emerson, Ralph Waldo 173
Engineer Corps 103
England 8, 9, 45, 10, 70, 75, 76, 138, 149, 154, 157, 159, 160, 166, 173, 181
Epernay 102, 166
Epieds 90, 99
Epinal 12
Episcopalian 160

Index

Esprit de corps 13
Essey 113, 117
Esternay 89
Ethe 140
Etoile 126, 188
Europe 155
Evacuation No. 9, 122
evacuees 140
Evige Lampe 160
Excelsior Hotel 187
Exermont 128
Express 167

F Company 1, 33, 57, 97, 98, 108, 162, 175
"Faiencerie" 39, 51, 54, 63, 70
Falinestock, Captain 68
Farley, Sgt. Maxwell 18, 32, 33, 40, 46, 48, 65, 76, 80, 95
Fathers and Sons 76
February 25, 26, 30, 69, 162, 163, 165, 173, 174, 192
Fennerville 35
Ferebee, Captain 192
Ferme du Haut d'Arbre 50
La Ferte 101, 102
La Ferte-sous-Jouarre 100
Fête Nationale 84
Field Officers 192
Fifth Division 139
5th Plattsburgh Company 20
1st Army Corps School 18
1st Battalion 1, 13, 18, 32, 51, 55, 57, 61, 90, 91, 94, 114, 116, 128, 132, 152, 158, 175, 179, 184
1st Division 1, 20, 23, 110, 114, 121, 134, 136, 139, 161, 172, 181, 187
1st Platoon 5, 12, 31, 37, 46–48, 61, 63, 91, 94, 100, 101, 110, 113, 179
Firth, Lt. Robert M. 144, 159, 160, 174
Flagler, Gen. Clement 144, 179–181
Flannigan, Pvt. John H. 48, 53, 93
Fleur, Cpt. Edward O. 61
Fleville 131
Flirey 110, 117
Flivver 177
Foch, Marshal Ferdinand 137, 139
Folies Bergere 126, 127, 166
Fontainebleau 166, 189
football 161, 162
Ford 38, 64, 117
Foret d'Argonne 85
Foret de Eliex 43
Foret de Fere, Aisne 90, 97, 98

Foret de la Reine 109, 110
Foret de Nesles 97
41st Division 122
45 106
42nd Division 20, 28, 114, 115, 117, 121, 126–128, 136, 138, 139, 168, 174, 178, 179, 185
4th Army Corps 181
4th Corps 179
4th Division 97, 139, 162, 164
4th Platoon 26, 48, 92, 94, 179
France 9–12, 15, 17, 24, 26–28, 30–33, 37, 38, 40, 41, 43–45, 47, 54, 55, 62, 64, 67, 69, 70, 72, 75, 78, 79–85, 87, 89, 99, 104, 110, 118, 127, 129, 132, 138, 141, 157, 165, 169, 172, 173, 175, 181–184, 188, 193
Francis, Major 186
Franken 154, 182
Frankie 32, 79, 132, 176
Fraser, Lt. Charles A. 186
Fraser, Nimrod 2
Fred 190
French Sixth Army Corps 28
Frenchman 101, 104
Friedensturm 85
Fulghum, Pvt. Milton D. (Dutch) 65–67, 86
Fullers 188
Fulton, Cpl. William E. 46, 48

G Company 1, 65
Gabrielle, Madame 102, 104, 105
Gannet, Pvt. Ray G. 128
Garden City 1, 3
Garden City Hotel 3
Gare 74, 127
Gare de l'Est 125, 127, 188
Gare de Lyon 170
Gare de Montparnasse 188
Gare des Invalides 189
Garner, Sgt. Carlos (Dot) 43, 46, 48, 65
garrison 35, 65, 70
gas guards 48
gas officer 13
Gay, Madame 12
General Order 189
George, King 185
Gerard, Pvt. Donald A. (Gertrude) 38
Germain, Lt. Georges 17, 18
Germaine 30
German P.O.W.s 20
German Zollverein 141
Germany 1, 16, 15, 20, 30, 31, 39, 40, 45, 50, 54, 55, 70, 72, 75, 76, 81, 82, 90, 92, 94, 96, 99, 115, 119, 120, 128, 129, 131, 133,

203

Index

135, 137–139, 141, 143, 146, 147, 149, 153, 156–159, 165, 172, 173, 181, 187
GHQ (General Headquarters) 143, 165, 184
Gibbons, Lt. Charles A. (Gib) 113, 157–159, 160, 163, 166, 170, 173, 175, 192
Gilbert 194
Gilbert and Sullivan 75
Gironcourt 107
Glees 149, 150, 174
Glines, Pvt. John A. 84
Gondrecourt, Meuse 18, 20, 23–25, 26, 42, 55, 75, 122
Gonnersdorf 176
Good Friday 169
Gothas 107
Gott 138, 148
Gout 105, 183
G.Q.M. 30
Graf Von Spee 154
Graham, Pvt. John B. 91
Graham, Lieutenant 172
Granatenwerfer 134
Grand Banks 4
Grand Hotel (Metz) 187
Grand Hotel (Paris) 166
Grand Rue 54, 55
Grandes-Armoises 132
Grant, Ensign 194
Green, Lt. Clarence R. 61
Greene, Lt. Douglas B. 98
Greenwalt, Sgt. Clyde W. 113
Greenway, Sgt. Claude W. 93
Grenadier Guards 160
"Grenier a foin" 105
Groupe de Combat (G.C.) 35, 37, 38, 42, 47–50, 51, 56, 57, 63, 65–68, 72
guardhouse 55
Gulf Stream 193
Gustine, Pvt. Clyde B. 43, 61

H Company 1, 35, 37, 98
Hagerman, Cpl. William 48, 92
Hagerty, Lt. Sheward 159, 160
Hain 157
Haley, Cpt. William M. 102, 128, 134, 156, 193
Halifax, Nova Scotia 3, 4
Hall, Cpl. Leroy B. (Tubby) 38
Hambourg 40
Hamilton, Pvt. Fred B. 48, 65, 92
Hanft, Pvt. Allen 90
Haraucourt, Ardennes 132–135
hardtack 134

Harker, Pvt. John T. 95
Harnoncourt 140
Harper's magazine 104
Harvard 8, 194
Hassinger 127
Hastings, Cpt. Thomas (Tommy) 190
Hatch, Lt. Roscoe C. (chaplain, Happy) 101, 102, 104, 106–108, 114, 116, 117, 120, 158, 161, 163, 192
Hattonchatel 114
Haumont 117
Haute Savoie 107
Hauts de Meuse 114
Hayden, Mr. 117
Haynes, Maj. Glen C. 21, 24, 179, 184, 192
Hazzard 21
Headquarters Signal Platoon 68
Hearts of the World 169
Heeckeren, Baroness de 170
Hegeman, Kate (cousin) 188
Heiden, Pvt. Lawrence E. 84
Heil Dir Im Siegerkrauz 149
Heilige Drei Könige 156
Heimersheim 154, 182
Heinies 70
Hempstead 154
Henderson, Francis 188
Henriette 185
Henry, King 175
Henry IV, King 55
Heudicourt 118
High Mass 160, 168
Hilbert 154
Hill 212 93, 95, 96
Hines, Pvt. Joseph 65
Hives 150
Hoar, Lt. George W. 35, 58
Hobart 101
Hobbs, Sgt. Clem M. 56
Holland 136
Holthausen, Eduard 153
Holthausen, Frau 152–156, 163, 164, 173, 174, 176, 177, 185
Holthausen, Herr 151–153, 176, 177, 185
Holthausen, Trautsche 152, 153
Hoover 168
Hope, Anthony 143
Hoply, Cook William (Bill, Billy) 105, 174, 186
"Hors de combat" 104
Horton, Arthur J. 21
Horton, Cpl. Floyd D. 68
hospital 7, 9, 11, 16, 25, 38, 39, 46, 61, 62,

204

Index

79, 82, 83, 96, 101, 103–105, 108, 122, 123, 133, 144, 154, 163, 173
Hotel de Crillon 126, 166, 168, 188, 189
Hotel de la Cloche 123
Hotel de la Gare 54, 55
Hotel Dieu 123
Hotel Disch 159
Hotel Dom 159
Hotel Kaiserhof 164, 172
Hotel Mertens 157
Hotel Regina Nice 170
Hotel Regina Paris 126
Hotel Ruhl 170
House, Edward Mandell 169
Hout, Captain 183
Howitzer 131
Hubbel, Pvt. Max L. 56
Hudson, Cpt. William S. 27, 28, 63
Huet, Madame 15, 16
Hull, Sgt. Carl E. 37, 87, 94
Hunting, Lt. Warren B. 87
Hupp, Captain Allen T. 4, 9, 13, 15, 17, 24, 26–29, 31, 32, 38, 39, 42, 55–57, 62, 64, 68, 69, 74–76, 79, 83, 87, 90, 91–93, 98, 166, 168–170, 174, 189
Hutchins, Lt. John 24
Hutchinson, Sgt. Isaac G. 35
Hutchinson, Lt. Colonel 25
Hutton, Pvt. Bert O. 48

I Company 1, 38, 48, 50, 68, 81, 887, 91, 102, 128, 134, 152, 163, 179
Iceland 5
I.D.R. (Infantry Drill Regulation) 174
Ihrie, Lt. Charles I. 63, 87
Imécourt 131
immigration 158
Indiana 87
Indians 10, 66
infirmary 75
infusion 135
Iowa 1, 110
Iowa Regiment 137, 183
Ire-le-Sec, Meuse 139
Irene Castle 123
Irish Sea 6
Is-sur-Tille 124, 125
Italy 10, 31, 34, 45, 59, 70, 77, 101, 140, 165
Ixe 126, 170

Jaignes, Seine-et-Marne 89
January 16, 18, 21, 22, 154–157, 159, 162
Jarvis, Lt. Robert Y. 50, 51

Jeanmenil 42
Jennings, Pvt. John M. 53
J.G. 55
Joffre, Marechal 106
John the Baptist (J.B.) 132
Johnny 22
Johnson, General E.M. 69
Johnson, Pvt. Ernest G. 117
Johnson, Cpt. Erney W. 118
Johnson, Lieutenant 165, 192
Johnson, Pvt. Skip 26, 32, 44, 84, 137
Johnston 193
Jones, Cpt. Theodore L. (Teddy, Ted) 13, 17, 18, 21, 22, 24, 25, 32, 43, 45, 46, 50–52, 57, 66, 76, 83, 98, 121, 143, 153, 155, 159, 162, 163, 166, 170, 174, 175, 177, 184, 192, 193
July 79, 80, 83, 90, 94
June 63, 65, 67, 68, 99, 192

K Company 1, 5, 8, 16, 24, 26, 31, 38, 47, 50, 55, 57, 59, 63, 68, 85, 92, 93, 102, 103, 106, 108, 109, 113, 114, 117, 128, 129, 135–137, 143, 145, 146, 148, 157, 162–164, 174, 175, 178, 179, 183, 194
Kaiser 136, 150, 156, 172
Kalles, Pvt. George 64, 65, 67, 68, 84, 137
Kelberg 148
Kelley, Cpt. William A. 116
Kempenich 162
Kenny, Sgt. Charles J. 49
Kenyon, Pvt. Leo N. 90
Killian, Pvt. Albert S. 84
Kim, Madame 58–60
King, Pvt. Norman L. 48
King, Pvt. William J. 86
King Arthur's Table 8
Kinselman, Pvt. Oral 48
Kloster 175
Knights of Columbus 157
Knowles, Mrs. Edith 59, 60, 63, 64, 73, 107, 108, 117, 119, 126, 154, 161–163, 182, 183, 188, 189
Knowlton, Lt. Bernard W. 13
Kocher 182
Kodak 76
Konigsfeld 152, 157
Krebs, Sgt. Charles 32, 46, 48, 97
Kripp 179
Kur Theater 182, 184
Kurhaus 154, 161
Kurort 154
Kurtz, Pvt. Ray B. 48

205

Index

L Company 1, 32, 50, 51, 55, 59, 61, 63, 67, 76, 82, 83, 88, 91, 94, 105, 113, 129, 133, 135, 162, 163, 174, 179
Laacher See 174
Lager 128
Lagney 109
Lainson, Cpt. Percy A. 13, 15, 32, 51, 53, 82, 96, 109, 113, 121, 133, 163, 173, 174, 184, 193
Lamorteau, Province de Luxembourg 139
Landblatt 141
Landladies 11, 12, 33, 78, 103, 141
Landres-et-St. Georges 137
Landreville, Ardennes 137
Lane, Pvt. Kit C. 12, 137
Langan, Sgt. Thomas E. 133
Langres 25, 27, 102, 103, 125
Lansing, Secretary Robert 168
Lapierre, M. 14, 18
Lapierre, Madame 12, 15
Lasseville, Marquis de 76, 77
Lasseville, Marquise de 75
Latour 140
Laura 156
Laval 190
Lavoir Ferme 133, 134
Lawrence, Pvt. Harold G. (Teddy) 68
Lazarett 39
Le Clere family 76
Lefferts, Lt. Marshall C., Jr. (Marshall) 3, 5, 7–9, 16, 17, 26, 27, 31, 32, 39, 51, 52, 62, 72, 79, 93, 98, 105, 106
Legion of Honor 192
Le Havre 10, 11
Lehrerinnen 149
Leijedal, Mrs. Maria 2
Lelotte, Reine de Cirque 172
Le Mans 190
Leonard, Miss 4, 5
L'Epine 77, 78, 87
Le Thiolet 99
Levers, Billy 25
U.S.S *Leviathan* 2, 191–194
Lewis, Pvt. Russell J. 48
Lewis, Lt. William N. (Bill) 3, 8, 9, 11–13, 15, 16, 17, 18, 24, 26, 27, 31–33, 35, 41, 42, 44, 47, 55, 57, 58, 64, 74, 75, 78, 81, 82, 84, 94, 95, 99, 104, 105, 107, 109, 113, 119, 121, 128, 130, 133, 138, 144, 156–160, 162, 163, 166, 170, 173, 174, 177, 183, 184, 192
Lewisburg 165
Liaison school 173
Life of Robert E. Lee 23

Liverpool, England 6, 7
Livingston, Pvt. John B. 91
Lloyd, Pvt. Chris B. 48
Lloyd-George 169
Locust Valley 26
Lohndorf 154, 182
Lombard, Lt. Richard (Dick) 153, 174, 176, 184, 192, 193
London 8, 26, 156
Loomis, Lt. Lynn A. 4, 5, 8
Lorraine 75, 158
Louis Martin's 15
Louis XIV 76
Louise 126
Louisville Farm 114
Louppy 139
Louvre 166
Lucas, Cpt. Albert K. (Luke) 24, 102, 108, 120, 134, 144, 162, 174–179, 183, 184, 192, 193
Lucy 125, 126, 166, 167, 169, 170, 188
Lucy-le-Bocage 99
Ludendorff 128
Luftkurort 147
Luneville, Meurthe-et-Moselle 28, 29, 30, 44, 47, 158
Lusitania 153
Luxem 149
Luxembourg 141, 143, 145, 161, 165
Luxusbad 144
Lyon 170

M Company 1, 11, 24, 33, 60, 82, 105, 111, 134, 162, 175, 179
MacArthur, Douglas 1, 138
Machine Gun Company 1, 61, 114, 152
Mack, Sgt. Mark L.J. 46, 48, 65, 117
Madelon 47
Magasins Remmis 41
Mainz 183
Manderscheid 147
Mantes 11
March 31, 33, 34, 38, 40, 41, 42, 69, 174–176, 178, 179, 181–184
Marchal, M. 46
Marchal, Mlle. 72, 73
Marguerite 30
Maria Laach 158
Maria Laach Abbey 174
Marie Adelaide, Grand Duchess 142, 143
Marie Feys, Mlle. 59, 64, 73
Marie-Louise 72
Marienstatter Hof 176

206

Index

Marinbois farm 116
Marine 7, 20, 131
Marne 76, 89, 100
Marseille 123, 170
Marsellaise 149
Marshal, Madame 60
Mary 78, 168
Mary Garden 189
Mason 76
Mathilde 33, 45, 47, 175
Matthews 7
Maurice, Lieutenant 183
May 54, 55, 59, 62, 194
Mayen 150
Mayer 177
McCann, Lt. James S. 113
McClure, Bill 22
McConnelee, Pvt. Irwin O. 56
McCormack, Lt. Scott (Mac) 3, 8, 14, 17, 18, 21, 22, 78
McCoy, Lt. Frank E. 23, 42
McHenry, Cpt. Harry C. 21, 32, 35
McHugh, Sgt. Leo P. 113, 117
McIlvaine, Lt. Francis A. 56
McKeon, Lt. Andrew J. 35
Means, Captain 133, 165
Means, Pvt. Orville B. 93
Meaux 89
Medaille Militaire 192
Medal of Honor 181
medic 177
Mediterranean 170
Mediterranee 170, 189
Memorial Day 63
Men-of-War 4
Ménage 12
Menoher, Gen. Charles T. 29, 138
Mersey lights 6
Metz 165, 172, 173
Meuse river 134
Meusieu 127
military police (M.P.) 46, 55, 62, 128, 159, 166, 170
Mintzer, Cpl. Lester P. 48, 93
Mirabelle 106
M.I.T. 8
Moderne 192
Moet Chandon 16
Mohn, Lt. Robert D. (Robbie, Robb) 100, 102–104, 109, 111, 150, 156, 188
Monk 175
Monopol 186
Monreal 150

Monroe, Mech. Ben H. 48, 162
Mons 25
Mont Sec 112, 115
Montagne de Reims 82
Montmedy 139
Monty 103
Moon, Pvt. Albert J. 94
Moon, Cpl. Woody C. 105
Moore, Cpl. Rennie L. 48, 92, 178
Mordor Haute Marne 25, 26, 31, 173
Morelmaison, Vosges 105–107
Morgan, Pvt. Glen A. 48, 50, 113
Morn Hill 7
Morpheus 43
Morphine 133
Morris, Cpl. Merle S. 29, 30
Morrow, Colonel 22
Moselle 186
Mother Earth 119
Motter, Pvt. Daniel P. 128
Moulin de Caranda 93
Mouvrey, Colonel 67
Moyer, Pvt. George A. 48, 83, 106
Mudville 31
Murphy 157
Murray, Captain 161, 163
Murvaux, Meuse 138
Muscat 46
Musson 140
mustard gas 60, 70

Nadine 103–105
Nancy 24, 27, 75, 165, 187
Napier, Pvt. Joseph B. (Joe) 133
Nash, Captain 190
National Army 13
National Guard 1, 13, 17, 44, 103
Nations, Pvt. James L. 113
Nazi 143
N.C.O.S. (Non-Commissioned Officers School) 162
Neale, Lt. Lawrence L. 48
Ned 105, 125, 126, 166
Neetz, Captain 154
Neichen 148, 149
Neilson, Cpl. Herman 46, 65, 67, 68
Nelson, Sgt. Caroll 14, 46, 84
Nesles 97
Neuenahr 154, 161–163, 182–184
Neufchateau 18, 25, 27, 75, 101
Neufmaisons, Meurthe-et-Moselle 32, 33, 35, 37, 38, 40, 43–45, 57, 60, 63, 64, 70, 72, 158

Index

Neunkirchen 147
Neuviller 51
Nevins, Sgt. Lee M. 113
New Orleans 75
New Year 16, 18
New York 1, 15, 26, 117, 138, 192–194
Nice 162, 163, 164, 166, 170, 172, 174
Nice Express 169
Nichols 113
Niederbreisig 152, 155, 159, 160, 162–164, 172, 175, 177–179, 183–185, 193
Niederzissen, Brohltal 150, 153, 155, 160, 164, 177, 183, 185
19th Division 139
Noble, Lt. G.B. (Bernard, GBN) 44–46, 50, 53, 54, 57–61, 63–68, 75, 76, 87, 98, 101, 116, 158, 166–170, 188–192
Noble, Lt. Heath B. 4, 5, 13, 16, 17, 23, 24, 72, 87, 98
Nonsard 118
Notre Dame 123, 124, 168
November 3, 4, 5, 42, 129, 132, 135, 136, 138, 140, 141, 144
Noyon 105
nuns 161

O7 22
Oberbreisig 152, 176, 186
Oberzissen 152, 156, 162, 183
Observation balloon 115, 122, 128–130
October 1, 12, 120, 122, 123, 126, 128, 140, 166
O'Dell, Pvt. Louis E. 85
Odorf 146
Officer of the Day 4
Officer of the Guard 4
Officers School 14, 154
Officers' Y 20
Oklahoma 103, 157
Old England 166
Old Soldiers and Sailors (O.S.S.) 182
"Old Soldiers Never Die" 91
Olizy 78
Olympia 166
Omar Khayyam 173, 177
On a Bank by the Ourcq 94
Once-and-Over 42
150th Seventh Army 161, 179, 194
150s 94
155 batteries (howitzers) 56, 82
151 First Army Band 59
151st Machine Gun Battalion (M.G.) 133, 165

151st Seventh Army 161, 179
101st Infantry 90
105s 80
149th Machine Gun Battalion 149th 165, 192
117th Engineers 30, 33, 45, 179
110th Infantry 94
168th Infantry Society 178
168th Regiment 1, 18, 22, 30, 39, 69, 121, 128, 137, 144, 179, 182, 194
165th Regiment 1, 30, 67, 92, 179
167th Regiment 1, 30, 174, 179
166th Regiment 30, 178, 179
120 118
O'Neale 193
Opera (Comique) 126, 143, 159, 166–168
O.P.W. (Office of Public Works) 127, 166, 170
orchestra 144, 153, 177, 184
Orney 76
Orphans home 173
O.S.S. (Office of Strategic Services) 1
Otello 168
Ourcq river 91, 93, 95, 98
Over There 4
Oxford 44

Pace, Sgt. Herbert W. 35, 48, 49, 84, 178, 181
Pachek, Pvt. Peter 114
Palmer, Lt. Newell 134
Pannes 117, 119
Pantheon de la Guerre 169
Pardee 11, 13, 59
Paris 2, 14, 20, 26, 69, 75, 83, 88, 100, 103, 107, 124–127, 158, 165, 166, 168, 169, 185–187, 189, 190, 192
Paris Express 125
Paris Herald 17
Pass in Review 181
Pathé 189
Patton 90
Patton, Sgt. Paul K. (Bud) 158, 164
Paul (cousin) 166
Pavillion des Officiers 51
P.C. (Post of Command) 49, 50, 55, 56, 65, 66, 70, 82, 96, 128, 134
Peace Commission 167
Peace Mission 158, 192
Peach, Pvt. Arthur 86
Pearsall, Lt. Francis S. (Tex) 24, 106
Pecham, Lt. Harold D. 166
Penitents 78
Pershing, General John 74, 144, 174, 178–181

208

Index

Persia 157
Petange 143
Petit dejuener 29, 168
Le Petit Parisien 17
Petite verre 106
Pettit, Captain 169
Pexonne 35, 38, 47, 52, 54, 60, 61, 63, 64, 72
Peyton, Lt. Charles (Charley) 128, 146, 152, 154, 155, 159–163, 174, 176, 177, 179, 182, 185
Philip 83
Phosgene 59, 65, 70
Picardy 43
Piggott, Lt. Albert T. (Al) 128, 130, 144, 150, 154–156, 158, 163, 174, 175
Pillessout, Madame 12, 13, 14, 16
Pink Chateau 47, 55
pinochle 103, 106, 119, 121, 130, 138, 156
pioneer troops 138
pitch 44, 59
Place de la Concorde 125
Place de la Madeleine 169
Place Jeanne d'Arc 18
Place Vendome 126
Plattsburgh 1, 22, 190
Plattsburgh Company 11
Platz 159, 172
P.O. (Post Office) 41, 149
Pogny 76
Poilu 172
Poincaré, Pres. Raymond 74, 139
Point 29
Point d'Appui (P.A.) 37, 50, 65–68, 70, 72
poker 83, 178
Poli, Lieutenant 72
Polk, Miss 29
Pont Mangis 134
Popote 33, 75, 77, 81, 141
Portuguese 10
Potts, Maj. Allen 28, 29, 30
Potts, Miss 177, 188
Pout-a-Mousson 171
Powell, Cpt. Clifford 17, 21, 32, 52, 53, 63, 76
Powers, Cpl. Estill 113, 117
Premiers 189
President Grant 1, 3, 12, 31, 192
Pretoria 194
Pretorian 192
The Price of Our Heritage: In Memory of the Heroic Dead of the 168th Infantry 2
Priddy, Lt. Wellborn S. 62
Prince, Lt. Harold A. 178

The Prisoner of Zenda 143
prisoners 8, 20, 32, 34, 42, 55, 63, 70, 75
Pritchard, Lt. Herbert 155, 159, 176
prohibition 157
projector 61, 63, 67
Protestantism 160
P.S. 5 (petite poste) 48, 49
Pugsley, Seargent 31
Purdue 193

quai 11, 29, 127, 190, 192; *see also* quay
Quai d'Orsay 169
quay 7, 9; *see also* quai

Rachecourt, Province of Luxembourg 140
Railroad Transportation Officer (R.T.O.) 27, 28, 127
Rainbow Division 1, 78, 159, 173, 181, 191, 193
Rambervillers 41
Raon-l'Etape 45, 52
Raon Road 59
Rapide 123, 188
Raubritter castle 151
Recicourt 127
Red Cross 3, 42, 95, 96, 117, 126, 161, 165, 184, 186
Reed, Walt 101
Reese, Cook Tom (Tommy) 148
refugee 12
Reims 26, 75, 78, 82, 89, 127, 141
Remagen 159, 179, 183
Rennes 190
Repos (rest) 126
Residenzstadt 186
Rest Camp No. 2 10
Reveille 13, 14, 20, 31, 100, 163, 174, 187
Rhein 152, 153, 155, 177, 186; *see also* Rhine
Rhein Hotel 178
Rheineck 158, 163
Rheinland 156
Rhine 136, 151, 172; *see also* Rhein
Rhodes, Pvt. Orien H. 86
Rhodes Scholar 44
Rhume 12
Rice, Pvt. Frank G. (Bud) 112
Richmond 30
Richmond Blues 30
Richthofen 85
Rigoletto opera 159
Riley, Cpt. Charles J. 168, 172, 173, 184
Rimaucourt, Haute Marne 11, 12, 15, 25, 53, 101

209

Index

Risse, Sgt. John E. 178
Ritz, London 8
Ritz, Paris 127, 167
Riviera 126, 162
Robb, Chaplain Winfred 2, 15, 63, 127, 161
Roberts, Cook Harry E. (Happy) 76, 81, 101, 102, 105, 108, 115, 146, 149, 152–154, 162
Robinson, Lt. Leo 128, 156, 162, 163
Roche aux Cochons 52
Rolampont 25, 27, 173–175
Rolandseck 163
Romania 59
Rome 82, 144, 165
Roosevelt, Kermit 30
Roosevelt, Pres. Theodore 157
Rosport 146
Ross, Maj. Lloyd M. 24, 161
Rotterdam 163, 178
Royce, Sgt. Maj. Willis G. 178
Roye 105
Rubel, Lt. Solomon G. 24, 98
Rue de la Paix 168
Rue de la Rochotte 60
Rue de Lorraine 37
Rue de Paris 57
Rue des Petits Ayeux 78
Rue Gambetta 53, 54
Rue Guibal 28
Rue Rivoli 125
Rue St. Anne 127
Rue St. Honoré 188
Ruggles of Red Gap 25
Ruisseau de La Verdurette 57, 58
Rumpelmayers 169
Runt 150
Rupt de Mad 113
Ruse 28, 30
Ruse, Madame 28, 29, 30
Russia 10, 11, 138, 158, 162, 169
Rust 132
Rutherford, Mr., and Mrs. 64
Rutledge, Pvt. Ralph A. 48

S., Jack 127
Sabin-Pasley, Mrs. 169
S.A.E. 8, 193, 194
St. Agnes 117
St. Arnaud 75
Saint Benoit 116
Saint-Brieue 190
St. Clement 28, 31
St. Die 188
St.-Dizier 102, 124, 127

St. Emilion 59
St. Georges 131
St. Gervais 169
St. Leger 140
Saint-Mard 140
St. Michel 124
St. Mihiel 104, 110–112, 115, 155, 184
Saint Patrick's Day 38
Sainte-Aulde, Seine-et-Marne 100, 102
Salonika 11, 27
Sam Browne belts 4, 57
Sambre et Meuse 18
San Francisco 29
Sandemans Port 189
Sanders, Cpl. Enoch A. 37, 48
Sanitary Detachment 1, 27, 49, 62, 177
Santa Claus 147
Santo Domingo 59
Sauer river 146
Saulxures, Vosges 105
Saveur 141
Saville, Randolph 126
Savoire 125
Savy, Louis 26, 27, 173, 178
scarlet fever 6, 7, 12
Schaefer, Lt. Walter B. 17, 50, 56
schlafzimmer 150
Schaumwein 153
Schleich (Gasthaus) 150, 153, 157
Schleich, Fraulein Therese 152, 153, 155, 157, 173, 185
Schleich, Ludwig 162, 173, 177, 183
Schleich, Marie-Luise 177, 183, 185
Schloss 154
Schloss Rheineck 155
Schmidt, Pvt. Jacob (Jake) 99
Schubert: *Wanderers Nachtlied* 67
"Schulmeister" 148
Schulmeister, Herr 149
Schuster, Pvt. Glenn C. 65, 70, 86, 91
Schwaller, Mr. Shannon 2
Schwester Ella 182
Scott, Lt. Robert F. (Scotty) 41, 46, 47, 59, 60
2nd Battalion 1, 32, 91, 94, 98, 113, 116, 128, 129, 132, 152, 158, 179
2nd Battalion Headquarters 47, 166
2nd Brigade 87
2nd Canadian Division 159
2nd Division 1, 121, 136, 139
2nd Platoon 68, 87, 179
2nd Training Camp 41, 44
sedan 134, 178

Index

Sefton, Lt. Earle (Eric) 17, 75, 98, 120
Seicheprey 110
Sentry 54
September 11, 16, 40, 103, 107, 108, 109, 111, 116, 118, 119
Serbia 10, 11, 59
Serge 103
Sergy 96, 97
Setzer, Lt. Walter K. (Setz) 13, 17, 18, 21, 22, 24, 25, 32, 51, 52, 75, 82
Seven Keys to Baldpate 182
7th Artillery (7.A. 1st Division) 22
78th Division 129, 132
75s 44, 54, 80, 83, 117
77s 50, 55, 66, 67, 94, 115
77th Division 66, 69, 72, 77, 132, 133, 137
Severe, Lt. William E. 62
Shakespeare, William 55
Shepard, Cpl. Curtis E. 29, 30
Shive, Pvt. Peter 48
Short, Pvt. John (Jack) 85
Short, Sgt. Walter S. 108
Siceloff, Professor 24
Siebengebirge 153
Sievers, Pvt. Oren M. 133
Sigma Phi 101
Signeulx 140
Simerman, Cpl. Wayne A. 46, 48, 92, 105, 137, 173
Simpson, Sgt. Webster G. (Fido) 40, 65, 84, 112, 113
Sinzig 154, 159, 179, 181
Sivrey-les-Buzancy 131
S.I.W. (Self Inflicted Wound) 46
16th Infantry 134, 172
Smith, Lt. 165
soccer 159
Soissons 70, 87
Somme 58
Somme-Vesle 79
Sommerance 131
Sorbonne 175
Souain 80, 82
Sous-chef de gare 11
Southampton 8
Spanish relief commission 140
Spealman, Major 162
Spence 22, 76, 114
Springfields 20
Springtime 22
Squadron Officers School (S.O.S.) 107, 108, 143
Squibb, Lt. George Sampson 4, 5, 8

Staar Hotel 143
Stanislas of Poland 30
Stanley, Lt. Col. Claude M. 35, 47, 57, 96, 161, 178, 184, 185
"Star Spangled Banner" 4, 180
Steinfort 145
Stellar, Cpt. Edward G. 24
Stephen Leacock: *Sunshine Sketches* 175
Stinson, Cpl. Sherman W. 65, 93, 178
Stonne 132
Storm troopers 64
Strasbourg 188
Strickland, Lt. Henry W. (Chaplain) 156, 157, 160, 163, 175
Subalterns 20
submarine 5, 6
Suippes 79, 80
Sultaine 12, 13, 15
Susie 68, 84
Sutton, Lieutenant 174
Sutton, Cpl. William M. 91
Suzanne 30
Swisher, Sgt. Claude D. 112, 113
Switzerland 31, 42

Taber, John Huddleston (John, Jack) 2, 21, 22, 42, 58, 113
Tank Corps 122
Tanner, John 152
"Taps" 63
Taupette 12, 13
Taussig 193, 194
Telegrafen Strasse 154, 161, 184
Tenor 144
La Tentation de St. Antoine 83
Texas 103, 188
Thaïs 189
Thanksgiving 6, 144
Thaon-les-Vosges 74
Therese 153, 155, 177
Thiancourt 110
3rd Army 139, 179
3rd Army Reserve 181
3rd Battalion 1, 3, 17, 32, 55, 74, 78, 82, 96, 102, 103, 104, 113, 114, 116, 117, 128, 129, 132–134, 144, 146, 148, 150, 155–158, 160–162, 172–177, 179, 184, 185
3rd Division 110, 139, 172
3rd Platoon 7, 113, 179
39th Division 67
39th Infantry 162
32nd Division 47, 59, 95, 139
37 millimeter (mm) 56

Index

Thomas, Major James (Jimmy) 127, 184
Thompson, Lt. Hugh S. (Tommy) 2, 32, 51, 58, 63, 82, 85, 103, 104, 113
Thompson, Lt. Ray 101
Thorpe 194
Thrasher, Cpt. Robert B. 24
308th Infantry 68, 190
310th Signal Battalion 175
356th Infantry 113
Timothy, Lt. Christopher S. (Tim) 14, 18, 24, 26, 27, 32, 33, 41, 42, 44, 47, 52, 55, 64, 66, 67, 72, 75, 77–79, 81, 83, 84, 98, 103
Tinley, Col. Matthew A. 67, 95, 97, 104, 107, 108, 134, 143, 161, 176, 178, 184, 186, 188, 190
Tittsworth, Lt. William D. 159, 161, 163, 184
Todd, Kenneth 166
Toul 27, 75, 108, 109, 165, 188
Tour de Nesles 97
Tour Eiffel 89
Toussaint, Mere 40, 42
T.P.S. ("telegraphe por sol") 64
trench fever 62
Treves 165
Treves, Lieutenant 187
trial 177
Trilport 89
Troubetskoy, Princess 30
Tucker, Lt. William J. (Tuck) 9, 24, 41, 63, 76, 78, 83, 99, 101, 103–106, 133, 144, 155, 160, 162, 163, 164, 175, 188
Tuileries Garden 125
Turks 119
Tushek, Lt. Randolph R. (Tush) 24, 26–29, 33, 38, 42, 44, 46, 51, 64, 66, 96, 100, 102, 103, 106–108, 110, 119–121, 130, 138, 139, 144, 146, 154–156, 159, 160, 161–163, 169, 174, 176, 179, 183, 185, 193
28th Division 94, 95
21st French Army Corps 79, 80
27th Division 101, 174
26th Division 20, 90, 121, 122, 139, 165
Twining, Sgt. Merrick C. 35, 37, 88
240 35

Umbarger, Cpl. Hiter B. 173
United States 4, 8, 10, 11, 24, 45, 51, 72, 77, 78, 79, 81, 83, 89, 104, 117, 125, 131, 133, 140, 141, 144, 150, 159, 163, 165, 172, 173, 181, 187, 188
U.S. Army Heritage and Education Center 2

University of Illinois 193
University Union 126, 188
Upton, Colonel 21, 25

Van Order, Cpt. Paul I. 50, 103, 177
Van't Hof, Lt. Bernard 33, 38, 98
Vantrot, Corporal 33
Van Zandt, Lt. George T. (Doc) 163, 184, 193
Varennes 121
Vaudville 182
Vaux 99
Veasey, Lt. Edward J. 87
Venizelos, Mr. 169
Verdilly, Aisne 99
Verdun 82, 118
Verrières 132, 135
Versailles 126, 189
Vidal, Lieutenant 122, 123, 125
La Vie Parsienne 76
Villa Carlsheim 155, 179, 186
Villa Lucia 184
Village Indien 57, 58, 60
Village Negre 54, 56, 61, 62, 64
Villagers 11
Villers-Cotterets 70
Vire 140
Vitrimont 29
Vitry-la-Ville 75, 76
Vitry-le-François 77, 102
Vittel 103
Le Vivier, Ardennes (Atraise) 135
volcano 153
Von Bethmann-Hollweg, Reichskanzler 155
Von Order, Cpt. Paul I. 97
Von Wetten Kampf, Baroness 181, 183
Vosges 28, 30, 52
Vreeland, Cpl. Cliiford C. 48, 65

Wages, Lt. H.W. (Hal) 162, 164, 174–176, 185
Wagner 163
Wagoner, Pvt. William H. 48
Waldorf 154, 157, 182, 184
Walferdange 144, 145
Wallace, Lt. Mahlon D. (Wallace, Wally) 13, 14, 18, 32, 51, 58, 63, 64, 75, 76, 113, 117
Wallace, Pvt. Floyd E. 92
Waterloo Station 8
Watson, Lieutenant 68
Wayland, Lt. Clyde (Doc) 176, 183, 193
Wehr 175
Weibern 163

Index

"Weihnachts geschenk" 152
"Weihnachts kuchen" 152
Welles, Major (grandma) 22
Wells, Lt. Edward D. 113
Wheeler, Lt. Karl H. 113
Wilhelm, Crown Prince 137
Whippet tanks 110
White, Ambassador 168
White Mule 134
Wiener, Lt. Frank W. 103, 106, 113
Wiesbaden 183
Wilhelm I 172
Williams, Cpl. Edwin (Ed) 46, 48, 93
Williams, Pvt. William H. (Billy) 43
Wilson, Miss 161
Wilson, Pres. Woodrow 2, 128, 141, 168, 169, 190
Winans, Col. Edwin B. 5
Winchester, England 7
Winnal Down 7
Winning of Barbara Worth 44
Witherell, Cpt. William B. (Billy) 58, 135, 155, 162, 163, 177

W.O.L. (Without Official Leave) 47
Wolcott, Lt. B.C. 51, 52, 58
Wood, Lt. Thomas L. (Rex Woody) 57, 58
Woodard, Pvt. George M. 44, 48, 53, 57, 66, 93, 137
Woods, Sgt. Merle 32, 35, 46, 48, 51, 65, 80, 91–95, 97, 112–114, 116, 120, 164, 178
Worthington, Major Emory C. 13, 16, 18, 91, 93, 128
Wurtenbergers 20

Yates, Major Orville B. 23, 133, 135, 155, 157, 158, 160
Ye God Begot Hotel 7
Y.M.C.A. (Y) 20, 21–25, 49, 58, 59, 61, 64, 76, 78, 90, 102, 114, 117, 125, 127, 157, 158, 174, 175, 177–179, 182, 183, 185
Younkin, Cpt. Frank B. 65
Ypres 119

Zike, Pvt. Everett R. (Cap Zig) 50, 176, 178, 182, 184–186

www.ingramcontent.com/pod-product-compliance
Ingram Content Group UK Ltd.
Pitfield, Milton Keynes, MK11 3LW, UK
UKHW041955140426
5217IPUK00015B/817